Tackling Dyslexia

Second Edition

Tackling Dyslexia

Second Edition

Ann Cooke
Dyslexia Unit, University of Wales, Bangor

W
WHURR PUBLISHERS
LONDON AND PHILADELPHIA

© 2002 Whurr Publishers
First edition published 1993 by
Whurr Publishers Ltd
19b Compton Terrace, London N1 2UN, England and
325 Chestnut Street, Philadelphia PA19106, USA

British Library Cataloguing in Publication Data

A catalogue record for this book is available from the
British Library.

ISBN 1 86156 065 6

Printed and bound in the UK by Athenaeum Press Ltd,
Gateshead, Tyne & Wear.

Contents

Preface

Helping dyslexic children to read and write is often a daunting prospect for a teacher. Everyone knows that a lot of hard work lies ahead for the children who have never made a start, for many others who have begun to read and then come to a halt, and for the people who must help them.

This book is intended especially for those teachers who are able to take pupils on their own, or in small groups, and so can tailor the work to meet each one's particular difficulties. The instructional approach has been described in some detail, so that teachers who are new to the business of helping dyslexic children may find plenty of guidance about procedures and about the sequence of work. Parents too may find this useful. Much of what we do is common to good educational practice: the difference with dyslexic children lies in the need for extra intensity at the point of teaching, for greater structure to help them learn, for more support while they practise, and for explicit instruction throughout.

Since the book was first written (1992) there have been a number of far-reaching developments in the way that children are taught to read and write in school. Chief among them is the introduction into primary schools in England of the National Literacy Strategy and the Literacy Hour as a method of delivering the National Curriculum for English. This has been followed by a similar initiative in mathematics, leading to the Numeracy Hour. The Strategies arose from concerns about children's literacy and numeracy standards and about the levels of these essential skills among school-leavers.

Anyone teaching dyslexic children in a specialized context has to take account of what is happening in the classroom. The Literacy Hour has changed the way that early literacy skills are taught. The concentration on learning skills and the new emphasis on phonics and phonological teaching means that mainstream practice is now much closer to the methods that are recognized as being effective for learners with dyslexia. The new approach is bringing other changes too, particularly in the kind of early reading books that are now available. Where books with a systematic phonic sequence were difficult to find a few years ago, there is now a wide choice.

Other initiatives are concerned with early years' teaching. The Department for Education wants children with difficulties to be identified and helped as early as possible. This is mirrored by projects carried out by non-government bodies, such as the British Dyslexia Association and other organisations concerned with children's speech and language. Teachers can now easily find out about such initiatives by using the internet, another change since 1992. The development of Information and Communications Technology itself holds out immense possibilities for dyslexic individuals and their teachers.

All this could mean that some of our would-have-been pupils may, happily, no longer need our help. For those who continue to have difficulties, our approach to the phonic work may need some adjustment, according to how much the children have learned and remembered – and can use – from their classroom teaching. To provide a little information, the lists of vocabulary and technical language terms from the Literacy Hour materials are reproduced in Appendix V and a brief account of the structure of the Hour is given in Appendix VI.

So what has changed in *Tackling Dyslexia*? New chapters have been added on testing, early years, mathematics, and games and multisensory aids for teaching. The mathematics chapter is intended as a guide for literacy teachers who note a pupil's difficulty and are able to give a little help, perhaps with counting, or telling the time; the updated chapter on using computers and information technology is similarly for non-specialists.

Other chapters follow the same pattern as before and some have been expanded. The detailed description of the teaching approach (Chapter 4) is developed further in Chapter 6, where topics in the phonic programme are discussed at greater length in relation to pupils at different stages of learning.

In this chapter a different way of presenting the programme is shown. This developed from thoughts about how dyslexic individuals like to have a global picture of their topic, and prefer to work with the whole. It is unfortunate that in learning how a language is written we have to learn the detailed parts as well – and that is what our pupils find so difficult.

In Chapter 8, Reading, material has been added to the section on working with older pupils and Chapter 10, Into the Classroom, is expanded to look at different ways of helping pupils to structure their writing, such as using writing frames. Here again, the Literacy Hour approach includes the same kind of work. The later chapters deal with topics such as handwriting (Chapter 11), learning the alphabet and telling the time (Chapter 12).

Technical terms have been kept to a minimum – though the Literacy Hour expects teachers to know them. However, some explanation is needed of how the terms 'phonetic', 'phonological', 'phonemic' and 'phonic' have been used. 'Phonetic' refers specifically to the acoustic characteristics of speech sounds, the production of these sounds by the vocal organs, and how we perceive them. The term 'phonological' is broader and concerns the the way that speech sounds are arranged in a language; in the present context it is most often used in discussing the auditory and oral analysis of spoken language, as in the term 'phonological segmentation'. 'Phonemic' is used to refer specifically to speech sounds as they are perceived, where there is no associated meaning, as in 'phonemic awareness'. Finally 'phonic', in popular usage, makes an association between the perceived sound of words, and the way that they are written down. This is the term that is most appropriately used to discuss points of teaching, for instance the 'phonic' principles of spelling. It is widely used of course to refer to a method of teaching, as in a 'phonics approach' to reading as distinct from one that is 'visual' or 'whole-language'.

Where the printed letter is intended to represent the phoneme, or speech sound, slashes have been used (for instance /k/ denotes the sound, not the name of the letter); voiced/unvoiced sounds have been described; and diacritical marks have been used to indicate vowel values: all this rather than use International Phonetic Alphabet symbols.

I must also provide an explanation – a less technical one – for the references to the dyslexic pupil and the teacher, as he and she. This style has been adopted mainly to achieve simplification of writing: alternative methods of never using singular pronouns, saying 'he or she' throughout, or the convention s/he, all make for difficulties of expression or of style. The new convention of always using the plural they/them still reads a little oddly when it refers to a single individual. Wherever possible I refer to 'pupils' and use plural pronouns; where I want to talk about a pupil individually, I use 'he'. Four out of my five case examples are boys, which reflects the greater number of dyslexic boys than girls (though opinions about this ratio are now changing.) There are also many more female than male teachers working in the dyslexia field (though the reasons are probably different!). I offer humble acknowledgements to all girls and women who are dyslexic, and to the men among the teachers, and hope they will tolerate these conventions.

Tackling Dyslexia has drawn much from the philosophy and teaching approach developed at Bangor by Tim and Elaine Miles from the mid 60s onwards. It complements the *Bangor Dyslexia Teaching System* (Third Edition, Whurr 1997) in which Elaine Miles documents the programme of work that has been followed in the Dyslexia Unit at Bangor for over twenty-five years. The approach that is described in both books is essentially 'phonological' since it directs the pupil's attention to the sounds as they occur in language. It is also 'linguistic' since it pays close attention to the meaning and the linguistic structures of words. For the convenience of teachers using the two books together, suggestions made in Chapter 6 about the sequence of teaching are cross-referenced to the *Teaching System*. While both books suggest an order of teaching, neither is insistent upon the teacher following a prescribed sequence of work. *Tackling Dyslexia* could be used alongside any 'programme' as it is essentially a methods handbook.

It would be impossible to produce any work of this kind without the experience that teaching children brings, and without the help and advice of a great many friends and colleagues. The first expression of thanks should go to the children, especially to those whose work I have used to illustrate difficulties, and to show the progress that can be made. I should like to pay tribute here to the hard work that dyslexic children and students put into their learning. We cannot really understand the efforts they have to make and how uncertain they can feel about schoolwork and study. This book is about helping them to overcome difficulties, but I wonder how far we allow them to learn in the way that makes use of their strengths.

Then I should thank Jo Westwood for her permission to use the illustration on page 43 which is from her early phonic readers, the *Zed Project*.

I owe a great deal to all my colleagues, past and present, for the sharing of ideas, for their relish of this particular work, and for their understanding of dyslexic children. The teachers who have attended courses at Bangor are also part of that company.

As before, I appreciate the help and comments of teachers who read and commented on drafts of different chapters. Liz Du Pré, Janet Chapman, Ivy Webster and Bob Evans read the chapters on Early Years, Reading, and Into the Classroom and Julia Keeves read and contributed to Games. Marie Jones has been helpful as always in discussing books and materials and again the checklist that she and Janet Chapman drew up for the first edition is included. (This and the other checklists may be photocopied.) Elaine Miles and Anne Henderson encouraged me to include maths and provided useful information. Dave Lane advised on the Computer chapter, designed some of the figures and helped with technicalities. I should also mention my daughter, Celia Osbourne, who commented on several chapters from the point of view of an infant teacher and kindly let me into her classroom to observe – and give a hand.

Once again I have enjoyed and valued the support and friendship of Elaine Miles, who has read and commented on several aspects of this second edition of *Tackling Dyslexia*, and most of all I would like to acknowledge how much I owe to Tim Miles, from whose knowledge and experience so many of us have had enormous benefit.

Finally, my husband Maurice has been very patient, as always, listened to the dyslexia 'stories', and given me constant encouragement. To him, my very special thanks.

Chapter 1

The dyslexia difficulty and the literacy task

Literacy teaching in schools

When children first approach reading at school it is often by direct experience of a wide range of books. They will also have formal teaching about reading through the work of the Literacy Hour, in which the alphabetic system and the phonic structures of written English are introduced along with a basic vocabulary of whole words. Writing is taught in a similar way, through phonics instruction and whole-class teaching about spelling and sentence writing, including simple punctuation and grammar. The curriculum of the Literacy Hour therefore results in every child having direct class instruction in phonic and phonological skills and word reading from the third term in the Reception Year and Years 1 and 2, with an emphasis on learning the spellings for all the consonant and vowel sounds of English. Working individually and in groups, with time allocated to reading and writing, children then put all this work into immediate practice. It is expected that by school Year 3 most children will be able to read and write at the average for their age group (7 to 8 years) (Note 1.1, page 251).

Some children have always been able to perform the earliest reading tasks well enough to get into books with little or no direct instruction; they are able to extract enough information about written language to further their own development. For these children, learning comes from doing and sometimes appears to happen without very much effort on their part. Their proficiency with oral language – already well developed – supports their early encounters with printed words in a way that enables learning to begin. Young writers have always developed through 'emergent writing'. They draw on a number of sources for their information: words in books that they can read; a memory (sometimes muddled) of letters and words seen or used before; asking the teacher or other children; and the sounds of the words that they want to write. Gradually they build up a sufficient lexicon of words to enable them to communicate on paper. These processes are still encouraged although there is more emphasis on 'getting it right' at an early stage.

Dyslexic children do not seem able to learn at the same pace, and in the same way, as their peers. They find it more difficult to absorb and recall information about the alphabetic–phonological code that we use to write down language. Consequently, they cannot make a start and they do not have the same opportunities as other children for implicit learning to occur. It seems that several major factors contribute to the problems that they encounter when they are learning to read, write and spell:

1. They have difficulties with phonology, that is, their capacity to abstract detailed information about the sounds in spoken language is limited, certainly in comparison with others of the same age. They also find it difficult to manipulate those sounds.
2. They find it difficult to learn and manipulate the symbols that represent sounds. (They may have similar difficulties with other symbols such as numbers, mathematical symbols and musical notation.)
3. A further difficulty seems to involve the way that language, and language information, is taken into and processed by immediate working memory, and thence stored in long-term memory (Note 1.2, page 251).

The approach to teaching that is described in this book is designed to take account of these problems, and also of the nature of the task that the dyslexic child is trying to master.

It is not easy to separate cause and effect when the processes that underlie literacy functioning are examined, and to say how far the skills that are involved exist independently of each other and of the larger activity (Note 1.3, page 252). It is probable that reading and the low-level skills required for accurate and fluent reading are interactive. Reading and writing are complex processes that require a great deal of information to be processed very rapidly. For proficiency, response to printed symbols or the production of the needed symbols has to be instant and automatic. Dyslexic individuals do not seem able to work at the necessary speed. However, teachers and parents often observe that it can help if complicated information is reduced to small segments and they are allowed to work at their own pace. They also need many repetitions of the same information, followed by plenty of revision practice over an extended period of time.

The nature of the difficulty, together with that of the task, calls for an approach that addresses directly and in detail the areas that dyslexic children find so troublesome, and at the same time allows them to learn in their particular way. Such an approach might be termed a 'nuts and bolts' method. It will:

- present, and teach explicitly, information about the alphabetic–phonic code
- help to develop skill at segmenting sounds
- teach the details of the spelling system
- present this information in small steps so it can be absorbed and remembered
- control very carefully the sequence of the work
- organise the work according to the phonological structure of English (or other) vocabulary

- teach children to construct words according to learned principles so that the need to memorise whole words is reduced
- give plenty of repetition and practice
- teach reading and spelling alongside, so that one supports the other
- use a multisensory procedure.

Much of this work is now part of the Literacy Hour syllabus. The problem for the dyslexic child is that the pace is too fast. There are not enough opportunities for over-learning, re-teaching, and practice and cumulative revision. Those who do not keep up with the majority have a second chance to learn in the revision programmes for Years 2 and 3 and some children will catch up. The dyslexic child with severe difficulties will still be in need of individual help.

Literacy as a multisensory activity

Almost all of our senses are involved in the tasks of reading and writing. As receptive and expressive channels respectively, hearing and vision, and speech and movement are in constant interplay. Of course we do not always say words aloud, but the contribution that knowledge of word sounds makes to literacy activity must not be under-estimated. In fact, would we be able to think in language without some knowledge of how words are pronounced (Note 1.4, page 252)?

It is difficult to separate the interaction of sight and hearing. What may seem to be a simple visual task may have underlying resonances of sound, whereas an auditory task may be helped by pictorial images. For instance, a child who cannot recall the sound for the letter *p* may get to it by remembering the picture of a pipe; another may remember the letters of a word visually, but place them in correct order by reference to the pronunciation.

When we work with dyslexic individuals who have difficulty in learning, retention and later recall of sound–symbol information, it is sensible to use all possible ways to make the task easier. Multisensory procedures are essential when we teach sounds and words, to aid the learner's immediate response and to help him to remember them. As often as possible, sight, hearing and movement are engaged simultaneously with speech. In this way the stronger sensory channels are utilised to the full, and each channel supports the others. If an individual pupil has a weak channel, it is not usually profitable to ignore this modality. By using it along with the others, a teacher would aim to strengthen it.

The visual and auditory properties of words are of little interest unless meaning can be attached to them, and here the cognitive activity of the brain is required. If it is to be understood, information about literacy coming through the senses has to be organised and processed in the brain, and linked with language information already stored there. Outgoing language expression also has to be organised mentally before the senses convert it into spoken or written forms. This is usually all so rapid and automatic that we are not aware of the processes, except when we have to struggle to understand, or when we speak without thinking and notice (or others notice) afterwards.

Figure 1.1 shows the way that sensory functions interact and overlap with each other and with speech in the learning of basic literacy skills. The receptive input from the senses is linked with the expressive output function of speech and writing to strengthen the learning experience. The brain

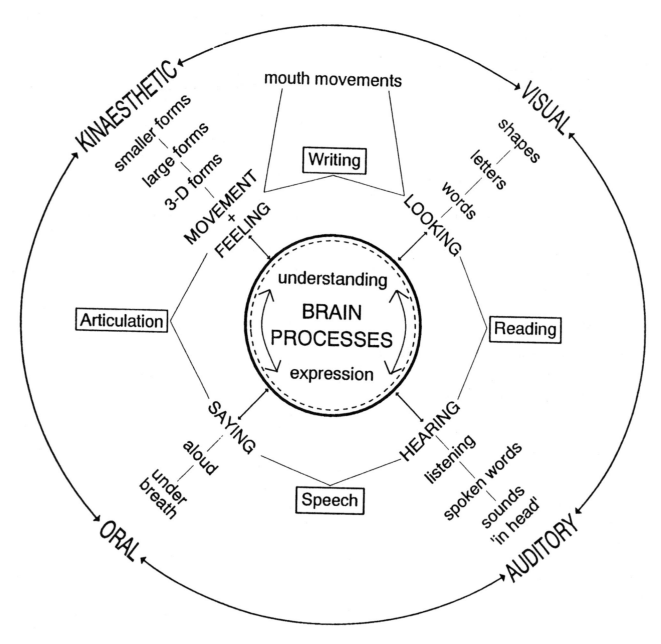

Figure 1.1 Multisensory activity in literacy teaching.

acts as a collecting and processing centre for the entire language activity.

The structured phonic programme

This is a remedial rescue programme to help children and young people whose literacy skills have not developed at the expected pace. It is intended particularly for children and students whose learning abilities in other respects are at least of an average level. Although the emphasis is placed on individual tuition, this does not, of course, imply a sealed box. Children may spend only 1 hour a week following a phonic programme and the crux is how well they transfer their learning to their classwork. If the work takes place in school, there must be regular consultation with other teachers, particularly class teachers and the Special Educational Needs Coordinator (SENCO). Teachers working in other situations are advised, wherever possible, to make early contact with teachers in school, and to keep in touch thereafter.

Many dyslexic children experience failure at school for some time, perhaps for several years, before the cause of their learning difficulties is recognised and help becomes available. They are often frustrated at their inability to succeed in class: they lack self-confidence, their ability to concentrate is poor, and many become either withdrawn or badly behaved (Note 1.5, page 252).

Very often these children have other kinds of skills, and are articulate and well informed; their teachers are frequently puzzled that they have such problems in basic literacy work. These pupils need to experience success immediately teaching starts, even if only in small tasks. Their self-confidence must be re-built by their being able to get things right, so they must not be allowed to fail. Although all pupils will follow the same broad structure, each individual's programme of work will be specific to his needs. Children need to be taught one-to-one wherever possible, and especially at the start. It is important to get the right environment for this work, away from distractions and without other pupils looking on. It follows that, unless the circumstances are exceptional, the pupil must be withdrawn from the classroom.

There are times when working with pupils in pairs or small groups has its advantages, as long as all the participants have made a good start and have skills at around the same level. Some children respond better in a shared lesson and it is helpful to take the individual spotlight off them. Competition from others can also be an incentive to work harder and there is a distinct advantage in a group when it comes to games. Such a situation needs careful management because a pupil's growing confidence can be shaken if he feels that he is the weakest member of the group.

When lessons start, success is often immediate and rapid: the early stages can be taught or re-built quite quickly. The rate of success is likely to slow down after a while, when the work gets more difficult and there is more to remember – and more possibility for confusion. As the work in class proceeds to new stages of the wider curriculum, the general demands on the pupil will change and increase; this may mean that different kinds of problems may emerge. In consequence, the teaching should usually be spread over a long period. A couple of terms' lessons may see a child through present problems – but it is difficult to teach beyond the point of current learning needs.

The immediate aim must be to give the dyslexic child a firm foundation in basic work; in the longer term his attainments in reading and writing must be brought as close as possible to his actual age. He must be helped to build methods of making new work easier to learn. Obviously, this will be more possible with younger children, for whom the gap has not become very wide; an early start is therefore of the greatest importance. However, support from specialist teachers should continue until it is clear that the new learning is well established and that he has developed strategies for coping on his own.

Part of the rescue programme can involve what might be called a 'counselling factor' and hinges on the relationship established between the teacher and pupil. Where this is relaxed and based on mutual esteem, it can give to pupils a sense of security that helps them to re-build their confidence. The teacher is a patient, understanding ally, and expects them to succeed because she does not demand impossible things. Pupils also feel able to confide in a visiting tutor, who is sometimes able to provide reassurance or act as an intermediary, precisely because she does not belong to the school 'establishment'.

One cannot make hard and fast statements about how long lessons should be, how many times a week and for how long they should go on. In any case, these are all likely to be affected by the conditions of local provision as well as by the needs of the dyslexic child. Whatever the variables, the essential factors must be the right kind of teaching, delivered in one-to-one lessons, to pupils whose needs are identified as early as possible. There will then be a good chance of success.

Chapter 2

The phonological approach

The National Curriculum and the Literacy Hour place the teaching of phonics and phonological skills at the centre of reading and writing instruction as soon as children start school. Although this may enable some dyslexic children to make a better start with literacy, those who have more difficulties with phonology and the processing of language information will still need a more detailed, explicit approach. These children will not learn as quickly as their classmates; they will need extra attention in the early stages and will take longer to internalise new learning to an automatic level. They will also need more systematic opportunities for practice before they are able to generalise their learning to a wider context.

The programme that is described in this chapter and those that follow, is intended for those children who need a very structured multisensory approach, and an approach that breaks down the learning into small units and provides cumulative revision. It should be flexible enough to suit children who are identified at an early stage of schooling as being 'at risk', as well as those who are not picked up till later on.

The phonic programme

The kind of phonic programme used in specialist dyslexia work has particular characteristics that go beyond the phonics needed by children who learn without difficulty and are different even from the work of the Literacy Hour.

Specialist programmes for working with dyslexic children, such as *The Bangor Dyslexia Teaching System* or *Alpha to Omega* (Note 2.1, page 252), analyse in considerable detail the sound structure and spelling of words. These are introduced and taught in such a way that the pupil can understand them as he meets the points one by one. It is not simply a matter of remembering the various patterns and principles: the pupil should understand the way that the writing system works so that he can learn to use it independently. At the same time, the programme will enable the teacher to work on the pupil's awareness of the phonemic structure of words and his skills with phonology.

Whenever possible the pupil should be helped to make discoveries for himself, but this must never be left to chance. The teacher has to know that every point is covered, that it has been learnt, that it has been remembered and that it can be used. Consequently such programmes should all be started at the beginning, with single sounds and letters and the associations between them, and with simple word structures – single syllable words of the consonant–vowel–consonant (*cvc*) form. The order of work is carefully sequenced, each step leading on to the next, particularly in the early stages. Gradually, more difficult sounds and spellings and words are taught, according to phonic regularity and frequency of occurrence. On-going revision of work is built in as the work continues, so that learning is practised until it is assimilated. At all stages the approach should be a multisensory one. This is particularly important for establishing the basic sound–letter correspondences and when the basic spelling work is being taught.

A teacher starting work with pupils who have already made some headway with reading and spelling must still make sure that there are no gaps in the early stages, so knowledge of sound–letter correspondences and early 'rules' needs to be checked. This must not be taken to mean re-teaching what is already known.

Order of teaching

The chart in Figure 2.1 shows in outline the major elements of phonic work that will form the core of the teaching programme and the progression of that work for dyslexic pupils (Note 2.2, page 253). It should start with short vowels in three-letter words – consonant–vowel–consonant (*cvc*). This is shown at the top of the chart.

The different consonant digraphs (*sh*, *th* – two sounds – *ch*) come next, then the consonant blends. Some children find the digraphs and blended sounds difficult. If they have had – or still have – problems with speech production they may have problems with /*th*/ or even with /*sh*/. (In children's acquisition of speech sounds, /sh/ appears later than /s/ and a child may say *sip* for *ship*.) They may not perceive the individual sounds of blends or reduce the cluster to a single sound (the earlier in order of acquisition.) Children who have difficulty with /l/ and /r/ sounds may find the *s* blends (*st*, *sn*, *sm*, *sp*) easier to start with.

There is a lot of work here and it is important that teachers should move through it as quickly as possible while taking individual needs into account. The different consonant clusters may be introduced in letter groups (blends with *r*, blends with *l*, blends with *s*) or three and four at a time. Triple blends (*str*, *shr* and others) may need extra attention. Work on the initial consonant digraphs and blends can be picked up again at the next stage, when the long vowels and vowels with *r* are taught. This is a convenient way of keeping them under review.

Some of the consonant blends that occur in final position (often known as assimilated consonants) are found mainly after short vowels, e.g. *mp*, *nk*, *ng*. Others, such as *nd* and *st* occur in more variable word patterns (*hand*, *found*; *last*, *most*) or have regional differences in pronunciation (*past*, *ask*, *bath*) Some are very unusual (*lb*)

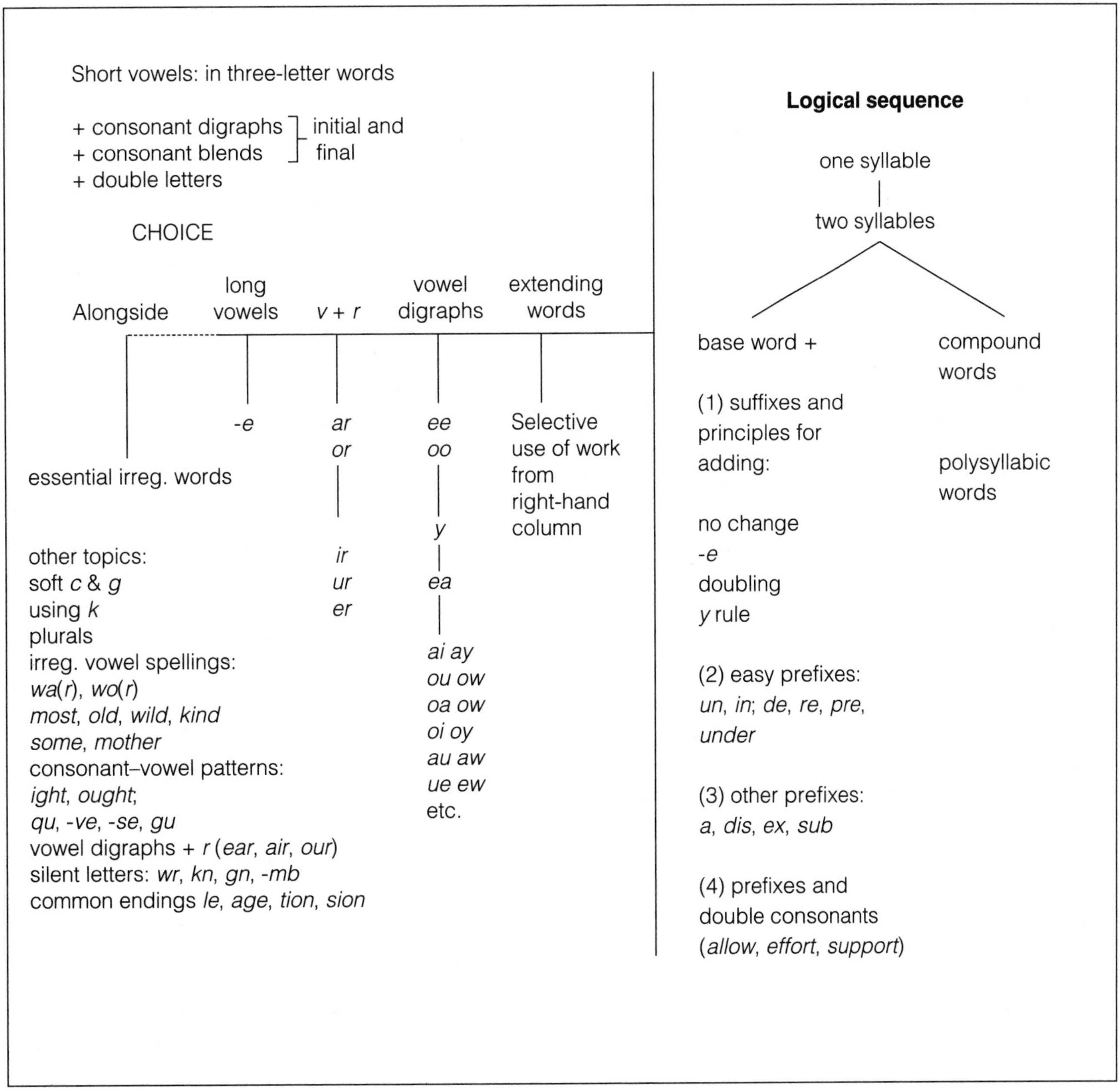

Short vowels: in three-letter words

+ consonant digraphs ⎤ initial and
+ consonant blends ⎦ final
+ double letters

CHOICE

Alongside	long vowels	v + r	vowel digraphs	extending words
	-e	ar or	ee oo	Selective use of work from right-hand column
essential irreg. words				
		ir ur er	y	
			ea	
other topics:			ai ay	
soft c & g			ou ow	
using k			oa ow	
plurals			oi oy	
irreg. vowel spellings:			au aw	
wa(r), wo(r)			ue ew	
most, old, wild, kind			etc.	
some, mother				
consonant–vowel patterns:				
ight, ought;				
qu, -ve, -se, gu				
vowel digraphs + r (ear, air, our)				
silent letters: wr, kn, gn, -mb				
common endings le, age, tion, sion				

Logical sequence

one syllable
|
two syllables

base word +   compound words

(1) suffixes and
principles for
adding: polysyllabic
                               words

no change
-e
doubling
y rule

(2) easy prefixes:
un, in; de, re, pre,
under

(3) other prefixes:
a, dis, ex, sub

(4) prefixes and
double consonants
(allow, effort, support)

Figure 2.1 Structured phonic programme – order of work.

or are found most often in irregular long-vowel words. The *l* clusters particularly are often associated with irregular vowel sounds (*wild, half*). When teaching the short-vowel word groups, it may be convenient to start by including only those consonant blends that are characteristic of short-vowel words and familiar words with less frequent clusters, such as *help*. Other blends and the more tricky endings – *tch* and *dge* – may be left till later for the pupils starting from the beginning of the programme. Use of a checklist showing every example will ensure that all are taught in due course.

After the short-vowel work, the order of teaching is less easy to prescribe in detail, as the needs of pupils will differ and a choice has to be made. For the youngest children, and others starting with little knowledge, it will be advisable to work next on long vowels, possibly starting with *ee* and *oo*, because these words have a memorable pattern; some children may already know them. Simpler words having vowels followed by *r* (*car, for*) might also be put in early on.

Long vowels with 'silent' final *-e* is a major topic. Children who have serious difficulties with identifying vowel sounds will need a lot of help here because distinctions between short and long sounds also involve decisions about spelling. Many teachers have their preferred ways of dealing with this and children's own learning preferences vary. Other vowel digraphs, and vowel + *r* combinations follow. There is a lot of work here, to be spread over several months.

Pupils who are a little further on when they start (say a spelling age of 8 on a standardised test) might begin with an introductory survey of short-vowel patterns, then proceed immediately to simple suffixing (where no modification of the base word is needed) and two-syllable words, before starting work on the long-vowel sounds.

With older pupils, who are competent with basic spelling but need more advanced work to meet the demands of the curriculum, the teacher should begin by checking that they understand the principles underlying short- and long-vowel spellings, and might then go straight to suffixing 'rules'. For them, the sequence on the right-hand side of the chart in Figure 2.1 could be followed.

At the left-hand side, a selection of other topics is shown, and here the order of teaching can follow the needs of the pupil. Some will dovetail neatly with other points, e.g. 'soft *c*' and 'soft *g*' are often introduced with *ace* and *age* words along with the long-vowel *-e* work. Work on irregular words (that need to be learnt as wholes) and groups of words such as the *wa, wo* spellings, is on-going. The order of teaching could reflect the vocabulary of the reading books.

At any time, teachers are likely to come across a word or spelling pattern that pupils know, but which they have not themselves taught. A check should be made on whether this is a 'one-off' or whether the pupil knows the word as one of a group. Since much spelling is learned by making analogies, the teacher has to decide how far to go at that point. If following up the word would disrupt the programme of work too much, it can be noted as a single, known word and followed up at a more convenient time. If the group or pattern is known, it can be slotted into place immediately and kept under review for a while, perhaps by being included in dictation work.

This kind of phonic work needs intense concentration and the pupil should not be expected to work in this way for more than 10 or 15 minutes at a time. If topics are selected carefully, lessons can contain material that is coherent yet varied, and which provides different kinds of support for the work on sounds. In this way the phonic work can advance along a 'broad front'. (Different ways of following the phonic programme at each stage, with more detailed comments on how points may be taught, are discussed in Chapter 6.)

A checklist of basic spelling work will be found in Appendix V. Along with this is another checklist of words, mainly irregular, that occur frequently in children's reading and writing. A few of these are regular and should be included also in the regular phonic spelling lists. (Both checklists may be photocopied.)

An alternative model of the phonic programme, which is more appropriate for planning work with older pupils, students and adults, is shown on page 97.

Promoting automatic response

Skilled readers and writers carry out the low-level, mechanical functions of literacy on 'auto-pilot' for most of the time. Response to written words is immediate and the processes of 'accessing the words' are working at a subconscious level. It is similar with spelling and handwriting; although words are written letter by letter, most of them appear correctly without the writer thinking about them. The details of language – grammar, punctuation and stylistic expression – need hardly any more attention. Full concentration can be given to the content of writing and points of style, and to

comprehension of what is being read. Dyslexic learners have to struggle to approach this level of competence and some manage with only limited success, especially in writing.

So while routines such as onset and rime exercises train generalisation skills (see page 13), the responses here will be considered and thought out. Other activities have to be put into lessons that can help to promote immediate, totally certain responses to the phonic elements taught in the structured programme. These often involve drilling specific knowledge and subskills, by presenting a visual or auditory stimulus (usually a letter, word or phoneme) for the pupil to give an immediate, automatic response. Such drills should be multisensory, especially in the early stages of work.

The Linkages practice described in Chapter 4 (page 34) and flashcard practice of irregular or high-frequency words are typical routines. As new spelling–sound correspondences and new words are taught, they can be added to a pack of cards for drill. Once learned, each point should be kept under review for a time – and re-visited if hesitations or mistakes crop up. Regularly saying the alphabet and the months, for instance, helps to keep the pupil alert to them. Precision teaching methods also aim at immediate recall of words that have been learned. (For maths, learning to say tables aims at making automatic the pupil's knowledge of the multiplication number bonds.)

A card pack for over-learning the spellings of phonemes and other word parts can also be made. In this drill the pupil is asked first to name the letters he would write for a given sound or syllable, then to give a keyword and to write the spelling and word. As he adds each new sound spelling to the phonic dictionary it is added to the appropriate card or a new card is made. In this way a bank of alternative spellings is built up. The practical outcome is that, when a particular vowel sound has to be written, the pupil knows immediately what the choices are. It is more difficult to establish correct responses for spelling than for reading, but the learning should result at least in a possible spelling for that sound, and it helps to take away some of the uncertainty. (By trying out a word with alternative spellings he might be able to recognise the correct one.)

Going through a drill routine

It is important to get off to a good start, especially if the task is being timed. To begin with, teachers should model the way they want the pupil to respond. They might also ask him to go through two or three practice items before starting the main drill. In that way, opening mistakes are not going to interfere with the learning process. If a card pack is being used, the pupil can set his own speed if he holds it and deals the cards himself (unless there is a difficulty with motor skills). Far from disliking this kind of activity, pupils enjoy their increasing success and it gives them confidence. It also helps to ensure that these basic elements of literacy can be transferred to other learning situations.

Setting targets

Teachers coming to this kind of approach for the first time are often uncertain about practical issues: how fast should they go through the work; how far should they expect to get; will the work suit every pupil? The answer to the first two questions is that it depends on the individual pupil. Although all dyslexic children need constant repetition and revision, the amount of over-learning needed will vary. Some will obviously move along faster than others. All should be expected to use their intelligence, although of course natural abilities will differ.

The teacher's expectations should not be low, however – the pupil has to learn. Good progress should be anticipated, especially in the early stages and especially in reading.

It is important to set targets. These can be revised according to progress, and it keeps the teacher looking ahead to the next set of needs. Although it is vital that pupils should be well grounded in the basic sounds work, there is a lot of work to be done. Except perhaps in the case of the very youngest pupils, of 7 years or under, who have a little time in hand, children must move on as fast as possible. If the child has an Individual Education Programme (IEP), it will be useful to check those targets so that, if possible, the work in the dyslexia programme can be coordinated with that of the classroom.

Work on long vowels, at least for reading, should be reached in most cases within the first year of work. This can be helped by teaching the vowel digraphs and other vowel sounds (such as ar, or) for reading, starting with ee and oo before tackling 'long-vowel -e' and building up a set of words related to the child's reading books. Reading will nearly always go ahead more quickly than spelling. When the more complex sounds are introduced into the spelling work, they will not be unfamiliar and links between the two can be made.

For the pupils whose difficulties are very severe, the pace of work will of course be slower. It takes an extra amount of time for each small piece of learning to become secure. They may be unable to remember the letter–sound associations. They cannot read whole words. Three-letter words have to be sounded out, but they have difficulty holding the sequence of sounds in memory and consequently they cannot blend them into a word. They cannot learn whole words either. (These children are sometimes better at spelling simple words than reading them. As they know the whole word, they are able to succeed with the task of segmenting the phonemes.) These children need extra reinforcement of learning in the form of daily supervised practice, particularly of letter–sound correspondences and of reading.

Different styles of learning

The third question raises the question of styles of learning. Although most dyslexic learners have difficulties with phonology, most of them do have an underlying aptitude for phonic work. (This can be seen in their many resourceful efforts at spelling.) With a multisensory approach and systematic help, most of them learn to improve their skills.

For children who have extreme difficulty with phonology and the auditory modality, so that perception of the constituent sounds of a word is difficult, an approach that channels learning through visual routes instead of a concentration on sound patterns will be needed. The visual and kinaesthetic pattern of the whole word, or successive parts of it, should be emphasised and linked to the pronounced sound of the whole word. Teaching will need to focus on larger units, such as sylla-

bles, on principles of word building, on visual spelling patterns, use of onset and rime, and much learning by multisensory tracing and visualising of individual syllables and whole words (Note 2.3, page 253). These children will need to learn more by memorising, because they are not able to utilize a phonic word-building strategy; they will probably need many repetitions to achieve long-term learning.

Even so, they still have to learn a method of writing and reading words that have never been taught or even seen. The visual presentation should still be linked to pronunciation; the pupil should be taught to generalise the visual patterns to other words that sound alike – even nonsense words – which will help to encourage them to link the words to their sound. Oral work should always be linked to kinaesthetic and visual modalities with letters, cards and drawings. Making words in clay can help to 'fix' the image of a word and link it to meaning. Words with low imageablility will need extra practice. The majority of the hundred most frequently used words fall into this category (Note 2.4, page 253). Work should still proceed in small steps through a spelling programme, but it will need to be structured more by letter patterns than by spelling-to-sound regularity.

Onset and rime

All pupils – including the 'visual learners' – will benefit from practice at building and reading words from onset and rime, which makes larger segments within the syllable (*b-at, cl-ock, d-amp*). In this method, the rime is introduced and taught as a sound unit alongside the single initial consonants, and the pupil practises making words that follow the pattern and reading them. (This is one of the approaches used in Literacy Hour work.)

A programme such as Phonological Awareness Training (PAT) would be particularly helpful for these children. This is designed for groups of children but it could also be used to follow up individual work, possibly in class time. The worksheets present carefully structured exercises in word making, using onset and rime, and pupils work by finding analogies. A set of target rimes is given along with the alphabet and selected onsets – consonant blends and digraphs. Children must make as many words as possible using the given word parts. It is suggested that they have 10 minutes word-making practice using the same set of sounds on three consecutive days. On day 4 a set of 20 words is given for reading and spelling, with five short dictated sentences on day 5. This kind of work is effective because it builds in plenty of repetition and it relies on the child to discover his own words. It links reading to spelling, puts the words into context and works within a limited spectrum of sounds at any one time. The first stage (preliminary) uses single sounds and letters, and the programme goes on through three other stages to syllable division and use of suffixes and prefixes (Note 2.5, page 253).

Making a record of the work: the phonic dictionary

The compilation of a record of all the work in the form of a 'phonic dictionary' is a core element in the *Bangor Dyslexia Teaching System* and it could usefully be adopted by teachers working with other programmes.

Pupils need a thick exercise book – preferably with hard covers for durability. In this book they keep a detailed account of all the structured work that they do with their specialist teacher. It is both a cumulative record that goes right through the course of the teaching and a reference book. Although called a 'dictionary', it is not arranged in alphabetical order. Essentially it is a book of word lists that are a record of each bit of phonic work as it is done. The pupil has a reminder of the spellings that he has learned; the teacher can refer back to remind him or to revise a point. It is best to keep the word lists short – they are examples of spelling, and of sound–spelling word groups, not attempts to write every word that the pupil can think of. When another example, or a related word, comes up in a later lesson, it can be put into the right list as a reminder of the spelling. The pupil should take charge of the dictionary and be encouraged to use it for his own reference. Other teachers and parents will be able to see what point he has reached in the work and therefore what he can be expected to know. (Only work done by the 'dyslexia' teacher is entered – it is not for phonic work done with anyone else.) Although it is best kept free of practice sentences and lesson work, the pupil can illustrate and decorate the pages with helpful drawings, mnemonic phrases, etc. In this way it becomes his own book, with its owner's identity.

The first couple of pages must be kept for a list of the contents (number the pages!), introductory work such as the alphabet, and essential terms such as vowel, consonant and syllable. Other terms should be entered as they are taught. The back pages might be used for words that the pupil needs or wants to learn, outside the sequence of the phonic work. The teacher must decide how the word lists are to be grouped although some general principles can be followed, e.g. spelling 'topics' such as 'consonant blends' can be shown together on one page. It is useful to put together on one page (or on a double-page spread) spelling patterns that exemplify major principles, such as short-vowel words (*cat*, *pet*, *pin*, *rod*, *mug*) and long-vowel -*e* words (*name*, *time*, *home*, *tune*). It is better to keep the different vowel digraphs apart, because they vary much more and they have to be remembered as individual spelling groups. The arrangement of the work is bound to vary at different stages and this is discussed further in Chapter 6.

The following guidelines should be followed:

1. Entries in the phonic dictionary must be correct.
2. Do not use it for giving tests.
3. When words are entered they should be written to dictation, not copied, although a cue card could be provided for the less confident child; practising the words before entering them should ensure success.
4. Words should be set out clearly with plenty of room.
5. The pupil will usually write the words in his dictionary himself.

Occasionally there might be exceptions to this last point. If the child's handwriting is very poor, with badly formed or uneven letters, it may be better for him to write word lists in a separate lesson-work book; he can dictate them afterwards for the teacher to write in his dictionary, and add some more words himself later. This is preferable to illegible and messy pages. As work will be going on to remediate the handwriting, this stage will probably not be prolonged. In cases of extreme difficulty, use of a word processor might get round the problem.

I make a practice of using only the right-hand pages for the lists when first entering a new point. The left page is then available for later additions or a related point, or for drawings, example sentences or mnemonics.

Generally, the time to begin compiling the dictionary will be when a pupil is able to write some three-letter words with short vowel sounds without undue difficulty. The first pages contain lists of these words, written in columns down the page (see the example on page 66). Until he is used to the method, and can identify the vowel sound reliably, the child should indicate the correct vowel column for each word before writing it, because this makes sure that he gets everything right. It also helps to ensure careful listening.

Chapter 3

Testing and monitoring work

When teaching starts, tests and checks should be carried out to find out what a pupil knows, what he is uncertain about and his general level of attainment. After that, monitoring of learning will be on-going while teaching continues, and at longer intervals some of the standardised tests should be given again as a more formal check on progress.

This chapter gives a brief account of the testing process for practical teaching purposes and discusses the way that work is monitored.

It also looks at screening tests that are used by teachers to look at children who have not been assessed as being dyslexic, but who they suspect might be within that group. A note on these tests is provided at the end of the chapter. Some of these, such as the *Phonological Assessment Battery* (PhAB), may also be useful for testing phonological skills before teaching is started.

A selection of tests and further references is listed in Appendix II.

Giving tests

By giving standardised tests and making informal diagnostic observations the teacher should be able to:

- establish a baseline against which progress can be measured;
- collect information about difficulties and skills so that an individual programme of work can be planned.

After about a year, the baseline (standardised) tests should be repeated. This will show whether there has been 'real' improvement, i.e. how much the gap between attainment and chronological age has narrowed. Standardised tests should not be repeated frequently; the gap between two administrations of the same test should not be less than 6 months. It is best to use tests that have alternative forms so that the pupil is not asked to read or spell the same words on a re-test.

Criterion-referenced tests will be used for regular monitoring to check on the pupil's understanding and learning, and whether it is being transferred to wider use in the classroom. These tests will be closely related to whatever has been taught, and to whatever targets have been set. The need for revision or re-teaching can be seen and the programme can be adjusted accordingly. In this respect criterion-referenced tests are quite unlike standardised tests; a teaching programme must not reflect the detailed content of a standardised test.

Tests at start of teaching should include some or all of the areas listed in Figure 3.1, depending on the pupil's level.

Finding a baseline

If the pupil has been seen recently by an educational psychologist or advisory teacher, some assessment or testing may have been carried out and scores for reading and spelling may be available that could be used as a baseline. Even so, scores give little information other than how the pupil's skills compare with those of others of the same age. They may even be misleading because only correct answers are counted; they give little indication about how the pupil tackles reading and spelling tasks and give no credit for 'near misses'. (If a report is available it should give information of this kind.)

Class teachers will be able to provide the pupil's level on different attainment targets of the National Curriculum but, again, this will not give sufficiently detailed information about skills. As soon as possible after meeting the child, therefore, the teacher will want to make her own investigation of what he can do.

Actual testing should be kept to a minimum: much of the diagnostic work can be done by

- Alphabet knowledge:
  alphabet order
  vowels and consonants
  letter sounds and names

- Writing of letters, lower case and capitals

- Phonological awareness:
  initial letter, final letter, medial vowel –
  and more detailed tests as needed

- Appreciation of rhyme

- Phonic knowledge:
  letter-to-sound and sound-to-letter
  correspondences
  letter name-to-sound correspondences

- Reading:
  single-word reading; continuous reading,
  including comprehension

- Spelling

- Free writing – spelling, use of punctuation,
  grammar

- Handwriting:
  letter formation – lower case and capital
  letters, relative letter size in printed and
  joined writing, position on the line, spacing

- Copying skills – handwriting and spelling

Figure 3.1 Baseline information: what do we need to find out?

informal observation during the first few lessons. Some systematic investigation will be needed, however, and there are a number of ways in which this can be carried out. It is necessary to keep in mind what can be shown by the various procedures.

Giving tests (see Figure 3.2)

Testing should be carried out individually by the teacher who will give the tuition. She should observe closely and note the way the pupil responds to both reading and spelling tasks. Every attempt can show the way that skills are developing and is therefore important for teaching. For instance, was a word read correctly on first attempt; how was it read – instantly, studied, decoded/blended or guessed? All incorrect answers should be written down as closely as possible to what was said.

This is valuable information for planning the teaching programme, and it can be used for comparison when the test is given again. Marking by ticks and crosses alone has limited value.

Standardised tests: working out the score

As well as testing to establish a baseline, it is useful to know how pupils compare with others of the same age. This can also give a rough guide to the amount of ground that must be covered to bring their reading and spelling up to levels that will meet the demands of classwork. For this purpose, norm-referenced, or standardised, tests must be used. Tests with up-to-date norms should be used although older tests can be useful for diagnostic purposes. Wherever possible it is preferable to use tests designed for individual administration.

Reading tests are available in different formats: single-word reading (word recognition); sentence reading; sentence completion (cloze); passage or continuous reading (reading analysis).

Scores can be shown in different ways which give different kinds of information. When working out a score, it is important to know which way will be most useful for a particular purpose, e.g. if the aim of giving a test is to find a suitable reading

---

- Explain:
  that you will be giving a test and how you will proceed; that the words will get harder as you go along; what you want the pupil to do
- Tell the pupil that you will not be saying right/wrong or giving any help – unless helping is permitted by the test instructions, in which case tell him what kind of help you will give
- Reassure and encourage but give no cues
- Use crossed ticks, or diagonal lines instead

of crosses for errors if the pupil can see the marking sheet, so it is not discouraging, but try to keep your record out of sight
- If the pupil is uncertain, or offers two versions, encourage him to make up his mind ('Which do you think it is? OK then.') but do not help
- Stop testing after 10 consecutive mistakes. Make an encouraging remark (well done, that was great) so the pupil doesn't think he has failed

Figure 3.2 Procedure for giving tests.

book, a reading age score will be more helpful than a raw score. If a comparison with other children in the group is needed, the standardised score will be the most helpful. The different kinds of scoring are shown in Figure 3.3.

Standardised reading tests

The conditions under which a test is given vary from one test to another, according to what kind of test it is, e.g. in single-word reading tests no help must be given, but in some passage reading tests (e.g. *Neale Analysis*) the teacher gives words that are not known and corrects mistakes. Instructions are always provided in the teacher's manual. It is important that these are read and followed exactly, so that the tests are given under the same conditions for everyone.

Single-word reading tests

These tests can give an indication of words that the pupil knows, and of his proficiency in decoding and word attack. As words are selected by frequency of use by individuals in each age band of the test, they will not be a systematic test of phonic knowledge.

In some word-recognition tests, the child has to match a word pronounced by the tester to a printed one, choosing from a number of printed options. This can show what use is being made of phonic cues. This kind of test can be particularly useful for younger pupils.

Sentence reading tests

Recognition of words in the context of short sentences may help with reading of individual words.

Scores can be expressed in different ways:

- 'Raw scores' – the actual number of correct responses
- 'Standard scores' – how the raw score compares with those of other children of the same age, expressed as a number in relation to the average for the age group. Average score is usually set at 100.
- 'Reading age/spelling age' – the child's level in relation to others in the age group, but shown in years and months.
- 'Percentile scores' – show where the child's score falls on a scale of 100 (e.g. if the score is at the 12th centile this means that 88 of 100 children in the same age group would gain a better score than he does)

Tables are provided in the teacher's instructions for each test for the conversion of raw scores to other kinds of score

A Reading Age/Spelling Age score shows years and months (up to 12) and the numbers are separated by a dash (e.g. 8–10) not a dot, which is a decimal score, 8.9. To convert a decimal score to a Reading/Spelling Age score the decimal to months ratio must be worked out (e.g. 8.5 = 8 years 6 months/8–6)

Figure 3.3 Different ways of expressing a score.

Sentence completion tests

These tests combine sentence reading and word-recognition tasks with a comprehension task. Sentences are presented with one word missing, to be completed by choice of one word from about five (a cloze task). The first few sentences may have picture cues and there may be 50 sentences altogether. These tests are designed for group administration and in such situations they will be completed silently. In the one-to-one situation, the teacher may prefer to hear the pupil read the sentences aloud, which can give additional insight into the reading skills and into the process of word choice. In some ways, this kind of test is more demanding than single-word reading because the sentence must be read sufficiently correctly to allow correct choice of the missing word. Only the correct target word is scored.

If the pupil has never before done a cloze reading exercise, he may be at a disadvantage unless he has some practice sentences first.

Passage, or continuous reading, tests (reading analysis)

These tests are closer to an actual reading task and can reveal more about a child's reading strategies than other tests. Short passages of increasing difficulty must be read, and questions answered. A number of reading skills can be assessed: accuracy, fluency, use of context and picture cues, and understanding. Scores are calculated for accuracy, speed (fluency) and comprehension.

A full record of the pupil's responses is kept on a prepared form on which the passages for reading are printed. This is later analysed to provide the scores and to indicate the kind of mistakes that were made – a miscue analysis procedure.

If the teacher is not experienced with giving this kind of test, it is advisable also to record the child's reading on tape for checking later.

Phonological awareness and phonological skills

Research studies and clinical observation provide a good deal of evidence that children with dyslexia have difficulties with aspects of phonology. This includes perceiving individual sounds within words, processing of the sounds (e.g. is the individual able to segment sounds within words and manipulate sounds orally?) and recognising similarities and differences (Note 3.1, page 253). As the phonological difficulty is partly a delay in development, a teacher might expect that pupils who are late being referred for help would have caught up, whereas the younger pupils would need more help in these areas. But all these phonemic and phonological skills, although necessary for literacy development, are themselves developed by reading and writing activities. Older pupils with reading difficulties will not therefore automatically make up for a late start.

It seems that the order of developing phonological awareness is as follows: first, segmentation at the syllable level, followed by initial letter, then onset and rime (*b/ed*; *spr/ing*) and, last, final letter and medial vowel sound. The teacher looking for evidence of ability to segment should present test items in the same order.

Valuable information about a pupil's perception of speech sounds and syllables can be obtained from free writing and from the child's spoken language even before specific tests are given. Particular mispronunciations, poor articulation (*th/v/f* is the most obvious), or particular spelling mistakes (e.g.

omission of '*n*' in '*nt*' words) should lead the teacher to check phonological skills more systematically and could indicate wider difficulties of development.

One of the published standardised tests could be used, such as the *Phonological Assessment Battery*, and this would be advisable if a child has a noticeable difficulty (see Appendix II, page 231). If an informal check is made it should include some or all of the tasks shown in Figure 3.4 as well as the tests of basic phonemic skills as shown in Figure 3.1.

These tasks are all quite difficult – especially the final, 'Spoonerism' task – and the teacher must make sure that the pupil understands what is expected. If a test is being given that will be scored, some practice tasks must be given with each item before scoring starts.

If the teacher is not familiar with particular test materials, or experienced in the procedures, it might be best to refer the pupil to a specialist teacher or to a speech and language therapist.

Non-standardised and informal reading tests

These look in detail at areas of competence; they are particularly relevant when a pupil is first referred for help. Although standardised tests can be found, many teachers follow their own informal procedures.

Phonic knowledge for reading and spelling

Systematic tests of phonic knowledge provide important information about knowledge of letter sounds, vowel digraphs and other letter clusters, and can include whatever aspect of phonic knowledge the teacher wishes to check. So beginner pupils might be asked to read (and spell) regular words of a consonant–vowel–consonant (*cvc*) pattern; those with a higher score on a reading test might be tested on vowel digraphs. For the latter group, this kind of test can be done as a revision exercise. The first couple of pages of the phonic

---

- Individual sounds: the pupil should be asked to listen carefully to pairs of words pronounced by the teacher, and to say whether or not these are the same. The word pairs chosen should differ by a significant sound: voiced and unvoiced consonants (*d*/*t*, *c*/*g*, *b*/*p*, *th*/*v*/*f*), medial 'n' sounds (*bag*/*bang*; *sad*/*sand*), *m*/*n* differences, etc.
- Segmentation of initial and final consonants
- Rhyming words: it is important to check first that the child understands what is meant by 'rhyme'. The ability to make and identify rhymes can be checked in many ways: completion of a known nursery rhyme, providing a rhyming word, rhyming games. Same–

different (*dad*/*mad*; *man*/*map*) and odd-one-out exercises (*pig*/*big*/*bin*; *pat*/*hot*/*rat*) can be given to check rhyme identification. Success with the odd-one-out kind of test may also depend on the child's ability to remember and recall the three words presented. If the teacher suspects that the real problem may be one of memory, the child should be given picture cards to sort into rhyming sets
- Ability to segment syllables and to transpose them (*cowboy* → *boycow*); ability to delete single sounds in initial position (*sand* → (*s*)*and*) or sounds embedded in the word (*sting* *s*(*t*)*ing*); and to transpose initial sounds of words (*fast car* → *cast far*)

Figure 3.4 Further tests for difficulties with phonological segmentation tasks.

dictionary can be compiled at the same time to provide the basis for the spelling system (see Chapter 6, page 75).

A test of phonic knowledge can be constructed by the teacher, using a checklist as a guide. A pack of alphabet cards, and a set of letters laid out in alphabet order, are needed. Letter clusters and words can be presented on prepared cards. It can be convenient to record responses on a prepared checklist, but then the cards should be presented in the same order as the marking sheet.

If the pupil has little reading skill it is preferable to test knowledge of letter sounds and names separately; those with some reading proficiency might be expected to cope with sound and name of letters together. Particular attention should be given to the short sound of the vowels.

It is most productive if a systematic routine is followed:

Teacher	Pupil
shows letter ------>	gives sound (and a keyword if possible) (and name)
says sound ------>	identifies letter from alphabet or letter-box
says sound ------>	(gives name and) writes letter
says name ------>	gives sound and writes letter (and capital letter)

(These correspondences are sometimes referred to as Linkages. Early work in the phonic multisensory teaching system aims to establish them to an automatic level – see Chapter 4.)

Such a detailed set of phonic points may take some time to administer and can be spread across two or three lessons. The teacher must judge how much is to be tested, possibly guided by how the pupil responds on a reading and spelling test. Similar information can of course be gleaned less formally from the pupil's reading and writing work, but this method runs the risk that areas of uncertainty or lack of knowledge are not picked up.

Many children will be able to make more correct responses in giving sounds for letters and reading words than in writing letters for sounds.

High-frequency word knowledge

A list of high-frequency words can be used to gain information about the pupil's knowledge of essential sight vocabulary. The National Literacy Strategy list for Years 1 and 2 would provide this (see Appendix V), or alternatively the Dolch list of basic sight words.

Reading 'miscues' test

An informal diagnosis of reading skills can be carried out by making a 'running reading record' sometimes known as an Informal Reading Inventory (IRI). This is similar to the standardised Reading Analysis Test (Neale) but is made by the teacher from the pupil's own reading book or one at a similar level. Applying a 'miscue analysis' routine will show how many words he reads without errors, the kind of errors he makes, the way he responds to the text, and how he sets about the reading task. Overall it will indicate whether a book is at the right level and show what kind of work is needed. For a brief account of this procedure, see page 27.

Spelling tests

Standardised tests

As with reading tests, these will enable a baseline score to be set and a comparison to be made with other children of the same age. The pupil is usually required to write single words, which the teacher dictates and puts into a sentence to make the meaning clear. The first words are usually simple regular words but, after the 7-year level, irregular words and high-frequency words are included which often have tricky spellings. They are not therefore a systematic check on what a pupil knows or on his phonic knowledge.

Errors can tell us about a child's knowledge of letter–sound correspondence and the kind of spelling strategies he uses – whether phonic (cueing to the sounds) or trying to remember the letters (what is often called visual strategy). Performance on a standardised test may also indicate the disparity between the child's skill level and what will be expected of his age group in the classroom.

Careful analysis of the mistakes is needed because the reason for a particular response may not be all it seems, e.g. what appears to be lack of knowledge, failure to recall a pattern or even an apparently bizarre spelling may in fact point to weaknesses of auditory processing. This is all valuable information for planning the work.

(In the National Curriculum Standard Assessment Tests [SATs] the words to be written are dictated within a story and are taken from word groups and spelling patterns that form part of the NC programmes of study for the Key Stage.)

Non-standardised and informal diagnosis of spelling difficulties

The tests of phonic skills described under reading (above) will be informative about spelling too, and the responses can be analysed to make a list of 'knowns' and 'unknowns'. This will be used in programme planning.

Free writing

When a pupil is referred for help he should be asked to produce a piece of writing as part of the diagnostic testing process – taking 10 to 15 minutes, preferably during an individual lesson. A topic should be suggested, something on which he will have plenty to say, or a picture can be provided as stimulus – anything to get him going. The teacher should watch, unobtrusively, how he sets about the task. If he gets stuck after only a few minutes, he should be encouraged to write a bit more – given a prompt, perhaps, or being asked a couple of questions to suggest ideas.

Careful analysis of free writing can help to show what a pupil can do, and what strategies he uses, as well as where he is uncertain or lacks knowledge. As it contains the child's own selection of words, it can also indicate where he feels secure. It will also show much more than formal word-spelling tests. It will show how the pupil copes with the complex demands of writing – generation of ideas, their expression in written language, spelling, punctuation and handwriting. Scanty writing might suggest an inability to organise thoughts and ideas, but fear of making mistakes could equally restrict a child's willingness to write.

However, free writing itself has limitations for diagnosis: the child is in control of the content and therefore of the range of words. He may not use some words that he can spell because he does not need them, and he might avoid others for fear of getting them wrong.

Some pupils can spell words correctly in a test which they then misspell in free writing: in the test situation they do not have to give attention to ideas and continuous expression.

> When I write, I can write; when I spell I can spell. But I can't do both together.
>
> *Comment by 12-year-old dyslexic girl*

Categorising errors of spelling

It is sometimes difficult to establish why a particular error has been made.

Hasty judgements about 'auditory' or 'visual' mistakes should be avoided and a closer look taken. The link between hearing and pronunciation should also be kept in mind when considering the reasons for mistakes.

Suggestions about how mistakes in spelling can be analysed are shown in Figure 3.5 and this might be a starting point. These are not infallible and it is possible for an error to fit into more than one category. The phrase 'phonetic' or 'phonic mistakes' can also be misleading. Mistakes based on the child's phonic understanding, i.e. a reasonable attempt to spell the word as he hears it, can lead to an absolute error, namely a non-English spelling or a word that looks bizarre, or to a logical phonic alternative (a reasonable transcription).

Summary of tests needed

In most circumstances, a minimum of preliminary testing will be enough to establish the level of attainment, and to check on areas of knowledge and uncertainty. It should normally include:

1. Standardised tests of reading and spelling.
2. A systematic check on basic knowledge of letters, sounds and their correspondences using alphabet letters or a pack of phonic flashcards.
3. Knowledge of the alphabet.
4. A check on high-frequency words.
5. A test of knowledge of written letter forms; ask the pupil to write each letter in turn, including capital letters.
6. A piece of free writing.

Checking other factors

A number of features could lead a teacher to suspect difficulties with visuo-spatial organisation and hand–eye coordination. These include poor spacing of work on the page, wrong orientation of letters, persistent faulty letter formation, very untidy or illegible handwriting, poor word-spacing or generally poor presentation of work.

Tasks of matching or copying, of picture completion by joining dots or of tracing can be given to check on these difficulties. The teacher should watch the pupil carefully while the tasks are carried out. If the same kind of exercise is given several times, improvement or lack of it could suggest whether the difficulty comes from lack of practice or from a sensory weakness.

If the suspicion of a weakness is further strengthened by these informal exercises, the

- Phonic:
  - i   *brane, dauter*: reasonable attempts; doesn't know/remember the *ai* spelling or the *aught* words
  - ii *rm* for *arm*, *bak* for *back*, *becos*: unacceptable phonic alternatives
  - iii *liv, rid* for ride, *liveing, stoped*; unacceptable phonic alternatives/doesn't know spelling rules
- Vowel errors:
  (phonic): *led* for *lid* – auditory perception or lacks knowledge of sound–letter correspondence; *thay* for *they*, *bruther* – lacks knowledge
- Letter order mistakes:
  felt for *left*, *gril* for *girl* – sometimes called 'reversals'. This term should be used only for actual 'reversals', i.e. where the letter form is written back-to-front as in *b/d* or the whole word is reversed, e.g. *saw/was*. Calling all incorrect letter-order mistakes 'reversals' can lead to misunderstanding about what is going on
- Letter–form errors:
  b/d; *p/b* either a confusion between the letters or a mishearing of the sound; *u/n*; *m/w*: uncertainly about the orientation
- 'visual' errors:
  ligth, thouhgt, buisness, hoilday, tounge, thier;
- mistake based on faulty recall of a pattern, possibly from attempts to learn by 'visual memorising'
- Consonant errors:
  nise, danse, dolfin – lacks knowledge of *soft c, ph*
- Letter omissions:
  belive, plese, hors – lacks knowledge of vowel spellings and *-se* endings
- *Groud* for *ground*, *sping* for *spring* – poor auditory perception/poor phonemic segmentation skills?
- Confusion between similar words:
  whent – visual confusion; *where/were* and other homophone errors – lack of knowledge
- Grammatical or semantic mistakes: *coverd*; *mined* for *mind*; *practice/-se*
- '*Must of*' for '*must have*', *are* for *our* – based on sound of words
- *Word* for *ward*, and other *o/a* mistakes: may be faulty letter joining
- Incorrect word segmentation: *a cross, some thing*; *ofcorse*
- bizarre and probably unclassifiable: *butleapalas* (*Buckingham Palace*), *cdmd* (unrecognisable)

Figure 3.5 Suggestions for classifying types of spelling error.

pupil should be referred for further investigation by an orthoptist or occupational therapist.

Difficulties with vision may be suspected if the pupil frequently loses his place on the page when reading, makes frequent mistakes of letter order, or habitually crouches over the desk or seems to prefer a head-down, sideways position. Again referral to an orthoptist or clinic for a full test of vision would be indicated.

Print distortion and other discomforts

Some children (and dyslexic students) remark on visual effects that make reading and other close work difficult. They report 'dazzle' or say that print is unclear – it moves around or words merge into each other; overhead light creates glare on the page or 'white rivers' down the page distract them from the text. They may suffer from sore or watery eyes (similar to hay-fever symptoms), dislike fluorescent light, and they may complain of headaches. Certain visual patterns can be disturbing, especially those with repeated, heavy lines close together.

A teacher may also notice some of these symptoms – especially if a child rubs his eyes continually, or shakes his head as though trying to clear his vision – although the child himself does not complain. These signs, or reports from the individual, should be taken seriously.

The child's parents should be advised to refer him to their doctor, and to ask for a detailed examination by an orthoptist and a check for Meares–Irlen syndrome (sometimes called 'scotopic sensitivity'). If this is suspected, a visit to an optometrist who specialises in this kind of diagnostic examination may be advisable.

Meanwhile using a pastel shade paper may help with writing and a coloured overlay with reading. Eventually, tinted glasses may be prescribed (Note 3.2, page 253).

Using the information

When the tests are complete, and all the scores and information are gathered together, what should be done with it all? The chief purpose of testing is to draw up, or modify and develop, a programme of work, its general aims and particular objectives; the teacher must decide where to start and what the sequence of work, or next work, should be.

Careful analysis of the samples – tests, free writing and reading records – will show errors but certainties are also important. It is convenient to make a list of all misspelt words – with a space alongside to note the kind of error. These can be grouped together and it may be possible to see how the different kinds of difficulty compare, or

whether one predominates. The secure points should be ticked off on a checklist.

Many teaching programmes for dyslexic learners specify in detail what must be taught, and in what order – but every pupil is an individual with particular needs. How can these factors be reconciled? It is fairly safe to assume that the pupil is secure with words read and spelt correctly up to a half-year level below his score on the tests and it might be tempting to start there, or even at the point that mistakes begin. A better option is for all pupils to start building their phonic dictionary from the very first pages to establish basic knowledge about the English spelling system. For a pupil with some spelling ability the first few pages can be gone through quickly, as a focus for revision or to enable the teacher to explain how the written language system works. After that there is a general course to follow, but the details can be adjusted according to what is needed. The essential factor is that a structure is established, work follows a carefully arranged sequence and nothing is omitted.

These points are dealt with in detail in Chapters 4 and 6.

Monitoring work

Spelling and written work

During the course of teaching regular checks will be made to monitor how the pupil is learning. These should be closely related to the child's programme. Every lesson should include a test of the previous lesson's work to make sure that it has not been forgotten or misunderstood. Progress through the programme is itself therefore a kind of monitoring.

Work from previous lessons also needs to be kept under review for a time. This can be done by a cumulative list of words that are tested at intervals, perhaps by being included in dictated sentences.

Criterion-referenced testing

If more formal, systematic monitoring is needed, lists of words for criterion-referenced tests can be drawn from the programme of work. Teachers can construct their own lists of words. These can include phonically regular words, basic rules (e.g. adding 's' and 'es' for plurals) and common irregular words. Progress can then be seen as the pupil works through the lists.

Obviously there is a difference between being able to spell words that are presented one by one in a list, and being able to get the same words right in written work, when content and expression of thoughts compete for attention. So performance criteria should also include spelling words in dictated sentences and in sentences of their own making.

Automatic or effortless spelling is essential if written work is to be fluent. To promote this automatic response, teachers might consider timed tasks, as used in precision teaching, in their regular monitoring procedures. The target might be for a number of words from a selected group to be written in a given time – with the time being reduced over perhaps three repetitions. Alternatively, a number of words (perhaps five) can be chosen, each to be written four times in random order, again in a specified time. (This can be an aid to learning as well as a test.)

Samples of free writing

Free writing can show how the spelling work is being assimilated and used, and it is useful for pieces to be collected regularly for detailed inspection. Examples from classwork and course books can also be used to monitor the way in which learning is being generalised to wider contexts. Different methods might need to be tried, perhaps in response to new insights into the pupil's learning needs. It is useful to look at the pattern of mistakes that the pupil makes in written work, to see where previous work is half-remembered, to identify particular or persistent difficulties (including handwriting problems) and also to note what he gets right.

The next steps in the teaching programme can be planned, or adjusted, according to what the written work shows.

Reading

Criterion-referenced tests

Precision tests of the kind described under 'Spelling' (above) can also be used to check specific areas of reading such as recognition of common irregular words, or even syllables. Words might be drawn from a cumulative list. Speeding up the response would be an important target.

Listening to reading: making a running reading record

Teachers monitor their pupils' progress regularly when they hear them read and errors can be noted down quickly. However, it is useful to take a more detailed look from time to time by a making a 'miscue analysis' record. The test is set up by selecting a passage of 100 to 150 words from the pupil's current book, or from a text at the same level. This is copied on to a page with plenty of space so that it can be marked; every word and letter that is read differently from the text is recorded there. (On the first occasions of carrying out such a test, it is useful also to make a recording on tape for subsequent checking.)

There are specific points to look for when examining the record.

1. Identify the type of 'miscue'
- Omission or insertion?
- Graphophonic mistake? (e.g. letter error, letter-order error, total misreading)
- Word not attempted?

Separate those that affect the meaning from those that do not.

2. Word recognition
- What proportion of words are read at sight?
- Are some kinds of word recognised less often than others?

3. Word attack strategy. What use is made of:
- phonic cues
- recognition of syllables
- blending of words
- context
- grammatical knowledge?
  Adjusting verb tenses and plurals to fit other mistakes would indicate that reliable strategies are being used even if they do not always produce the correct word.

4. Does he make use of/observe punctuation? If not, does this reflect lack of understanding?

These observations will suggest the kind of reading strategies that the pupil is using. It should

be possible to estimate how close to the meaning of the passage the reading has come.

Reading behaviour should also be noted.

5. Fluency
- How many hesitations and repetitions are made? These are not necessarily a negative sign; they may indicate care, or a need to take some extra time.
- Is it held up by word recognition problems?
- Does it show comprehension?
- Does he try to read with natural expression?

6. Speed
- How much time is taken to read the whole passage?

Very slow reading may affect comprehension.

7. Comprehension
- Can he retell the story or the information?
- Can he answer simple questions about the passage?
- Does he put information together to make deductions?
- Is he able to make a sensible guess at what happens next or give an opinion about what he has read?
- How well did he engage with the text – did he seem interested?

This information can help to show areas where specific help or practice is needed.

It is also a guide to whether the reading book is at the right level for teaching and developing reading competence. If the child makes almost no errors, and his comprehension is good, this indicates that the pupil should be able to read this particular book without help, i.e. independently. It will help to consolidate the present level of skills but, for teaching, a slightly harder book is needed. This should produce, on the same kind of scrutiny, about 5 per cent error in word recognition and 75 per cent correct answers to questions asked about the passage. If, overall the frequency of error is greater than 10 per cent, an easier book is needed. This is 'frustration level' and the pupil will not gain anything, even if he is obliging and willing to struggle on (Note 3.3, page 254).

Estimating progress

More formal tests: re-running the baseline tests

The original standardised tests, or other versions of them, should be given annually and certainly not more frequently than twice yearly. Comparisons can then be made and progress charted.

Scores alone cannot tell the whole story about a pupil's progress. There will nearly always be progress that cannot be counted: an incorrect answer can still reveal that the pupil makes a better attempt at a word than on the previous occasion, e.g. he might write 'fittid' for 'fitid', or 'brane' for 'bran', in each case producing a spelling that is a possible phonic alternative. For the same reason, the recording of actual responses in a word-recognition reading test is most important.

Confidence is another factor that cannot be measured easily. A child may be more ready to attempt words – even completely unknown words – after a period of teaching and this is hugely important. The number of words attempted can be

revealing: children who, on the first test, would not risk making mistakes, or who perhaps did not have a clue about tackling unfamiliar words, might still make errors, but the change in attitude can be a significant mark of progress. Noting the time taken over the tests can also provide useful information about immediacy of responses.

So when teachers report the results of tests, they should always comment on how the pupil coped with the task, not merely record the scores.

Understanding the learning process

It is important that the teacher should help the pupil to make explicit for himself any successful strategies that he is using, or conversely to identify why he is not being successful. Older pupils especially should be helped to explore the methods that work best for them.

Samples of writing and criterion-referenced tests can be used positively and can help to raise a pupil's self-esteem and self-confidence. Comments about work should be fed back to the pupil with due praise for successes (however small) and encouragement to keep on trying.

Other kinds of tests

This chapter has been concerned mainly with finding the pupil's level of skills in reading and spelling. Test material of a wider kind may be needed if a teacher wants to look for the underlying causes of a child's difficulties. There are a number of tests which look for points of difficulty that are characteristic of dyslexia: phonological discrimination and segmentation tasks; phonic blending, including non-words; facility with naming and word retrieval; 'working memory' tasks, such as remembering shapes, sequences of movement and numbers (digit span tests); and knowledge of letters and sounds. (These are screening tests that indicate the possibility of dyslexia, but they should not be taken as giving a firm diagnosis. Positive indications would suggest the need for a referral to an educational psychologist.)

Dyslexia screening tests

Dyslexia Early Screening Test – for children aged 4;5 to 6;5 years (DEST)

Dyslexia Screening Test – for children aged 6;5 to 14 years (DST)

Dyslexia Adult Screening Test – for individuals over 15 years (DAST)

The tests consist of 10 or 11 items and look at phonological skills, access to words, rapid naming, word reading, spelling and copying, digit span, reading nonsense words in a short passage, bead threading and postural stability. The items in the DEST include tests of letter naming, order of sound, phonological discrimination, rhyme detection and first letter sound, and shape copying. The DAST includes tests of reasoning ability. The results of the tests give an at-risk estimate for dyslexia.

Bangor Dyslexia Test

The items on this test look at left/right discrimination, and at various aspects of memory and working memory. It notes difficulties with *b*/*d* and asks whether others in the close family have difficulties of a similar kind.

Aston Index

Items from this test could help to assess different aspects of the child's working memory skills, e.g.

memory for sequences of pictures and shapes. Sound discrimination (same or different) and sound-blending items test phonological skills whereas a copying task tests graphomotor skills. Reading subskills and underlying ability are assessed with a letter-naming task and vocabulary knowledge test. Different subtests are provided for children of different ages in the 5 to 14 age range.

Phonological Assessment Battery (PhAB)

A set of tests which investigate the development of phonological skills – segmentation of sounds, and rhyming – and word-naming speed.

Children's Test of Non-Word Repetition and Graded Non-Word Reading Test

These tests of non-word repetition and non-word reading look at aspects of phonological skill and working memory – both important as indicators of dyslexia as well as essential subskills for literacy. As the words used are nonsense words, the child cannot call directly on his knowledge of vocabulary or sight words to get the answer.

Cognitive ability tests

Logical reasoning tests look at the child's thinking skills in verbal and non-verbal reasoning contexts. Vocabulary knowledge gives an indication of a child's verbal intellectual ability.

As dyslexic children can be disadvantaged by their poor reading skills, it is especially important that they are given non-verbal reasoning tests. The test formats may, however, present difficulties. The test items are often diagrams which might themselves be confusing, and the response form may be set out in a grid with very small 'boxes' to be ticked.

These can both create problems for a dyslexic learner, especially one with poor visuo-spatial skills, Meares–Irlen syndrome or poor motor skills, particularly if the test is timed. Any of these factors could affect the score.

NFER Cognitive Abilities Test, Cognitive Abilities Test (CAT) and Ravens Matrices

These tests are all non-verbal reasoning tests of the above kind.

The Cognitive Profiling System (CoPS) (5 to 8 age group) and the Lucid Assessment System for Schools (LASS) (11 to 15 age group)

These are computer-administered tests designed to assess the cognitive abilities that are needed for literacy learning. They concentrate on phonological awareness, memory and auditory discrimination, which are also important indicators of dyslexia. The tests are presented in the form of games. As all the responses are made via the computer, the difficulties of some paper tests are avoided.

The tester would need to check that the child is competent with the mouse.

Vocabulary tests

It is important to note what kind of language skill is being tested. Is it understanding of words only (receptive vocabulary) or does it include the ability to explain the meaning of a word by giving a definition or using it in a sentence (expressive vocabulary)? If the second kind of test is given, the score may be affected by a child's difficulties with word finding and his ability to give clear explanations, which does not mean that he does not understand the target word.

A vocabulary test that depends on the child's ability to read is (obviously) not suitable for dyslexic learners unless the tester is permitted to read it aloud. (Test instructions must not be ignored because this affects the reliability of the scoring.) It should also be remembered that the extent of a child's vocabulary knowledge may depend on the kind of word-learning opportunities that he has had, e.g. his reading ability or his home environment.

British Picture Vocabulary Test

This test requires the pupil to select the most appropriate picture to match a word pronounced by the tester. No reading is included, and no verbal response is expected from the child.

The Mill Hill and Crichton Vocabulary Tests (for older and younger pupils respectively)

These tests have two forms: verbal explanations and a multiple choice format. Both tests may be administered orally so no reading is expected.

Although all these tests can add useful information about a child's knowledge of words and his thinking skills, they should not be taken, on their own, as proving that a child is either 'very able' or 'not very bright'.

Details of all the tests mentioned are given in Appendix II pages 229 et seq.

Chapter 4 Approaches and procedures for teaching

This chapter contains an account of teaching procedures used with dyslexic pupils in the context of the first stages of phonic work. It ends with a brief look at teaching dyslexic children whose first language is not English.

At the early stages, reading and spelling should be complementary activities; in fact, reading at the beginning is best approached through spelling and word building. Pupils are trained explicitly to use their phonological skills first to build, then to read, words, so that reading and spelling proceed together: 'What I write I can read' and vice versa (Note 4.1, page 254).

In later work, the procedures remain the same, although different amounts of detail will be appropriate according to the stage that pupils have reached. Throughout, success is essential to build up the child's confidence and enable him to take full part in the work.

The pupil's first learning need is to become familiar with single letters and their regular sounds, and to practise these until associations are mastered and response is immediate, automatic and 100 per cent accurate. While this learning is going on – a few letters at a time – simple one-syllable words with short-vowel sounds are built and read, using separate letters or onset and rime segments. The pupil is shown how to (or helped to) arrange the letters in the correct order to make a given word, and then asked to 'read' the word he has just made. The task must be presented in such a way that it is impossible to fail. The next step is to write the words in a list in the phonic dictionary and read them. Finally, the same words are used to make a sentence, which is written then read aloud. The aim is to show the child a reliable method for writing and reading these short words, and to give him confidence to use it. In due course (quite soon in many cases), he can be asked to write words without preparatory building work and to read words that he has not built up first (Figure 4.1).

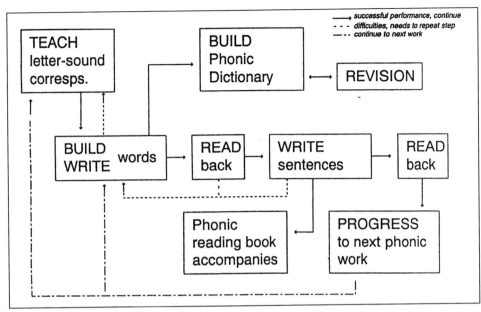

Figure 4.1 Flow diagram: sequence of procedures in teaching.

Teaching the letters and their sounds

The use of keywords

To help the pupil to learn the letters and their sounds, and to aid later recall, each letter is given a keyword. This can be chosen to relate to the letter shape (as in the Letterland system, Note 4.2, page 255), but it should always be a noun that is easy to show by a drawing. It must also be an exact representation of the first sound or combination – not *tree* for *t*, for instance (where the first combination is the blended *tr*). The association of letter–sound to picture–word remains the same while the pupil is learning these correspondences, and naming the keyword is part of the learning procedure. (Sometimes the link between keyword and picture can remain, for letters that have been found difficult to learn, as an important trigger to recall of the letter sound, or the correct letter form.) A pack of flashcards with a letter on one side and picture on the reverse is needed. It is almost impossible to practise the sound–keyword correspondences without such a visual aid.

For the youngest pupils, or others whose basic skills are minimal, I consider it preferable to concentrate on the letter sounds alone at the outset, and leave the letter names till later. Letter names are needed for alphabetic oral spelling and for learning sight words, but for early word building, and teaching blending skills the sounds carry the important information. Introducing the names as well could be confusing and give the pupil too much to remember. Attention can be given to the letter names in the routine for learning the sequence of letters in the alphabet (see pages 41 and 174). Particular attention should be given to the vowel letter names, because these are the long-vowel phonemes (unlike consonant names) and therefore important for reading and spelling. They will need different keywords (/ă/ is for *apple*, but /ā/ is for *acorn*).

Teaching the 'Linkages'

The correspondences between each letter, its sound, its name and its written form are sometimes called the Linkages (Note 4.3, page 255). These should be taught using a multisensory procedure:

1 Sound: show the picture and ask the pupil to give the word for it. Ask for, or help him to identify, the first sound.
2 Letter: show the letter on the reverse. Say the word and letter sound. Ask the pupil to repeat this.
3 Letter form: show how this is made. Discuss the letter shape and the writing movement.

This is particularly important when confusable letters such as *b/d*, *p/q* are introduced, and other forms that a child might reverse, such as *s* and *z*. Use large letters for clarity, printed on card or written in marker on large paper, or on a board. The pupil should then:

- trace the letter with his index finger saying the sound at the same time
- trace over, or write, the letter himself, starting in the right place and working steadily with a smooth movement, again saying the sound.

Repeat these steps as often as necessary for the pupil to remember the sound and the written form, and to recognise the letter when its sound is given.

The first practice of the written form should be large, perhaps on a blackboard, to get maximum arm movement. Later, writing in the air, and writing the letter shape with the eyes closed, enable the child to concentrate on the movement sequence, but at the outset the visual image needs to be part of the learning process.

The letters for finger tracing could be sandpaper or felt covered, to give extra tactile emphasis to the shape. Three-dimensional wooden or plastic letters may be used for feeling the shapes as concrete objects. Many other letter-learning activities can be devised. Children can make letters in Plasticine, identify letters in a 'feely bag', draw in a sand tray, or write with finger paint or in glitter glue, or select letters from ready-made cut-outs to stick on card. The cards can be taken back to the class for further practice, or home for parents to help.

Letter style

The style of the letter is a matter for the teacher's own judgement and the policy of the school. The pupil's age, class level and degree of pen control will contribute to the decision about whether to start with the printed form or to teach a cursive style immediately. It is now usual for joined writing to be introduced very early, but this may be difficult for children who are struggling at the basic letter–sound level. The intermediate stage in which letters end with a hook will be more appropriate for some pupils, e.g. *h*, *d*. For the youngest it may be sensible to teach a form that most resembles the style they meet in the first printed books (but keeping to the simple *a* and *g* styles.) (See Chapter 11 for a further discussion about handwriting.)

The guiding principle should be to avoid anything likely to cause confusion. Whichever form is used, it is important to emphasise that all letter forms except 'd' and 'e' start at the top. (Flashcards with the conventional printed style of a and g should be changed to ɑ and g.)

At the Linkage-learning stage, the letter can be taught in the first place without additions, or as it appears on the card, to establish the form. Joining lines can be added afterwards, in preparation for using the letter in words. Make clear that it is the joining strokes that start from the line and go up, not the letter itself; also that the small hook at the end of the letter is really the start of the join to the next letter. This will help to explain the differences between the appearance of handwritten and printed letters.

Linkages drill with cards

Routine practice of the Linkages with the pack of flashcards is an essential part of every lesson, particularly at the early stages. Letters and letter clusters are added as they are taught. The names of letters can be included as appropriate for the individual pupil.

The Linkages drill, in which the letter–sound associations are rehearsed in three ways, is shown in Figure 4.2. Use just lower case letters at first. Capital letters have very specific uses that can be omitted in the first stages of learnings to reduce memory load – except for the capital letters for the child's name. Some teachers like to start with capitals because they are somewhat easier to form, but we do not use capitals for word making. Recognising and writing capital letters can be added later.

The Linkages drill should aim for speed – as fast as possible without mistakes – to promote immediate response. When the pupil is used to the procedure he can deal the cards for himself in the first drill.

1. The teacher presents the card, letter-side up; the pupil says the letter sound (and name) and gives the keyword
   This is the important link for reading
2. The teacher says the letter sound; the pupil writes the letter (and gives the name)
   This is the important link for spelling
3. The teacher says the letter name; the pupil says the sound and writes the letter
   This is the link for writing words to alphabetic dictation

Figure 4.2 Drill for practising the Linkages.

As the teaching progresses, significant letter–sound combinations are added to the pack: consonant digraphs and blends; blends for assimilation (final blends); vowel digraphs; vowel + r combinations; soft c and g, etc. The aim here is to help the pupil to learn the basic building blocks of words and to respond automatically to each one by reading and writing. For the more complex sounds, such as vowel digraphs, a keyword can be substituted for a picture. For older pupils, this kind of pack can be extended to cover common syllables and affixes.

A ready-made pack (such as the *Alpha to Omega* flashcards) is an invaluable teaching aid, and the pupil should also build a pack for himself as the work goes forward. He may enjoy illustrating the cards and his pack can go back to class or home for practice. The cards may serve also as cue cards whenever word and sentence writing is going on.

Oral/Auditory work

All pupils will benefit from attention to phonemic and phonological skills. Some will need a good deal of saying and listening work while they are learning letters and word building. Many pupils will need practice with oral segmentation and blending of sounds. This can be accompanied by letters to give visual reference to the sound and to strengthen the association between the two.

Counters or some other kind of marker are useful in segmentation work because they give extra emphasis to the individual syllables and sounds; they also help the child to concentrate on the segmentation job without worrying about finding letters. (Letter–sound matching can be a separate activity.) It also helps him to count the number of separate segments identified. Clapping and counting at the same time may be difficult for the younger children, especially if there are also difficulties with number (Note 4.4, page 255). Use a visual method of recording separate syllables and sounds by placing counters for each one. Provide a prepared card, with a picture or diagram for placing the counters (Figure 4.3).

The cards can be drawn as any shape with horizontal segments – caterpillar, train, strings of beads, etc. – or as a picture – a house with windows and door, or a flower; counters can be presented as parts of a picture that are added one by one until they are all used – spots on a ladybird, buttons on a coat. Pupils can practise on their own if given pictures of the words to be studied.

This is not a test, but a method of learning to distinguish individual syllables and sounds and of training segmentation skills. As word patterns with more complex sound clusters are met, they can be practised with diagrams made to correspond to each one. Thus *band* will have a four-box, and *tramp* a five-box, diagram. The exercise should

1. Give the pupil a simple diagram or picture (e.g. a caterpillar) marked into squares/segments to match the number of sounds in the target word and the same number of counters – so no mistake can be made
2. Pronounce the word slowly and carefully, so that each separate sound can be heard
3. The pupil repeats the word, placing a counter in each box to represent each separate sound as he says it
4. Finally, the whole word should be said again in a natural way

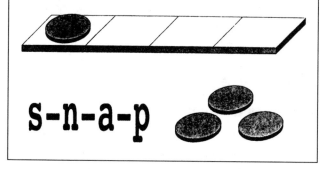

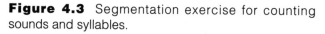

Figure 4.3 Segmentation exercise for counting sounds and syllables.

not be complicated by introducing digraphs, where one sound is represented by two letters, because this brings in spelling knowledge and children may have picked up spellings of /sh/ and /th/ (/ng/ is also a single phoneme). As the skills begin to develop, a random number of counters could be given; later, to emphasise the sequence of vowels and consonants, these could be represented by red and black counters.

This kind of visual representation can be helpful at any stage where extra attention to separate sounds is needed. It can be especially useful if one letter is frequently missed out when a word is written, e.g. a penultimate /n/. Comparison of the diagrams for *sad/sand* helps to emphasise the sound structure.

The amount of oral work needed will vary according to the age of the pupil, and other factors such as his verbal fluency, his capacity for dealing with phonological information, how quick he is to grasp the idea of representing a sound with a symbol, and so on.

Production of speech sounds

If pupils articulate sounds poorly, extra attention should be given to careful listening, and to the way the sounds are produced by mouth movements and by the voice. A mirror is useful to watch tongue and lip position: /f/th; m/n; b/d; s/sh; sh/ch; l/r.

Voiced and unvoiced consonants can be distinguished by sensation: the pupil's hand can be placed on his – or the teacher's – throat to feel the different sensations in, for example, /f/ /v/, /c/ /g/ or in front of the mouth to feel the different amounts of air blown from the lips when sounding /f/ /th/ and /b/ /p/.

Later, the 'under-the-chin' check for syllables can be useful: each distinct syllable produces a slight downward movement, although it is not easy to detect some unstressed syllables such as /le/ in this way.

It is important to make very 'clean' consonant sounds, with no additional /uh/ sound (the linguistic term is 'schwa') and to teach the pupil to do the same. Thus /h/ will be no more than a breath, /m/ a closed-lips hum and /s/ a kind of hiss. The voiced sounds, especially /b/, /d/ and /g/, are impossible to pronounce without a following vowel and need practice to keep a clean sound.

Much can be done through games and word play and suggestions for this kind of work are given in Chapters 5 (page 56) and 14 (page 211). They can be adapted according to the age of the pupil. The sound segmentation exercise (see Figure 4.3) can be helpful for older pupils who have difficulty with the longer-consonant clusters or vowel/consonant order. Older pupils may also need some attention to articulation of phonemes. The routines outlined above can be used, suitably adapted.

Using first letters for building words

Letters should be taught not in alphabetic order, but selected according to usefulness for first word making. Three or four consonants and one vowel should be taught together so that the step to making words can follow immediately: *h, d, t, p, c, n* and short-vowel *a* give a number of possibilities. Whichever letters are chosen it must be possible to make rhyming words. It must also be possible to show how altering the letter order will produce a different word – *pat, tap* – while combining them with others will give further words – *hat, cap*.

The terms 'consonant' and 'vowel' should be used straight away; this makes it possible to talk about the processes of spelling and word attack. Pupils should understand why the vowel is especially significant, and learn the important concept that every syllable needs a vowel. Colour can be used to stress this point: red is often used for the vowels. (This is fitting because the vowels are usually the 'danger-zone' letters for children with reading and spelling difficulties.)

The concept of a short-vowel sound may also be introduced at once, because all the first words will have the *cvc* structure and no irregular words will be included. Pupils often seem to have difficulty deciding whether a vowel phoneme is short or long, but the trouble may be caused by confusion about which label to apply, not with 'hearing' the vowel itself. Learning one label, before 'long vowels' are introduced, can be helpful. The diacritical mark ˘ should also be shown. For pupils coming back to trying to read after some years of failure, these more technical points help to present the basic work in a new, more mature way.

Before the pupil writes words he should first build them with plastic letters or letter tiles. This enables the teacher to apply some important teaching principles:

1. It reduces the task of spelling to small segments – each letter can be found, and placed correctly, before the handwriting task is attempted.
2. The letters can be moved around until the word is correct. The child is thus enabled to be successful from the start – vital for someone who has previously failed – and it will help to build his self-confidence.
3. It is easy to demonstrate how letters can be rearranged to form different words – showing that the details of letters and letter order are important.

A box of letters arranged alphabetically is an essential tool for this work.

In the procedure for word building, the relationship between the sequence of sounds in the spoken word and the letter order in the built word should be emphasised. However, two factors may influence the way that the words are segmented –

the child's age and the instructional practice of the school – and the teacher may decide to vary the details of the procedure. In the Literacy Hour work of Year 1, the focus moves from single phonemes (taught in Reception Year) and onset and rime are introduced. A young pupil who has worked extensively with this intra-syllable approach may be confused if the specialist teacher begins work with the smaller units. For these pupils – probably those in Key Stage 1 – the teacher may want to prepare cards with rimes for the first work. At each step make sure that the pupil listens attentively, repeats the word and says the phonemes or the unit.

However, single phonemes have to be mastered and, for many dyslexic children, a single phoneme approach has its advantages: there are fewer units to learn and not all children are good at making analogies – the basis for the onset and rime approach (Note 4.5, page 255). Onset and rime may have an advantage for reading in that two units make less demand on memory than three or more single phonemes, so that blending is easier.

Whichever model is followed, the procedure will be similar – the child must segment the word, identify the phonemes and find the letters (Figure 4.4).

Many pupils will be able to carry out the first word-building task unaided; some will need to work with the teacher, and a few may need to have the activity modelled for them before they can attempt it. (In the latter case, it might be best to wait until the letter–sound correspondences are more secure before doing much word building.)

After the first word has been built successfully, another word can be made that rhymes with the

---

1. Say the word to be built and ask the pupil to repeat it
2. Identify the first sound, find the right letter, place it in a space on the table
3. Say the rest of the word. Segment the vowel sound and find that
4. Say the whole word again. Separate the last sound; complete the word and read it

OR

2. Identify the onset and rime. Find the right letter for the onset . . .
3. Say the rime. Find the letters (the last letter, then the vowel), complete the word and read it

---

Figure 4.4 Building the first words.

first. This should be placed underneath so that they can be compared easily:

hat

mat

Hearing and appreciating the rhyme is important. It helps to train the pupil to isolate separate sounds in words, and to show him how phonic information can be generalised from one word to another. Development of these key skills should be started in the first lessons by this simple word play. It is more effective if the pupil can be led along by appropriate questions to make discoveries for himself: how many letters have been changed to make *mat*? Does it rhyme? What happens if we change the last letter – does it still rhyme? Children who find it difficult to say words 'in one', without sounding out the letters, can be helped by getting them to read down a list of three or four

rhyming words, i.e. changing just the first consonant sound each time.

The next step is to change the final consonant: *man*, *map* and, after that, to change both ends of the word: *mat*, *pan*, *bag*. How fast you proceed in this depends entirely on how successful the pupil is at each level of the task.

Drawing attention to, and working with, the rhyme in a single-letter approach is not the same as working with the larger rime unit. The procedure can easily be adapted for an onset-rime focus but, if so, a single-letter approach should be introduced as soon as the pupil is able to carry out the more detailed segmentation.

In all this work, attentive listening and repetition of word and phoneme are of the greatest importance. Pupils should form the habit of looking at the teacher while she says the sounds and words, to enhance attention and concentrate fully on the task. Some teachers like to emphasise this with hand gestures that help to hold the eye contact.

Writing words

The preparatory work with separate letters is followed by writing the same words in a list. The pupil should write without copying. Again, the task is approached in stages:

1. Look at the word and read it aloud.
2. Write it saying each sound (or onset and rime) in turn as the letter is written. Cover the word while this is done. (A peep is allowed if needed – let the pupil decide.)

When he is confident with this first task, he can try to write the next rhyming word without building it up or reading it first. In this way, he can be shown that he can write simple words just by listening to the sounds and writing the letters in the order in which he hears them.

In an onset-rime approach the importance of the rime analogy should be stressed. If there is any hint of uncertainty, help should be offered. Mistakes and failure must be avoided, especially in the early lessons. (If the learning steps have been carefully graded, the risk of failure will be minimal anyway.)

Writing sentences

Writing and reading sentences is the last step in the basic teaching sequence whenever new sounds and spellings are introduced. Even at the earliest stages of word building, it should be possible to construct a simple sentence that the pupil can write without help. The words that have just been taught should be used – the pupil should be able to write these; it should not be assumed that any others are known: *the* can be copied from a card (unless there is good reason to think it is known already).

The very first sentences might seem strange, but these phonically regular sentences are an important part of the learning sequence. The point of the exercise is to show the child that he can write these simple words. Using the first few letters taught (*h, d, t, p, c, n, a*) he could write:

- *I can pat the cat.*
- *Dad had a cap and a hat.*
- *The cat had a nap in the hat.*

(Sentences should make sense though! The capital letters and full stops would not justify examples such as '*I can tap*' or '*Dad can pat*'.)

The procedure for sentence writing (shown in Figure 4.5) uses the same kind of routine as the earlier word-building work.

After listening to the sentence, the pupil should always repeat it before beginning to write. This is important for several reasons:

- It encourages attentive listening; there is some memory training. It is surprising how often a detail gets changed, even in a simple sentence.
- It also helps the pupil to internalise the sentence, which is useful for comprehension.

During the writing, the teacher should watch carefully so that mistakes can be stopped before they occur. If a mistake is made, it may be desirable to work on a correction immediately in the early stages. Later it can be left, so that the pupil can learn to check his own work. Pupils who are not very confident may like to build the first sentences with letters before writing.

1. Say the whole sentence while the pupil listens
2. The pupil repeats it exactly
3. Dictate the sentence, grouping the words sensibly
4. The pupil should say each word as he writes it. If he has difficulty, encourage him to say the whole word, listening to the sound, then to say each letter sound as he writes. A capital letter and a full stop must be used
5. When the sentence is finished, the pupil reads it aloud
6. He should look along the words carefully to make sure it is right, or check it against a model

Figure 4.5 Dictating sentences.

The next work

It is best to teach the short vowels in an order that keeps apart the sounds /ĭ/ and /ĕ/ as these are the most easily confused; a, i, o, e, u is convenient for word frequency. y as a vowel is not taught to beginners at this stage. The child should be shown the ˘ mark (breve) that indicates a short vowel, and later the ˉ mark for the long vowel (macron) although the terms need not be used. These give a visual cue about how a vowel should be sounded, which is particularly helpful when the pupil is learning to distinguish short- from long-vowel sounds. These should also be used to mark vowel sounds in the words heading the lists in the phonic dictionary.

Consonant blends and digraphs and, later on, vowel digraphs should be shown together on the flashcards, but can be assembled for spelling from their separate letters. However, it is important that they are pronounced as 'units' and not as separate letters. This is particularly important for the digraphs sh, ch, th, etc. because they produce a new sound unrelated to their component letters. If joined writing is being used, this can help to emphasise their distinctive character.

Letters and sounds that are easily confused should be taught on separate occasions – especially ee and ea and vowel digraphs with long vowel -e counterparts. If there are problems to sort out, such as b/d, it can be helpful to concentrate on one only, noting a distinguishing feature.

The letter d is the only letter with an upright that is to the right of the letter and therefore – unlike b – it does not start at the top. A mnemonic can help ('Start d with the round bit') or point out that it follows c in the alphabet and also starts with a c shape. Multisensory work is essential here.

As the work goes on, each new step is introduced with detailed attention to letters and sounds, and with multisensory tracing. If teachers find that a pupil does not need this minute attention to detail, it can be reduced: it is for the teacher to judge. However, should difficulty arise at any stage, it is good practice to take information down to its smallest elements again, and to put in more multisensory work.

During all the teaching and practice procedures visual aids in the form of cue cards should be used, e.g. the flashcard for a consonant or vowel digraph can be on view as long as the pupil needs it, or a short-vowel card with picture cues when the child is learning to distinguish between these sounds (Figure 4.6). This is especially useful in the first stages of building the phonic dictionary (see Chapter 6, page 66).

Learning the alphabet

The alphabet sequence of 26 letters makes considerable demands on pupils' memories. Plastic or wooden letters are ideal for this work. Sets of upper- and lower-case letters will be needed, but it will be best to select one to begin with and teach or check the correspondences later. If upper-case letters are used, care must be taken that these do not become linked exclusively with the letter names.

From the start, the whole alphabet should be set out in correct order each time, saying the letter names from A to Z, at first with the teacher taking the lead. Gradually the pupil can be helped to remember the order of the letters – a few at a time – until the whole sequence can be repeated independently. A rainbow shape is a convenient format for setting out the alphabet: it fits into a limited space, as well as looking attractive.

Figure 4.6 Short-vowel cue card.

The alphabet routine provides a useful focus for all kinds of letter–sound association work and pupils usually enjoy games for practising alphabet order (see Chapter 12 for suggestions). This kind of activity can help to break up a lesson and give pupils a rest from concentrated phonic work. It is important that a pupil masters the alphabet as early as possible, but it can take up a lot of time in the first few lessons. Teachers must make decisions about priorities, which will be different for every child.

Revision and review

As the pupil works through the short-vowel work and beyond it, adding new information, it is obvious that he has more and more to remember. Revision of previous work must therefore be an on-going part of the procedure. This can take the form of

letter–sound drill with the card pack, setting out the alphabet, and games and exercises. Words from previous lessons can be carried along and included in sentences for dictation. Work should also be reinforced through reading.

If parents are able to help, children should be expected to do some reading at home, along with learning of spelling work through exercises and games. This is especially important if the child has only one lesson a week.

Reading

It is important that the pupil should begin to think of himself as a reader as soon as he can. While he will be gaining practice from reading back what he has written, a published book – with a printed cover and numbered pages – is important for his self-confidence, as well as for the development of his learning. Reading books that use the same kind of vocabulary should accompany the detailed work of constructing words from sounds. The emphasis throughout the early work is on teaching reading and spelling together as two sides of the literacy task, so reading at the earliest stages needs to reflect the work that is done in word building and sentence writing; the two activities are parallel. Figure 4.7 shows an example of reading material that is suitable for this purpose.

Reading should also be about the enjoyment of reading a story. Even at this level, the book should be approached by teacher and pupil as something that is interesting and worth talking about. As the story develops, the characters and what they

Look, in the bog we can see a big log. Zom's rocket has landed on the log. In the box at the end of the pond we can see a fox.

Zom hops off the log and has a good look at the pond and the bog. Zom can see a big box, but he cannot see the fox in it.

4

5

Figure 4.7 Early reading material. *Zom*: Book 3 from the Zed Project by Jo Westwood IEC Books Ltd. (Reprinted by permission of the author.)

do can be discussed, guesses made about what might happen next, or thoughts and opinions exchanged.

Early reading subskills: decoding and word-attack strategies

Decoding a word can be thought of as the reverse of word building; yet word building is involved here too – in this case from the sequence of sounds (or syllables) that emerges as the pupil responds to the letters. The two skills, although not inseparable, are very closely associated and they benefit from being taught together

At the earliest stage, children often read words by saying the sounds of letters one by one, then running them together into a whole word. If they cannot recognise words as wholes, this kind of phonic analysis and synthesis is an important technique. Some children find it difficult to make the step from sounding letters individually to saying the word 'in one'. An onset and rime approach could be helpful here because there is less to blend. Teachers may need to give these particular children concentrated practice at whole-word pronunciation, particularly if the 'sounding out' persists, as such a habit can be difficult to break. Some routines for helping with this skill are shown in Figure 4.8.

It may be that the onset + rime division is easier to hear when a child is learning to segment words into sounds, but blending may be easier with the *cv + c* segmentation. Both ways can be tried to see which is easier for the individual.

---

1. Read down a list of words. The words should change gradually as described on page 39. In the first stage of practice, make sure the pupil is aware of the pattern and where the changes occur. This will give him confidence to try the words as wholes. Colour could be used as a guide in the first stages
2. Aids such as flip cards, strip cards with a sliding consonant and word wheels can be used for variety. These also help to focus attention on the changing letter
3. Be explicit about what the child has to do, namely focus attention on the whole word before thinking about any individual sound
4. Limit the 'looking' time to encourage the pupil to take in the whole word quickly. He can often do this much more quickly that he imagines

5. Help the child to speed up the 'collision' between the first part of the word and the end. Label two objects with word parts, e.g. onset and rime *r* + *un* – and make them collide

   Show the child how he can get his mouth ready to say the first sound, but not let it go until he is ready to say the last part. The collision is the signal for saying them together

   Or slide a finger along a line, e.g. *h———at* – and say the parts together at the end
6. For the alternative segmentation, first consonant + vowel and (single) final consonant, e.g. *ba/t*, *ski/p* (*cv + c*), again use a collision as the signal for saying the whole word. This time the first part of the word can be pronounced and the last sound added – but the process must be quick to get the word as a whole

Figure 4.8 Some routines for decoding and blending words.

Four or five words may be enough in the first stages. A child often starts off well then begins making mistakes. If this happens, stop the exercise. As the skill develops, the number of words can be increased but success needs to be maintained or confidence will be at risk.

Further discussion of early reading will be found in Chapter 8.

Some activities and games to follow up phonic work

Word recognition

- Snap; Phonic Rummy – collecting and sorting game.
- Memory (Pelmanism) game – find the pairs with cards face down. Less confident pupils can assemble pairs from cards presented face up.
- Sorting games are useful for attention to detail; words can be put into groups according to vowels, first or last consonant, consonant blends, rhymes, etc.

To ensure multisensory processing, words should be read aloud at the time and/or afterwards. For sentence building and reading using whole words, write a simple sentence (short for beginners) on card and cut it up. The pupil can read it first or not, as appropriate. Reassemble and read.

Word-recognition and vocabulary development

- Pairing games and finding sets – synonyms and opposites
- Finding categories – on separate cards write fruits, furniture, birds, etc.
- Word- and sentence-tracking exercises

- Sequencing words and sentences. Put jumbled words into sentence order, or sentences into the correct order to match a given cue – a series of pictures or a known story.

If word recognition is hesitant, the pupil should read the sentence first (or it can be read to him) then cut it up and reassemble it. Encourage quick reading and thinking by timing the activities.

Early work on syllable division and word attack

Write two-syllable words on card. Read them and mark the syllables then ask the pupil to cut them up: read each syllable separately and then the whole word:

1. Use compound words first (*sunset*, *drumstick*), then others (*bandit*, *trumpet*).
2. Do this with three or four words and shuffle the syllables. See how quickly the pupil can reassemble them.
3. Make words from separate syllables without seeing the whole words first.

This activity helps pupils to deal with syllables and word parts as wholes.

English has six common syllable types. This kind of word play can help to emphasise their characteristics (see Chapter 6, page 83 for further discussion and an approach to syllables for pupils who are further on in the work).

Games

Snakes and Ladders, and race-track and 'obstacle course' board games can make use of all the above tasks.

Children should be encouraged by all possible means to engage in word play. Five-minute games with a simple format can be fitted into a lesson to follow up a new point or for revision:

- 'Word steps' where the last letter of one word becomes the start of a descending word, and this leads down to start the next step.
- Simple word grids where words have to be fitted into the correct number of squares.
- Games of dominoes with three-letter words, consonant blends or, later, two syllables.
- Crosswords; short, regular words can be combined with reading practice (the clues) while at the same time close attention to word meaning and vocabulary is required.

(See Chapter 14 for more suggestions.)

Teaching dyslexic children whose first language is not English

There is increasing realisation that specific learning difficulties are often overlooked in children whose first language is not English when they are at school in a bilingual or multilingual environment. Learning difficulties may be ascribed to the language factor, or the children may be thought to be 'not very bright' because they are unable to communicate well enough in the classroom or in an assessment situation. Being taught in a second language has its difficulties for any child. Many learn enough English to communicate well orally, but more work is needed if they are to read with full understanding and to be able to function effectively right across the curriculum. Writing has additional problems – the chief being spelling and grammar, but mastering the script may be difficult for children from some cultures.

For the dyslexic child learning English as a new language, the specific phonological and working memory difficulties bring added problems. Just how seriously these will affect their learning will depend to some extent on the characteristics of the child's first language, particularly on its phonology and written form. There may be distinct differences between the sounds of the first language and English. Children may have difficulties perceiving the detailed phonemes of the unfamiliar language and the phonetics of their own language may be an obstacle. But they must be able to hear and pronounce English words as well as possible before they can segment the new sounds. They must then be able to remember them, learn to recognise them in written form, and finally spell them.

The nature of the pupils' own writing systems is also a factor in how well they learn to read and write English. A child whose first language is written in the Roman alphabet should have less difficulty than one who sees (and may already be learning) a different script at home, e.g. the right to left script and flowing characters of Arabic languages.

A teacher working with any child whose first language is not English will want to find out more about her pupil's first language and think about the way that this might affect the specific learning difficulty. The usual questions about early development should also be asked, e.g. ear troubles in infancy that may have affected the development of their early spoken language may carry over to the task of segmenting sounds in a new tongue.

Competence in English will vary from one pupil to another, and this will affect the kind of teaching programme that is set up. By the time the pupil is referred for specialist help, he may be able to speak English well and may already have some reading and writing skills. If this is so, the work may not differ greatly from that done with an English-speaking child of the same age and a similar profile.

If the child's English is poor, a lot of work on oral language will be needed with an emphasis on phonological skills. For some children, onset and rime may be more appropriate than a single phoneme approach, especially if their first language has a syllabic structure.

The teacher may like to consider the following linguistic points:

- How well the child speaks his first language.
- His knowledge of English.
- The phonetic and phonological characteristics of the first language.
- The written script and writing conventions of the first language.
- Particular ways that the spoken and written language might affect the learning of English, e.g. auditory processing, saying the sounds and the conventions of writing.

Although phonology will need to be given particular attention, a combined phonological and whole-word approach may be needed for children whose English needs a lot of help, so that early reading and word acquisition go along together. Meaning should be emphasised throughout, especially at the sentence level; books with plenty of illustrations will help with understanding and language learning. Systematic teaching will be needed with a multisensory approach for all parts of the work. This can make use of many of the materials, games and visual aids that have been mentioned; the segmentation exercise (see Figure 4.3) might be especially helpful because it is independent of letter knowledge. It could be useful for helping to segment words and syllables before the phoneme level is reached.

Consultation with other teachers is especially important, e.g. the pupil may be placed in an English as an Additional Language (EAL) or similar programme. This teacher may be able to provide the necessary information about the child's first language. If there is a teaching assistant who speaks the home language, it might be possible for her to attend some of the child's lessons, especially in the early stages. The usual communication with the class and subject teachers will be helpful. In science and practical fields the pupil may be achieving more than in the language-based subjects. Targets and objectives will need to be set carefully; it may be necessary to concentrate on oral language skills, both speaking and listening, to meet the pupil's immediate needs.

Sources of information on multilingualism and dyslexia are given in Appendix II.

Chapter 5

Teaching the dyslexic pupil in Key Stage 1

This chapter looks at the kinds of help that children may need if they are referred to a specialist teacher at an early age, before school Year 3, while they are still at the early stages of literacy learning in their class. The length of time that a child spends in the early years of schooling varies according to local policy and the date of his or her birthday. In some counties, children may begin at 4 years, in others in the term preceding the fifth birthday. A child aged under 7 years may already have been at school (including nursery school) for between 2 and 3 years or just over 1 year when he is referred for help. The summer-born child may have had at least two terms less at school.

Formal teaching of letter and sounds starts in the third term of the Reception Year (YR) so he may have an assortment of knowledge about reading and writing and possibly some skills – but all unreliable. This means that the teacher is already carrying out a remediation job. This is so for an older pupil too, but for the Key Stage 1 (KS1) child the work will be approached in a different way. For an older pupil the first teaching procedures will have a more narrow focus on word reading and spelling, and these are described in detail in other chapters. Although the same principles of structured and systematic work and a multisensory approach are essential for the younger beginners, the procedures will need to be more flexible. The 'summer-birthday' children may not have made any kind of start. For all these children (and the last group especially) a good deal of oral and auditory work will be needed for them to become confident and to make a start with reading and spelling. Development will be between 9 and almost 12 months behind their older peers.

There will be differences too in the way that teaching is organised. It is more likely that the youngest children will be taught in a small group with short teaching sessions spread through the week. For those with greatest difficulties individual attention will also be essential. Teachers should look for the child's particular competences and develop their strengths while working to improve and enhance the weaker areas.

General pointers to difficulties with learning

It is well established that certain phonological difficulties in school entry pupils (such as difficulties with rhyming tasks) are reliable predictors of poor reading progress.

It has also been shown that early training in phonological skills helps to avert such failure or reduce it (Note 5.1, page 255). Knowledge of letter names and recognition of letters at school entry are also strong indicators of how well children will progress in early literacy work. Figure 5.1 illustrates checkpoints for early language and motor development.

There is also much reported evidence that children who later are found to be dyslexic have earlier had noticeable difficulties of other kinds, although these may seem to have been overcome at the time of diagnosis. (Some examples are given in Figure 5.1.) Information about these factors can be a useful pointer for a teacher working with a young pupil whose difficulties have not yet been fully identified. Parents may need to be asked specific questions, or there may be information in reports from nursery school or playgroup.

Checking the development of language skills and literacy subskills

The conversational language of most dyslexic children might not seem different from that of their friends, but even mild difficulties in an area of expressive and/or receptive language can affect the way the child responds to early reading

- Oral language development (late talking; some may have had help from a speech therapist)
- Naming and word finding (knowledge of colours; use of wrong words)
- Ear problems (glue ear; sometimes insertion of grommets)
- Spatial and motor organisation (getting dressed, using a spoon, using pencils, painting, pouring)
- Sequencing of tasks (putting clothes on in the right order)
- Laterality and direction (persists in putting shoes on the wrong foot)
- Late establishment of handedness (uncertainty about preferred hand for eating, scribbling, etc.)
- Fine manipulation (piling up bricks, handling small toys, doing up buttons, threading beads)
- Balance and control of larger movements (late walking, clumsiness, climbing, running, hopping, skipping)

Figure 5.1 Checkpoints for early language and motor development.

and writing work. Such difficulties might also underlie problems of inattention, poor concentration, inability to settle, or social and behavioural difficulties. The teacher should make an explicit – if informal – check on the major areas of development. Some children, particularly the younger ones, may need a good deal of saying and listening work while they are learning letters and starting first word building – and before they can be done successfully. Even mild difficulties may be affecting progress and the teacher should watch out for awkwardness and inaccuracies.

The National Curriculum Statements of Attainment can be used as a framework, but one of the specific published tests will provide more detailed guidance for observation (see Chapter 3 and Appendix II). Informal checks can be made by observing the child individually and among the group and looking at the following areas.

Spoken language

- General speaking and listening behaviour:
  - organisation of spoken language
  - comprehension of the language of others.
- Awareness of language structure and segments:
  - sentences
  - question and answer
  - words
  - sounds.
- Memory:
  - does the child not remember what he has just heard?
  - does he remember details of often-told stories?

Particular points that might be observed include:

- Difficulty with word finding
- Use of wrong words
- First letters transposed and other mispronunciations
- Poor articulation or difficulty with saying particular sounds
- Poor control of language (e.g. high-grade chatter, words tumble out)
- Undeveloped grammar (e.g. past tense mistakes, difficulty with prepositions).

Phonemic awareness

A particular check should be made on the development of phonemic awareness (individual sounds in words) and phonological skills, (the segmentation and manipulation of language sounds). These will probably need to be checked by doing puzzles and games with the child on his own.

- Saying nursery rhymes
- Identifying rhyming words
- Repetition of non-words and longer words
- Awareness of individual speech sounds
- Separating initial sounds
- Oral blending of syllables and sounds.

Writing and pre-writing skills

- Can the child write any letters?
- Can he copy letters, or shapes; does he orientate them correctly?
- Does he draw, or scribble, or write 'notes' or 'letters'?
- Can he 'colour in' shapes and pictures?

Awareness of print and the conventions of reading

- Does the child know how to handle a book and the way that a book is organised – front and back, top and bottom of page?
- Is he aware that we read the printed marks, rather than the pictures?
- Does he know that a book is read from left to right?

Motor and visuomotor skills: development of pencil control

The reason for poor development of handwriting is often put down to carelessness, hurry or lack of persistence in the child; the child who knocks things over, or cannot sit still, can be judged as generally fidgety or clumsy. That there may be a physical or visuospatial reason for these 'personality traits' is often not considered. Teachers might bear in mind the following points:

- A child who has even minor difficulties with more general movement may need to develop greater control over balance, to increase his spatial and body awareness and to gain control of larger muscles, before the fine motor skills needed for handwriting can be developed successfully.
- Consistently poor posture and arm position (slumping and a need to support the head and body) may be related to a more general motor problem, or to lack of practice at early pencil work. Can the child sit – and sit up – comfortably? Is he generally 'floppy'?
- Are the shoulder and arm muscles sufficiently developed for forearm and wrist movement to be flexible and independent?
- How does he cope with non-writing tasks, e.g. fitting things together, water play (can he pour from one container to another?). Does he prefer painting to drawing?
- A child with an unusual or awkward grip may have weak finger or hand muscles.
- Persistent wrong orientation may indicate a visual difficulty.

Consultation with a PE specialist, children's occupational therapist or orthoptist may be advisable, and a referral for assessment made if the difficulties seem to persist.

A programme of exercises for individual work may be needed but some helpful routines can be included in lessons by the specialist teacher. Choosing suitable exercises and writing implements for particular children depends on identifying the reason for the difficulty. The following suggestions might be tried:

- For improving poor grip: strengthening exercises and warm-up exercises before writing starts – stretching and scrunching fingers, pressing small balls or spring clips; playing with toys that need manipulation and fitting together by pressing and pulling.
- If the child has developed a dislike of drawing and writing, novelty pens and pencils can help to overcome this.
- Teachers routinely check a child's pencil grip. It is usual to try to correct it by giving a plastic pencil hold but a variety of shapes should be tried. It may be enough to wind a rubber band around the pencil as a reminder of where it should be held. A child who wants to hold the pencil too far up can be given a very short pencil – even a stub. The thickness of the pencil or pen is important.

Guidelines and detailed suggestions can be found in a number of sources which are listed in Appendix II.

Useful pointers can be obtained by observing what a child prefers to do, and noting the areas where he has good skills. Does the child seem to prefer jigsaws, Lego and other construction toys? This may be a sign that they are more comfortable with global, spatial tasks. Parents can provide important information about all these points.

Suggestions for working with younger pupils

Terms for talking about language

Teachers should check whether a child understands the words and concepts that are being introduced in the Literacy Hour. Dyslexic children may be confused about these abstract words – if they are aware of having heard them at all. In Y1 and Y2, the Literacy Hour programme includes word, sound, first and last sound, syllable, consonant, vowel, phoneme, grapheme, and onset and rime (see Appendix V for a list of terms). Other words – for instance, prepositions before, after, up, down – may be more familiar in other contexts.

Speaking skills

Some young dyslexic children need extra practice in conversation and social communication skills. The reluctant talker needs help to express himself and develop his spoken self-expression. Toys and puppets are useful aids here. A child might more readily answer questions from a puppet, soft toy or doll, and talk to it, than respond to a teacher, particularly if he is a shy individual. Directed play of all kinds gives excellent opportunities for communication skills: shops, home corner or dolls' house play, or other play focused on small toys and characters: Play People, Thomas the Tank Engine, etc.; talking through building and construction work; interactive computer programs; and board games. Talking in these kinds of situations can be directed to the activity and allow the child to be less self-conscious.

In a one-to-one or small group situation, the teacher has opportunities to encourage clear spoken language:

- A child who 'rattles along' can be asked to slow down, 'tell it' more clearly. Encourage the child to take his time.
- It can help to place him at a distance, or turn away from the listener, so that he is conscious of the need to be clear.
- Pretend the teacher speaks another language, or ask the child to explain something to a 'Martian' or to a puppet.
- Picture books as a focus of interest for talking may help a child to speak more slowly.
- Topics of importance to the child can encourage clear speaking.
- Short poems and nursery rhymes, said or sung, will emphasise the rhythm and encourage steadier, more controlled speech.

Listening, looking and paying attention

Dyslexic children can find listening difficult, especially in a large group or class where the teacher's attention cannot be focused entirely on them, and eye-to-eye contact is sporadic. Background noise can interfere with the actual hearing of speech or distract attention. Many other stimuli can distract in the same way: movement, pictures and displays, and other children's activities. This is so for many children of course, but dyslexic youngsters seem to find it more difficult to re-focus attention after a distraction; the loss of attention means that meaning is lost too. Work with a small group, and particularly with an individual pupil, might be best carried out apart from the main group, or in a separate room.

- The pupil should be encouraged to look straight at the speaker who should develop ways to keep his attention and eye contact, e.g. hand signals.
- Purposeful short 'talk/listen' sessions can train the maintenance of attention.
- Specific talk-and-respond work: games such as Simon Says; question and answer routines; oral games, e.g. 'spot the silly mistake' (teacher makes deliberate mistakes in story titles, saying *Four little pigs*; *Goldihairs and the two bears*, etc.).
- Following instructions and directions: general class instructions may be difficult for the dyslexic pupil. He may not take them in at all and, even if he listens carefully, he is likely to forget before the message is complete. Sequences of instructions for practice and games can help to develop good habits of attending, listening and remembering. To begin with, instructions and directions should be given in the order in which they will be carried out (e.g. 'Get a hoop, then find a partner' rather than 'Before you find a partner, get the hoop'). The order may be reversed later, but this should be signalled very clearly.

Listening and remembering skills could be developed through:

- PE routines – although children may get excited and distracted by the activities.
- Action songs; circle games.
- Games such as Simon Says, Follow my Leader.
- Listen to an instruction and repeat back – or tell another person – what he has to do.
- Games and play of all kinds give excellent opportunities for practice.
- Turn-taking is important; this can be developed first with the teacher, then in a small group.

The sharing and turn-taking in all the above activities provide opportunities to develop language forms and to ensure correct usage – use of past and future tenses, prepositions, asking questions, using negative forms, etc., and to extend a child's vocabulary knowledge. Opportunities for practice can be planned within the Speaking and Listening Attainment Targets of the National Curriculum. This kind of work is particularly important for children who have wider language difficulties and in these cases it is important to seek advice from a speech and language therapist.

Phonological awareness: oral and auditory work

The ability to segment word parts and sounds begins to develop before the child encounters reading and writing, and it continues to develop as literacy teaching begins and skills increase. Children are able first to recognise and segment syllables, then intra-syllable word parts – initial letter(s) (onset) and word ends (rime). Segmentation of the last letter and middle sound (vowel) are the last to develop. So, in this early oral/auditory work it can be helpful to follow the same order when planning the sequence of activities.

Syllables and word length

Understanding of syllables and of word length go together. Syllables can best be shown and explained through movement and singing.

- Show how a word has a number of beats as you might beat a drum.
- Clap hands or tap for each syllable.
- Explore names. Clap each syllable in your name. Who has the longest name?
- Singing songs can emphasise words and syllables as units of speech. Nursery rhymes have mostly one- and two-syllable words (by far the greatest number are single syllables). These are sung mostly one syllable to a note. Dyslexic children might know some first lines such as 'Hickory dickory dock' and 'Humpty Dumpty sat on the wall.'
- What's the longest word you know? An illustrated alphabet book, an animal picture book or a dinosaur book works well for this. It will show what long/short words look like on the page. Repeating long unknown words is often difficult for dyslexic children but they may enjoy practising some of the dinosaur names especially if the plastic models are used.

Segmenting sounds in words

The child may find it easiest to begin by dividing first consonant(s) (onset) and vowel + final consonant (rime) thus: *h* + *at*. This can help to train the recognition and the production of words that rhyme, which may need a lot of practice. Much of this kind of work can be done through games and word play.

The method of using counters to mark the number of phonemes in a word (described in Chapter 4, page 36) is used in the Literacy Hour so children might already be familiar with this approach. For the KS1 pupil, different pictures can be made and it can be turned into a game or puzzle. The words should be spoken slowly and stretched out – although not so much that the sense is lost. (Say the word naturally first, so the task is not changed to 'Guess what word I'm saying'.) Syllables should be practised to begin with because they are easier to segment. If there is particular difficulty with segmentation of phonemes, more practice with syllables can be given. Placing the counters helps to emphasise each separate syllable or phoneme and helps the child to stay focused. It can be useful to watch how he sets about the task. Does he need a lot of repetition, or is he able to carry the word in his memory; does he say the separate sounds? Figure 5.2 illustrates pictures that can be used for a phoneme segmentation game.

Production of speech sounds

Children should be encouraged to listen carefully and to watch the mouth movements for particular sounds. Younger pupils may still be at an early stage in the development of some sounds; /l/, /r/ and particularly /sh/ are late to develop, and /th/ /v/ /f/ are easier to see by the position of the tongue. It would probably be a mistake to pursue slight difficulties with these more difficult sounds, but the stage of development should be noted. It may be

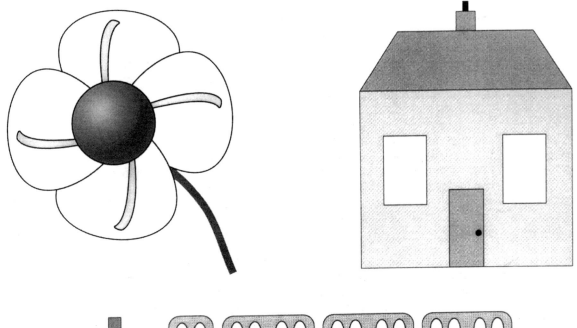

Figure 5.2 Pictures for phoneme segmentation game.

more important to check whether the child is able to identify the different sounds when they are spoken by the teacher, as single phonemes and in words.

'Same–different' games can be played (Am I saying the same word, or two different ones – *sip*, *ship*; *shell*, *self*?) or, with older children, segmentation games. (What word do you get if I say *frog* but leave out the /r/?)

It is important at this early stage to show the child how to say the consonant phonemes as 'pure' consonant sounds, with no additional /uh/ sound. Figure 5.3 illustrates more games for sounds play.

Blending sounds into words

This depends on memory. However quickly the sounds are pronounced, they are still a sequence

Quick responses can be encouraged in the sounds play – but this must be done with care and will depend on the individual pupil

- First consonant games:
  I Spy – initial sound identification (letter names can be used later)
  I Went to Market – alliteration – production of words beginning with the target sound. (There is no need to insist on the pupil memorising the growing list, which is an extra task and one that he is likely to find difficult)
- Discrimination:
  Odd-One-Out – listening and discrimination of rhyming words, first or last letter, or vowel similarity (*ring, fish, dish; cap, rat, cot; pin, book, man; man, rag, pit*; make sure that children know what they are listening for). This can be done with pictures, which takes out the memory factor. Give the pictures in groups (as above), to be sorted into the required category The words should be said aloud

- Bingo – pictures/alphabet/sounds/words – all kinds of variations
- Rhyme games – with and without pictures: Odd-One-Out and Which-Words-Rhyme? are different ways of responding to the same task. Find-a-Rhyme – listening and matching: children can be encouraged to invent words
- Splitting up words:
  be a robot: say the syllables/onset–rime/each sound separately
- Memory games can encourage attention and concentration, and also help to develop memory strategies – such as verbal rehearsal and pictorial imaging
  I went shopping – listening task (this may be easier with non-alliterative words). Encourage the child to make a mind-picture of each item
  Kim's game – looking task. Encourage the naming of each item
  Finding pairs – looking task. The usual 'rules' can be adapted, e.g. one card can be left face up each time or three cards can be turned up

Figure 5.3 More games and activities for oral/auditory phonological work.

in time. Each must be heard and remembered correctly before the whole sequence is recalled from the start. The 'trick' is to recognise the sequence as a whole word. Some children find this more difficult than finding the individual letters for a word they already know, when they can hold the whole word in immediate memory while they work out the separate sounds. (These children often surprise teachers by being able to spell simple words before they can read them). Remembering and recalling one unit (a whole word) is

easier than working with three or four units, especially when these must be assembled not from the last-heard sound, but from the first. For this reason, blending practice is usually carried out with letters as memory prompts. However, auditory blending practice can be useful. It encourages children to listen and try to remember, it raises awareness of sounds and the way they combine, and it is independent of letter knowledge. It requires concentrated attention and helps to train memory skills. Some children find this task very

- Give the exercise a play context: explain that you are a robot/Martian or use a puppet, and turn the exercise into a guessing game; you can also ask the child to talk in the robot's language. Use clipped consonant sounds for words (*buh + a + tuh* could be *batter*!)
- Start with syllables as two-syllable words also need to be blended. Care is needed to give the whole-word stress pattern (*car + pet* spoken with equal stress do not make *carpet*)
- Onset and rime words should be next; use two or three rhyming words before changing the word pattern. This will help memory and encourage generalisation – an important skill in reading new words
- The alternative segmentation of consonant + vowel and final consonant(s) can also be practised – especially for words that have a voiced first consonant such as *b*, *d* where a clipped consonant sound is almost impossible. It may be better to add a distinct vowel for blending, because this will come closer to the whole word. (Contrast the sounding of *b + at* and *ba + t*.) Experiment beforehand to see which is easier
- If the child works on segmenting a few words himself, before being asked to blend, he may have less difficulty. Use a picture to start off. Show how the word can be said slowly then ask the child to say it. Say it with him to show what you mean
- Picture cues: using three or four pictures, say the sounds and ask the child to find the right picture
- Say: 'Think the sounds in your head then say them all together when they are ready', e.g. *r + un*. This is necessary for words with a voiced first consonant: *b + a + t*
- It is also useful to practise blending consonants, to produce the sounds typical of blends *br, st, fl, sm*. Again make sure the child does not say *bruh, stuh, fluh, smuh*

Figure 5.4 Practising auditory/oral blending.

difficult and may need to be given a lot of support and some helpful 'tricks'.

Figure 5.4 suggests ways to practise auditory/oral blending. Five minutes might be plenty for oral/auditory work – certainly in one-to-one teaching. It can be followed up naturally by reading; poems are good for this purpose, especially short verses with good rhythm and strong rhymes. Children can also be encouraged to produce their own rhymes and illustrate them. Drawing can be used to give a break from the concentrated listening activity. The pupil might make his own book of letters with a brightly coloured letter on each page, thus merging sounds work with letter recognition.

Teaching letter–sound correspondences

The main routines for teaching are described in Chapter 4. With a young pupil it is especially important to emphasise the multisensory work: routines for teaching and practice, activities and games all need to combine the visual, auditory, oral and kinaesthetic modalities. Letters are symbols – with no logical connection to the sounds they represent. The sounds themselves are transient and some – especially the vowels – are difficult to distinguish. The means of linking them must therefore be as concrete and tangible as possible. Objects as well as pictures should be used as references for initial sounds. More play activity will help to consolidate the learning, e.g. making the letters from clay, making and feeling the letters with tactile material – felt, glitter glue, etc. – and use of solid letters – as large as possible. Learning without looking should also be practised: the child should be able to identify letters by shape – feeling them hidden in a bag or with eyes closed.

Opportunities will need to be created for children to use the sounds they learn in writing. Much of the writing may have to be done by the teacher, but the content should be of the child's own invention. Whether stories, or simple word books, they should be tailored as far as possible to the individual story maker. The pupil can claim the final work as his own by adding drawings, and colouring letters and pictures. Making books in the shape of individual letters, and illustrating them with appropriate pictures, is an effective way to consolidate learning of sounds and letters. Little books of this kind may become part of the child's first reading material.

Teaching and learning first words – including children's names

In the early stages of reading it is usual for children to work through whole words and for alphabetic skills to develop slightly later than these 'logographic' skills. (This would make sense as words are essentially meaningful wholes.) Understanding that words are formed by complex collections of sounds (phonemic segmentation skills) and that these are written as separate symbols (alphabetic skills) follows later (see Note 4.1, page 254).

Even so, learning whole words is a difficult memory task and multisensory work will be needed. Tracing is one way to learn words, but it may be difficult for the younger children who cannot yet control a line or form good letter shapes:

- Work with separate letters: find and arrange the letters for a word, copying from a card that also has a picture cue; or build words with card letters that fit together to make a picture jigsaw of a word.
- Feeling the letters: the child pulls out letters from a 'feely bag' in the right order for a given word; or he pulls out letters for given sounds (working one by one) and recognises the completed word.
- Flashcards: all words will need frequent practice. Aim for immediate response and build up speed. For some children the difficulty may be in saying the word – even though they recognise it. (This may result partly from lack of confidence.)
- Games: use the words in phonic games.

Teaching the letter names and the alphabet

The younger pupils will probably need a lot of help, and much practice, to learn and repeat the alphabet and they may not master the whole sequence till later. The important point now is that they should know the letter names. Work done in the classroom may be half remembered and confused so that some explicit teaching will be needed to straighten it out.

Individual letter names can be checked before the whole alphabet is tackled, and these linked to the relevant sounds. Children may know a random selection of the letters, especially if they can write their own names, and they often know some letter names from car number plates.

Some children may be able to recite or sing the alphabet, which the class will have learned, but they may not have understood that letters have sounds as well as names. They will also need to learn that each letter has a capital and a lower-case form, and that the name and sound belong to both forms.

Alphabet learning can be a discrete activity using names, because the reading and spelling work will be done through letter sounds. They should be shown that there are 26 letters and that we arrange them in a fixed order for some jobs, e.g. arranging words in lists according to the first letter, finding information in some parts of books, including a word book (dictionary) and a telephone directory. Plastic or wooden letters should be used for the layout, in each lesson going as far as the letters the child knows.

Colour the vowels in red if possible. This will help to show their importance, and be a reminder that, when consonants are used in words, they need a vowel to help them 'speak'. The vowel sound of *y* need not be included until the child meets *my*.

The Letterland method of making the letters into characters with stories can be useful to help children remember the characteristics of letters and their sounds at the early stages, e.g. the snake with a hiss, clever cat, the yoyo man, etc.

Handwriting

Younger pupils may find great difficulty not just in mastering the individual letter shapes but in the integration of correct letter forms into spelling and writing. If joined writing is expected at an early stage, this makes the further demand for continuous movement through the letters, which presupposes phonic skills and some spelling knowledge. Emergent writing shows that young children can apply their phonological skills in a purposeful way before they learn how to spell (e.g. *the gbred man jumt of the chwa*: the *gingerbread man jumped off the tray*), but they would not be expected to combine this kind of spelling with joined writing.

For a child with developmental difficulties, the separate skills will need much more direct attention before they are secure. Explicit teaching of letter forms will be needed, and a great deal of practice for them to become automatic. If a child has further difficulties of movement or body/spatial awareness, he may not be able to work on handwriting until some of these problems are addressed. Attention to the subskills for reading and writing can continue with the use of plastic letters, letter tiles or even a computer with a suitable keyboard overlay or on-screen keyboard. (Joined handwriting is a Level 3 Attainment Target, i.e. it should be achieved early in KS2 and by the more able children at the end of KS1.)

Learning letter forms

Multisensory activity is at the centre of handwriting learning. Making letter shapes requires integration of motor movement with visual monitoring of the letter and its production. However, at the stage of individual letter learning, it should not be dissociated from the sound/name of the letter. Later it may be linked to the learning of spelling and the pronunciation of words.

The teacher should make clear that writing is not 'drawing'; letters have to be correctly formed, correctly orientated, the right size – especially in relation to each other – and written in the right place on the line. They also have extra lines for joining up into words.

Letters should be made in different media – sand-tray, Plasticine, 'walking the shape' – so that the movement and the shape become familiar. Large muscular movements give stronger input to kinaesthetic memory, so big letter forms should also be made – in the air, against a wall, on a board or on paper of A3 size. A thick pencil or painting stick gives a good line. The child should also practise with eyes closed to get feedback from feel and movement.

Use of blank paper gives the child freedom to concentrate on the letter form. Later a line should be drawn so that the letter position relative to the line is made clear. This will also show that, although the joining strokes for individual letters start from the line, the letter form itself (except for *d*, *e*) always starts at the top. Comparison of different letters will also make the relative shapes and sizes clear: /f/ /t/, /m/ /n/, /h/ /n/, /m/ /w/. It is useful to compare letters that can be confused because of the orientation *m/w, n/u, b/p/d/q/*, although it is better to teach them separately in the first place.

Talking through the letter form can be useful and it adds to the multisensory learning experience. It can also provide a rhythm for the child to learn the flow of the letter. The number of 'stops' or changes of direction can be counted and this also emphasises the flow. So *h* can be 'start at the top, down to the line (1), back up, round and down to the line (2)'. (If joining strokes are added, another instruction, e.g. 'and flick', can be put in.) The teacher should be clear about the need to close the circle in the *o* group of letters.

Joining the letters

Many children with learning difficulties may be not ready to start joining letters until they have begun to be more confident about letters and sounds. However, the continuous movements needed for joined writing can be practised before letter joining is attempted. Typical patterns can be traced in the sand-tray or on a board, or done with a brush on large paper. The medium can vary, and the size gradually reduced until the child's pencil control allows them to be done at handwriting size.

If the exit line is included as a 'flick' when the letter forms are taught, it will be in place when the child is ready to join letters into words.

Figure 5.5 illustrates useful resources to use with younger children.

- Lots of picture cards – large, small
- Pictures for short vowel words, including rhyming sets
- Pictures to arrange in sequence
- Puppets and other toys for speaking and listening work and sounds play
- Small toys or objects for initial letter work
- Picture cards and counters for phonemic segmentation work
- Sets of capital and lower-case letters for first learning and alphabet work
- Sandpaper/felt/glitter-glue letters, plasticine, etc. for tactile work
- Letter–sound correspondence cards, with and without cue pictures
- Boxes of letters for word building, with vowels coloured red
- 'Feely bags'
- Jigsaw words
- Illustrated books, including alphabet books
- Poems, stories in rhyme, for listening skills
- Squeezy balls, spring pegs and clips, small 'assembly' toys and other items to strengthen fingers and practise fine manipulation
- Different kinds of pen and pencil of varying thicknesses, writing points and colours, including fun pens
- Pencil grips of different kinds
- Different surfaces for writing – large paper, lined paper, whiteboard/blackboard

Figure 5.5 Useful resources for working with younger children.

Chapter 6

Teaching phonic work at different stages

This chapter is concerned with how the phonic programme is taught to pupils at different stages. Although the content of the work remains broadly similar overall, the approach and the progression of the reading and spelling work are bound to vary to suit the needs of individual children. This relates not only to the level of each one's skill, but also takes into account the demands of the classroom and curriculum work at a particular time.

The first section looks at pupils who have no reading and spelling skills when they are first referred for individual tuition. It also touches on working with older beginners. The second section is concerned with those who have acquired a measure of basic skill, but have not progressed very far. The third section considers the needs of pupils in secondary school whose difficulties with reading, writing and spelling – although not extreme – are below the level that they need to cope with the curriculum and the demands of examinations. In the fourth section a new way of looking at the phonic programme is presented – the Spelling Wheel – and suggestions are made

about how this might be used with an older student.

Each section has notes on the phonic topics to be taught and the use of the phonic dictionary is discussed. The way that the work might progress is illustrated through examples of pupils' work.

Starting up: the younger pupils

Many phonological subskills contribute to competence in literacy, most of them so interdependent that it is difficult to separate them into individual processes. Yet these have to be intact if learning is to go ahead. By the time they are in the third year of school, many children who are still non-readers should have picked up some information about sounds and letters; however, it is often a 'rag-bag' of knowledge, with muddled scraps that cannot be used profitably.

They need to start at the very beginning and will probably benefit from a good deal of oral/auditory work. Some of the approaches discussed in Chapter 4 can be used, although these may need to be adapted to suit an older pupil.

The most important points that need to be checked and where work may be needed are shown in Figure 6.1. It is not possible to prescribe exactly the order of teaching of these points, and many will be taught simultaneously in the multisensory work.

Ability to separate individual words in the speech stream

Ability to segment sounds heard in individual spoken words

Ability to identify rhyming words

How to blend heard sounds into words

Knowledge of letters and sounds: correspondences between these

Automatic response to above

How to form letters correctly

Knowledge of vowels and consonants and the terms for these

How to build up words from consonants and vowels

Correspondence between sequence of sounds in spoken and written words

Ability to recognise whole words in reading

Skill at blending letters into words for reading

Ability to read words not previously seen by saying them 'in one'

Names of letters

Correspondence between sound and name

Capital letter forms

Alphabet in sequence

Figure 6.1 Basic phonic knowledge: points to be checked at start of teaching.

Knowledge about the conventions of print might be assumed in a 7-year-old child but they should still be checked:

- the significance of letters and words
- front and back of book
- top and bottom of pages
- left–right direction of reading and writing
- the relationship between pictures and print, etc.

Children who have not made a start must be taught the sound–letter correspondences in a systematic way. To reinforce learning there should be plenty of auditory-to-visual matching tasks, with listening exercises to identify first and last consonants, short-vowel sounds and rhymes in spoken words. They should begin to build simple words as soon as a few letters and sounds are securely known.

It is advisable to delay embarking on the phonic dictionary for a while; it can be started when the pupil is becoming more confident about writing words without much preliminary work. Instead a 'First Sounds' book might be used to record the detailed work of learning letters and letter–sound linkages. This can be full of drawings (or pasted cut-outs) as well as letters, and in this way the child can make his own book which will give a sense of achievement. Other work, e.g. on consonant digraphs and blends, can be entered in this 'First Sounds' book and recorded later, more briefly, in the phonic dictionary itself. The two might even proceed alongside each other for a time.

The phonic dictionary can be started when the child is confident about two or three short-vowel sounds and the teacher intends to continue working through the others (see Chapter 2).

Zoe: 8;0

When teaching began in September, Zoe knew hardly any letter–sound correspondences and did not understand the relevance of letters to sounds. She had no score on reading or spelling tests. She knew how to form a number of letters – in the sample in Figure 6.2 she uses 13. Her teacher had told

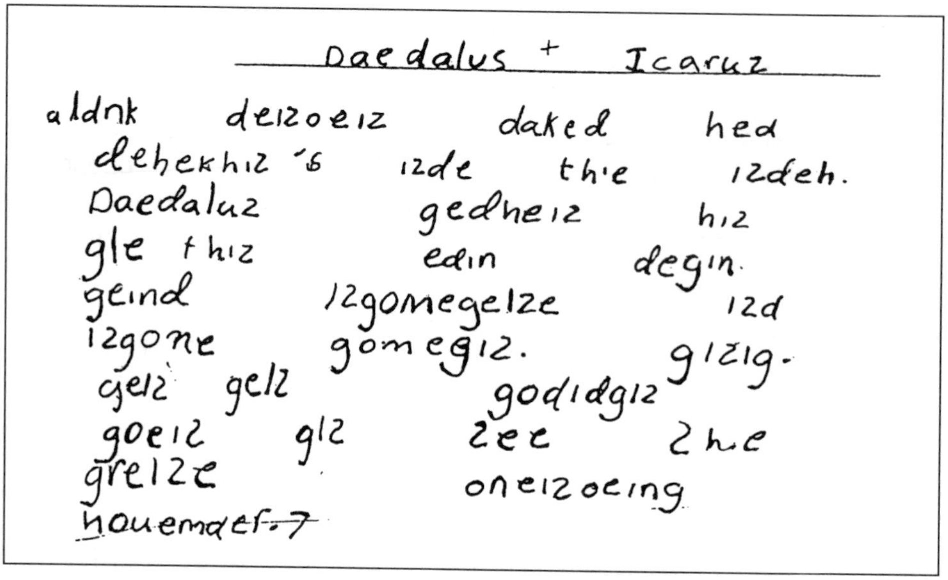

Figure 6.2 Zoe's first writing.

the class the story of Daedalus, and written the heading for the children to write their own version.

Careful examination of the writing suggests that she remembered how to write a few whole words: *his*, *this*, possibly *the*, the syllable *-ing* and *one*. An interesting feature is the occurrence of her own name in various places. This may account for her frequent reversal of *s*. She has also put in some punctuation, which suggests that she has looked at books. She has copied November – but reversed *b*. It is not possible to understand what she is saying, though there was probably a story there somewhere. Another piece of writing done on the same day has the same characteristics.

The first work was to teach the letter–sound correspondences. This involved a good deal of listening, selecting the letter to match a spoken sound, and writing the letter. The work was rein-forced with games. By February, Zoe was able to write without mistakes the sentence *Did the man run to the bus*? In March she was beginning to write 'notes' to her teacher. The first of these (Figure 6.3) shows her still struggling to make a reliable match between sound and letter. Her teacher had discovered that she knew the word *car* and she used this to help Zoe to correct *park*. (However, some time later, *park* was written *prck*, showing that she is still using the letter name to stand for the sound, although she is remembering some letter strings visually.)

The next month brought the note in Figure 6.4. Here it looks as if she was beginning to get a much better idea of 'letters for sounds' and even the trou-blesome *nt* is correct. The word *siu* suggests a tele-scoping of *sit in*, with the *n* inverted as happened also in the first *gadun*. Her teacher commented

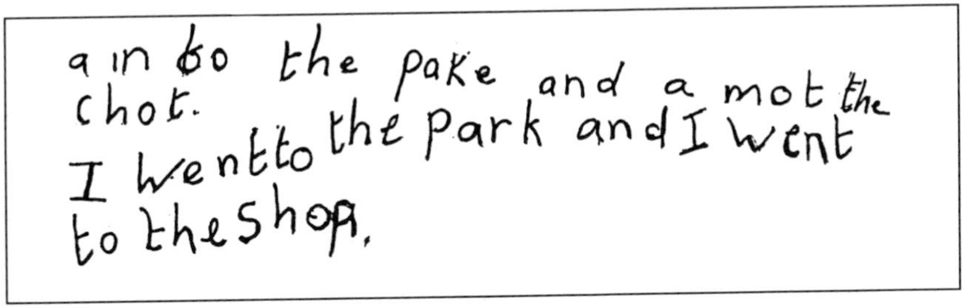

a in to the pake and a mot the
chot.
I went to the park and I went
to the shop.

Figure 6.3 Zoe – *I went to the park..*

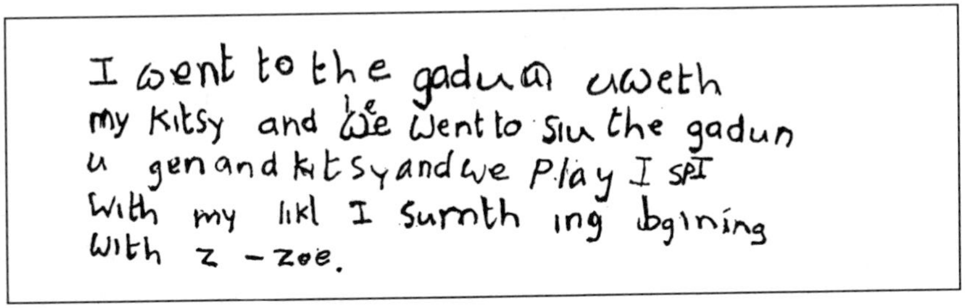

I went to the gadun uweth
my kitsy and We went to siu the gadun
u gen and kitsyandwe Play I spI
With my likl I sumth ing bgining
With z - zoe.

Figure 6.4 Zoe – *My kitsy.*

at this time that Zoe had a lot of trouble distinguishing final sounds – and tended to write *t* and *n* at random. She was given plenty of opportunities to practise final sounds with worksheets to follow up lessons. By June she was able to write a letter nine lines long describing a school trip. She could write *was*, *good* and *my* correctly, appeared to know *sh* and *th*, but had constant trouble with blends: *wet* for *went* and *cass* for *class*. Although she was still struggling with spelling, it was possible to see what she wanted to say. One of her difficulties was keeping her ideas clear; it is possible that, if someone had helped her by doing the writing, the expression would have been less tangled. Both tasks together were too much.

The immediate need at this point is to continue the short-vowel work, and begin building the phonic dictionary. This will help to practise the identifying of short vowels. Detailed work on consonant blends and digraphs can come next, followed possibly by adding *-ing* to words ending in two consonants. This would build on a pattern that she appeared to know. Reinforcement of common words such as *in*, *with*, *on* and *at* should be included. After that the *ee* and *oo* spellings, and possibly *-ay*, can follow. Words such as *my*, *we* and *she* need to be revised and will lead to others of the same pattern. The word boundaries are occasionally uncertain; oral work could help here, using a method where the pupil listens to a short sentence and places a counter for each separate word. (See the description of work on sound segmentation in Chapter 4, page 36.)

Jon: 8;6

The second pupil described, Jon, had made no start with reading and could write very little at the outset. He knew few letter–sound correspondences, although he learned these fairly quickly. Even then he had great difficulty remembering the sounds that some letters represented, which made decoding difficult. He could not remember whole words. He had less difficulty writing the letters for sounds, but he continued to use remembered picture cues when stuck for a consonant sound. He began building the phonic dictionary after a term. The first page is shown in Figure 6.5. The consonant blends occupied the next two pages.

The following describes the work being done just over a year later. In contrast to Zoe, Jon was a reluctant writer. He had great difficulty knowing where to start and how to express his ideas in sequence. The writing in Figure 6.6 was produced after a discussion about what he wanted to say, and he had been asked to write each idea in a separate sentence. (He was helped with the underlined words.)

In this sample he has little trouble with blends and he can write regular short-vowel words with

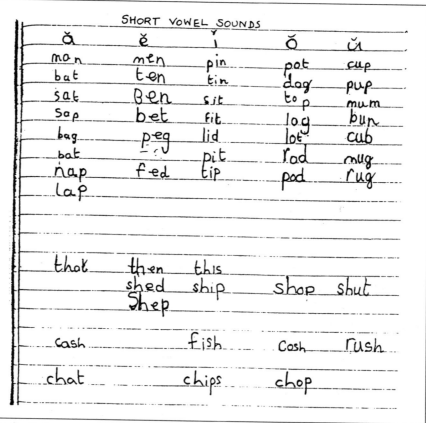

Figure 6.5 Jon's phonic dictionary, page 1.

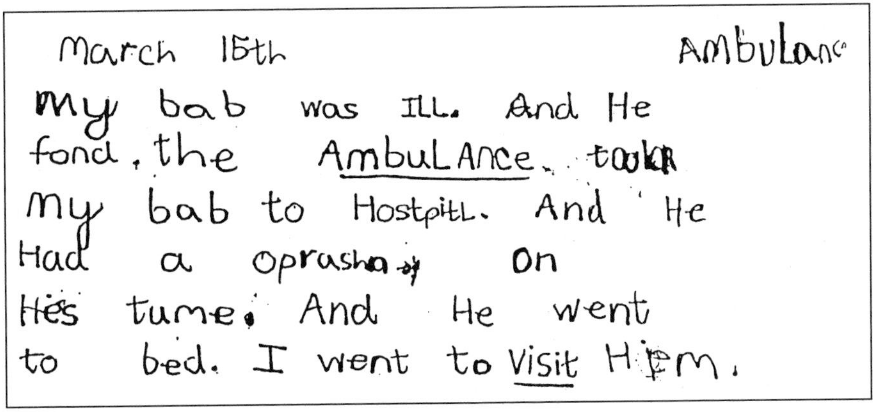
March 15th Ambulanc

my bab was ILL. And He fond, the AmbuLAnce took my bab to HostpitL. And He Had a oprasha on Hes tume. And He went to bed. I went to Visit Him.

Figure 6.6 Jon – *Dad and the ambulance..*

few mistakes. He does have to think about most of them, however; the spelling is rarely automatic. There is still difficulty over the short *i* and *e* sounds; *b*/*d* was a persistent problem in spelling and reading; 'finger tracing' helped when he was reminded about it.

The phonic work went ahead gradually, with much revision. The short-vowel and long-vowel -*e* work was extended to two-syllable words and some easy suffixing to help his reading. The vowel digraphs '*ee*' and '*oo*' were introduced before -*e*, chiefly so that his reading could go ahead. Irregular words were taught by multisensory tracing, working through a list of common words and in response to his needs.

Jon's first reading books were a set of simple stories with short-vowel words. He quickly learned to blend letters into a word, but had persistent difficulties with saying the words as wholes. The *Magic Key* books of the *Oxford Reading Tree*, and later the *Trog* books were introduced to help him acquire some sight vocabulary and discourage the habit of sounding out words. (See Appendix II for details of all reading material.)

The next work took him on to 'soft *c*' (*ace*, *ice*) words for reading and spelling, work on two-syllable words and simple suffixing for reading and spelling, and vowel digraphs and '-*ight*' chiefly for reading, For reading, he used the first levels of books designed to develop skills of comprehension and the finding of information, as well as a variety of readers at the 7;5 to 8 year level. (The lesson plans in Chapter 7, pages 105 and 106, are both from work with Jon.)

Starting older pupils

This section considers how reading and spelling might be approached through a phonic programme for a teenager with little literacy attainment. Older pupils whose reading and spelling have never got off the ground may view the prospect of starting all over again with some dismay. After several years of failure, they may be convinced that it is all boring, impossible and not worth the effort. It is also a different prospect for the teacher. The pupil in Key Stage 3 (KS3) or KS4 is faced with extensive demands in the classroom. It may be thought that the pupil's greatest need for help is with the curriculum, but this depends in turn on a basic level of literacy skill. The teacher will need to think about targets and priorities and what is possible in the time available.

The first consideration will be how to present it so that the pupil does not feel that he is being treated like an infant. Materials such as letter picture cards and separate letters are not likely to appeal, yet they can be very helpful, and it is important that they should not be rejected out of hand. (It might be less difficult for adult non-readers, who could take a more objective view of such visual aids.)

One way is to present the phonic/phonological approach as a rather scientific way of learning to read and write. Reference to the 'system' of spelling, and use of technical terms, may help to present the work as an adult study. It may also help the pupil's self-image to explain that these terms, and the detailed attention that he will give to sounds and word patterns, would be used by university students of linguistics and phonetics. When the work has begun to advance, explanations such as how adjacent sounds affect each other, how we use orthographic markers (such as silent -e) to indicate pronunciation, some account of the historical derivations of language, etc. can lift the whole area on to a mature level. Teachers can truthfully say that they would never teach infants in such a way. Of course too much explanation can be confusing and will not suit everyone; teachers must vary the approach to suit the needs of different pupils.

The usual teaching procedures of sequential, structured work should be followed, including multisensory methods. Pupils should be encouraged, for instance, to say words aloud, to say letter names, or to use sound cues when learning or trying to recall spellings. 'Finger writing' can be useful to try out a spelling pattern or b/d. The teacher should explain why these methods are recommended and adapt them to the individual pupil. He should be encouraged to explore which way he prefers to learn.

Boxes of letters might look childish, but presented in the right way can be used effectively. Scrabble letters might be acceptable. Even the Edith Norrie Letter Case, with its colour-coded sections, fits well with the linguistic/phonetic explanation, see page 211, Figure 14.1. Technology might help: the range of Spellmaster-type spellcheckers might be used to try out words before writing; they can be used to practise word patterns, just as well as to check uncertainties. A computer keyboard – especially if it has a suitable alphabetic order adaptation – is a splendid 'box of letters'.

Working on a computer is recommended for all kinds of reasons. It may be more motivating to work at spelling and writing if at least part of the work is through a medium that gives a presentable result. Older non-readers often feel very uneasy about their handwriting. They might still be using printed letters, or using capital letters inappropriately. Poor is made worse by crossings out and corrections. With a computer, the work can be saved, printed out – neatly presented – and filed for reference or further work. Any basic word-processing programme can be used (see Chapter 13 for further discussion).

The plan of work

Classroom demands cannot be ignored, but they should not drive the main programme. Basic work can be taught in a framework that uses some easier curriculum vocabulary and aims to move as quickly as possible to writing and reading words of two or more syllables. The pupil should be encouraged to write using basic phonic principles and aim for communication. If the work can be seen to have an immediate use it should be self-motivating. Easy information books and adapted curriculum worksheets can be used for reading.

Spelling and writing

The programme should be started from the beginning, because at best there will be gaps at the basic level and the level of skill may be very low. The pupil may be uncertain of the short vowels and attention to this area can take in a lot of basic spelling patterns – including *ck, ss, ll, ff* and consonant digraphs. Consonant blends and assimilation can be checked over or taught at the same time. Phonemic and phonological awareness may need some work; distinguishing between long- and short-vowel sounds is often difficult and produces a lot of mistakes. If the pupil learns to identify a long vowel and consistently spells it with final *-e*, that is a success! The vowel digraphs will have to be taught later – except for *ee/ea* and, here again, the aim should be to get an appropriate spelling for the vowel sound; *y* as a vowel, with its two final sounds (*my, body*), is another priority and will help to prevent the use of final *-e* as a sounded vowel.

Looking at the outline of the phonic programme on page 9, it would be appropriate to start work on the sequence to the right of the line as soon as possible, so that the written vocabulary can be extended. Suffixes themselves are not especially difficult. The pupil should be encouraged to use *-ing* and *-ed* (its three different sounds may have to be taught) without worrying too much about the tricky doubling and *-y* rules. Longer words are not as difficult as pupils think; they need to be taught how to break a word into syllables and work through the sounds. This can be done orally and with letters. The suffixes, and other common end syllables (e.g. *-ly, -le, -tion*), are stable units and, again, not as difficult as pupils think.

The teacher must also be useful! The pupil can be asked which words he wants or needs to learn and they can be covered one by one. If he cannot think, a look at his classwork may reveal the most frequent and obvious mistakes. He can be shown a number of strategies for learning and helped to find those that suit him best (Figure 6.7).

- Mnemonics: silly sentences, e.g. *-ould – O U lovely duck* words *because: big elephants can always upset small elephants* Illustrate with drawings if possible
- Little word in the big word: *they – he* is in *they*
- Visualisation: study the word then close eyes and try to see it. (It is sometimes suggested that looking up and to the left is effective)
- Multisensory tracing (see Figure 6.13)
- Saying words as they sound can help: *Wednes-day; pe-o-ple; fr-i-end*
- Alphabetic rehearsal in a 'rap' rhythm
- Cue card in handy place

Figure 6.7 Different strategies for learning spellings.

For pupils who find phonological work very difficult a different, more visual approach will be needed.

Handwriting

This will almost certainly need attention, if only because tests and exams nearly always have to be handwritten, although older pupils can be resistant to changing their writing habits. If the pupil is still printing, he may be willing to attempt joined writing.

Although this can be done as a separate exercise, it is better to approach it through spelling work. Encourage the pupil to adopt a simple style. A 'remedial job' needs a slightly different approach and it may be more practical to tidy up rather than attempt a complete overhaul. The pupil should be involved in the decisions and in the target setting (see Chapter 11 for further discussion).

Materials

It is important to make use of equipment, games, and means of recording work, that will help the pupil to accept the way he is learning. Pupils with a flair for drawing might make their own letter/sound cue cards and mnemonic sketches, and pack them in a plastic pocket-sized wallet. Some games are popular, e.g. the SWAP sets that practise vowels and spelling patterns. Instead of an exercise book for the phonic dictionary, a loose-leaf file, or a pack of file cards, hole-punched to go into a Filofax cover, could give a more adult image. All these devices should be presented as tools that have a useful function.

Reading

It can be difficult to find acceptable reading material that will not produce yet another failure. It is preferable to introduce something new; it is demoralising to have to go back to books tried before. It may even be necessary to hold back from a reading book until some sight vocabulary has been acquired and some word-recognition skills have been built up. Instead, reading can be practised by reading back sentences that have been written for spelling work. These could be extended with workbooks such as *Exercise your Spelling* that use a structured, small-steps approach, although this is far from ideal. Practice with other vocabulary could come from the learner's own ideas and self-expression, which the teacher could write down for him. The words on the 'most frequent usage' lists (Dolch, or the Literacy Hour materials) should be taught and practised for immediate recognition.

As soon as possible, one of the series for older beginners such as *Trend* (Ginn), *Spirals* (Ginn) or *Chillers* (Adult Basic Skills Agency/Hutchinson) might be tried. Information books have more to offer than stories, but easy books at the right interest level can be difficult to find. Size of print and the general layout will be important features. The pages in illustrated books are sometimes crowded with detail, which can be confusing.

It is especially important that this kind of work is offered in a private setting; pupils will be very sensitive to others seeing their struggles.

Catching up: the strugglers

This section is concerned with the slightly older children who have had very little help, or none at all, from specialist teachers.

By the time they are 9 or 10 years old, these children, even though dyslexic, may have picked up enough knowledge of the alphabetic–phonic system, letter sounds and simple word patterns to manage written work at a basic level. Their writing, however, is usually peppered with mistakes, showing confusions about spelling and phonic attempts that are often ingenious and sometimes bizarre. Some might actually be enthusiastic writers – producing work that is only half-comprehensible. More often they write little, and confine themselves to words that they know they can spell.

They have often acquired some reading skill, although their reading remains laboured. They cannot easily tackle ordinary books because of the longer, more complex sentences, and the hard words that break the fluency of the reading. Getting information from books for topic work is similarly difficult – although there the pictures help – and they may copy whole paragraphs that they cannot read accurately.

Class teachers sometimes do not worry unduly about a pupil at this stage because they seem to be coping. A child who has a basic competence might pass simply as one who does not try very hard; he might in fact be careful but be considered careless! Others might be more of a puzzle, e.g. the child who has plenty to say, but lacks the skills to get it on paper efficiently. Geoff's work (see page 74) fits the first description whereas Danny's writing (below) will serve as an example of the second.

Danny: 9;6

The adventure of Capten Zap (Figure 6.8) is part of a story covering several pages that Danny wrote over about 4 days. It is well structured, with ideas expressed in a lively way and convincing details that add interest. He had not had any special help. A look at the work shows that he knows a number of individual words; some mistakes occur in letter order (*nigth*, *firends*) and others either by omission or because he does not know the relevant spelling principle (*brak*). It looks as if Danny needs help on consonant blends: *srtis* (*starts*), *firends*, *bommrags* (*boomerangs*) and *samm* (*swam*). There are difficulties with tricky words such as *when*, and where he is uncertain he has two or three tries (*thre*, *ther; ovre, orve*). Long words are attempted more confidently, and he uses *-ed* and *-ing*. He also experiments with spelling in an inventive way; he explained that he intended *u geeeen* (*again*) to show that Capten Zap's song was a long one that went on and on. Danny was not happy about the way the song had worked out; he wanted it to rhyme but couldn't get the right words. He knew about 'rhymes' and liked reading rhyme books. Some testing will show more about the extent of his knowledge.

Although it is informative to look carefully at Danny's work, it would not be profitable simply to select mistakes for correction. Instead, a teacher should start by carrying out some systematic tests including letter–sound correspondences (he writes *grnied* for *journeyed*) and consonant blends. Does he hear the details of blends?

After that, the early work (regular words with short vowels) can be reviewed by building the first pages of the phonic dictionary, with as much detailed teaching as he needs to understand the principles.

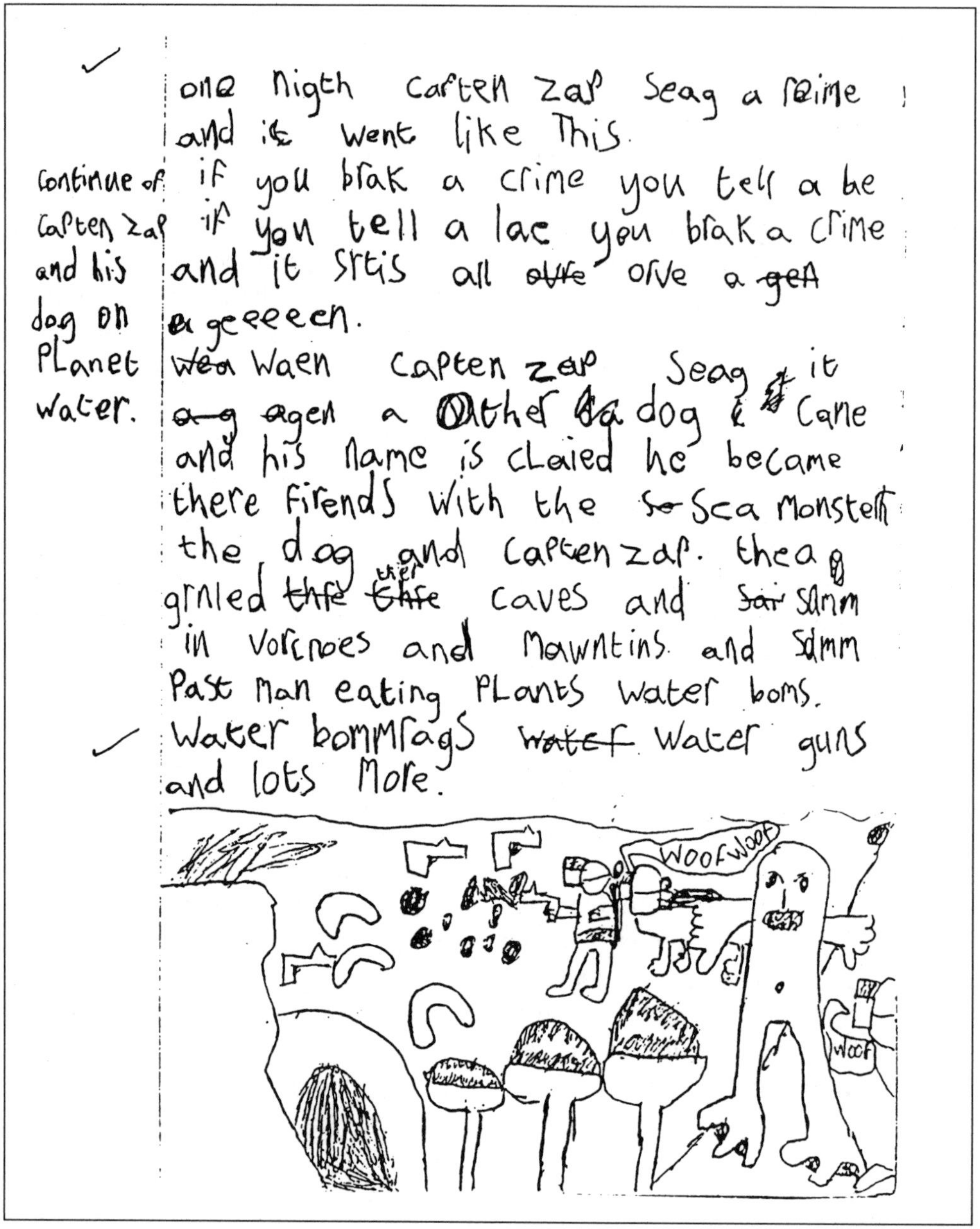

✓ one nigth carten zap seag a reime and it went like This.

continue of if you brak a crime you tell a be
capten zap if you tell a lae you brak a crime
and his and it srtis all olve olve a gea
dog on a geeeeen.
Planet wea waen capten zap seag it
water. agen a Other dog cane
and his name is claied he became
there firends with the so sea monsterl
the dog and capten zap. thea
grnled the the caves and san samm
in vorcnoes and mawntins and samm
past man eating plants water boms.
✓ water bommfags watef water guns
and lots more.

Figure 6.8 Danny – *The adventure of Capten Zap.*

It is important that he should understand the principles of short-vowel word structures and be sure of short-vowel sounds. In the sample illustrated, '*seag*' (*sang*) is a curious mistake, because he gets most of the simple words correct. There may be spelling patterns that he is not too sure about (e.g. *ck*). This work can all go on one or two pages if he seems secure; more space might be needed if there are numerous uncertainties (Figure 6.9). The teacher should explain that she is going to teach him the spelling system and this is the foundation work. Pupils do understand that 'everything needs a good foundation if it is to stand up without props'. (A note can be made of the mistakes in the story so that these can be given special attention over the first few lessons, either as isolated words or in due course with others in the same group.)

Unless this short-vowel work comes first, it is difficult to teach the principle of long-vowel sounds and their spellings logically and effectively. After that, long-vowel -*e* could follow; Danny knows some long-vowel -*e* words and it can link into these. The sentence-writing procedure will monitor his learning.

Danny had trouble with *start* (written *srtis*) so *ar* might follow. One cannot tell from one mistake whether or not this is general uncertainty. Again, the use of the phonic dictionary will provide a format for checking, revision or teaching, whichever is needed; *ar* spellings will have to be included in any case, so, if it is an isolated mistake, nothing is lost.

Geoff: 9;3

Geoff produces work (Figure 6.9) that is different from Danny's. It is factual and informative rather than imaginative, yet there are similarities. The numerous corrections show the ideas and the spellings being worked out – *because* was a small triumph. The different versions of the same word (*pound, pond; corut, cort*) indicate uncertainty and probably some lack of awareness of what he had actually written.

For Geoff too, the phonic programme must start at the short-vowel work. The pace of the work will probably be different from that of Danny, but the progression is likely to be similar.

The plan of work

It is likely that work with pupils such as Danny and Geoff would be planned as follows. (For teachers using the *Bangor Dyslexia Teaching System* [BDTS] references are given for the appropriate section for each part of the spelling programme – see Note 6.1, page 256.)

Spelling

Immediate objectives
- Sort out obvious confusions
- Consolidate early work, re-teaching where needed
- Teach remaining work in the basic programme. (*Bangor Dyslexia Teaching System*, Part 1)

Improve confidence so that more writing can be attempted.

Medium and long-term aims
- Teach a technique for learning irregular words
- Begin work on more difficult topics
- Continue into work to prepare for secondary school and the needs of a broad curriculum.

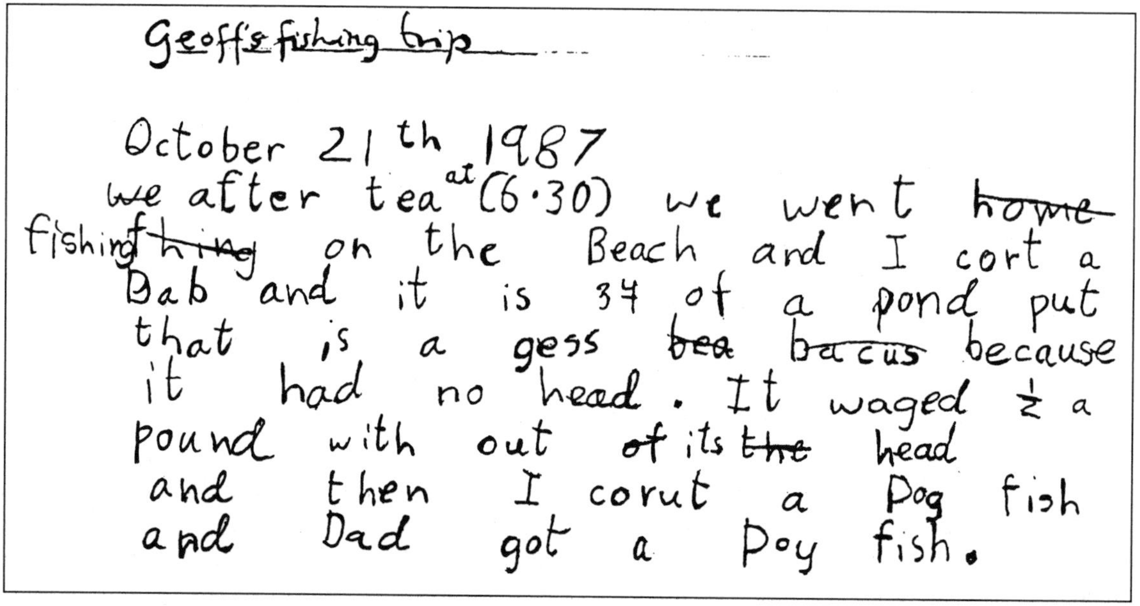

Geoff's fishing trip

October 21th 1987
we after tea at (6.30) we went home
fishing thing on the Beach and I cort a
Dab and it is 3¾ of a pond put
that is a gess bea bacus because
it had no head. It waged ½ a
pound with out of its the head
and then I corut a Dog fish
and Dad got a Doy fish.

Figure 6.9 Geoff's writing: *Catching a dab.*

Reading

Improve accuracy and fluency through:

- Direct teaching of more difficult sound spellings
- Development of word-attack skills.

Work on comprehension by development of strategies

- Use context
- Focus on meaning
- Engage with story or other text.

All these should interrelate, each helping development of the others. Provide guidance in choice of books, for enjoyment and interest. (For more detailed suggestions, see the end of this section, page 82 and Chapter 8.)

Further development of the phonic programme

Curriculum needs should be taken into account from the start. Pupils in the last years of primary school, and especially those already in secondary school, will need to write longer words than younger children. The suggestions that follow do not make up the whole spelling programme, but they include the most important. (See the BDTS or other manuals for a more detailed account of the phonic work.) They amplify the outline phonic programme shown in Chapter 2 (page 9).

Two-syllable words

After one-syllable words with short vowels have been checked, and the main patterns noted on

ă	ě	ĭ	ŏ	ŭ
hat	leg	sit	log	run
cap	pen	wig	pot	mud

Consonant digraphs: sh; ch; th; wh

mash	shed	ship	shop	shut
chat	when	fish	chop	rush
that		chips	moth	chug
		whip		
		which		

Consonant blends: beginnings

stab	step	spin	stop	stun
crag	dregs	slim	flop	plug
pram		grim	frog	drum
clap		skip		scum
		twins		

Consonant blends: ends

sand	end	sink	plonk	skunk
stand	tent	ring	lost	stung
lamp	best	fist	pond	chunk
	help	hint		jump

ck *end*

slack	deck	flick	rock	truck

Triple blends: spl; shr; scr; thr

splash		shrink		thrush
scram		spring		

Twins and triples

mass	bell	stiff	cross	dull
match	ketchup	hitch	scotch	hutch
badge	hedge	bridge	dodge	sludge

Figure 6.10 Phonic dictionary: first page for 'second stage' beginners.

page 1 of the phonic dictionary, some common two-syllable words with short vowels can be introduced.

- Two-syllable words with short vowels, e.g. *dentist*, *dustbin*, *ticket*, *instant* and the addition of simple suffixes (*-ing*, *-er*, *-ed*) to words where the root word needs no spelling change (*fish*, *fill*) might therefore follow on immediately from the first pages of the phonic dictionary. The vowel sound in a second (unstressed) syllable can be difficult to identify (e.g. *ticket*) and probabilities should be suggested; *et* is the most common ending; *rabbit* and other words with *-it* endings can be taught as exceptions.
- They may need help over syllable division – oral/auditory work will help. If they then work logically, such words should not prove too difficult. Systematic practice will help with both the reading and spelling of two-syllable words (see BDTS, Section 7). Pupils may need to be alerted to the final consonant in two-syllable words such as *dentist* which they may not pronounce clearly.

Long vowels; long-vowel '-e'

This is important both for new spelling work and to help to remove confusions. Many pupils have heard of 'magic *-e*' but are hazy about what it means. They can spell a number of words correctly, but have no knowledge of the principle to fall back on. (This can be seen in the example of Danny's work.) The important principle to drive home here is that two vowels are usually needed to make a long sound; they may be separated by one consonant and very occasionally by two. (In the Literacy Hour work 'long vowel *-e*' is

referred to as a 'separated digraph' and 'marker *-e*') (see BDTS, section 2.)

Two groups of words should be specially noted:
- *-ke* endings used with long vowels: this should be distinguished from the short vowel + *ck* ending to sort out the common confusion between *ck/ke*.
- *-ce*, *-ge* endings: these should be included as an introduction to the principle that *-e* softens *c* and *g*. Make a point of contrasting *-ce* and *-ke* words.

Two-syllable words may be introduced here too (e.g. *invite*, *excuse*, *alone*, *engage*) which will also help reading (see BDTS, section 7). Work on consonant blends and digraphs should be extended over the *-e* vocabulary.

Vowel + r spellings: -ar and -or

These early spellings may need to be checked.
-ir, -ur, -er

These are best spread over a few lessons, to keep like sounds with different spellings apart. Pupils should know the probabilities: *er* is the most usual spelling for a final, unstressed /ur/ syllable because it is a suffix. It is not so common as ir and ur in one-syllable words, but *her* and *term* will be needed frequently; *ur* is very unusual as an ending in a two-syllable word (*murmur*) (see BDTS, sections 2 and 4).

Adding suffixes

Simple suffixing with short-vowel words ending in two consonants (e.g. *fish*, *call*, *jump*) can be introduced almost immediately because no change to the root word is needed.

As soon as knowledge of short- and long-vowel principles is secure, and pupils can respond correctly to distinctive spellings such as *rip – ripe, not – note,* the next two suffixing rules can be introduced, namely the dropping of an *-e* used to lengthen a vowel, and doubling principles.

Practice in the form of word sums is useful, e.g. *fish + ing; time + er; nod + ed.* This can help a pupil to become aware of the parts from which many two-syllable words are built and of the procedures for adding them together. He is then in a position to check words as he writes, or after finishing the work.

Teaching the principles for suffixing

Suffixing can be taught simply as a pattern to be followed, but it is preferable for the teacher to explain the principle by reference to short- and long-vowel sounds: a short vowel in the first syllable must be followed by two consonants so the vowel sound does not change. If only a single consonant is used, the vowel will change to its long sound.

Pupils can see this by comparing words, e.g. *better/Peter, hopped/hoped, tapping/taping.* (Words in the vowel + r group have a slightly different sound, but behave as short/long vowels, e.g. *furry/fury; scarred/scared; sorry/story.*) Knowing the principle will enable the pupil to apply logic and follow the 'rule', instead of having to rely on memory or to recall the relevant pattern. This is one of the few 'rules' of English spelling that is almost 100 per cent reliable. A more technical explanation can be given by reference to closed and open syllables. (See

Figure 6.15 for notes on the six kinds of syllables in English words.)

Many teachers have their own preferred story about doubling, and draw pictures and diagrams to make the point more forcefully, for instance:

> The consonant must be doubled to make a wall that will 'protect' the first vowel from the vowel that follows; this means that the vowel will keep its short sound.

The portcullis must be dropped to keep out the invading vowel

The doubling/single consonant pattern is also found in many other words, where root and suffix are not involved but the principle is the same, e.g. *supper/super, letter/meter, giddy/tidy, hobby/robot,* etc. Here there are numerous exceptions that have to be learned – *robin, comic, habit, limit* – and many other words. Figure 6.11 shows a guide to suffixing.

As each suffixing rule is taught, all the vocabulary that follows can be extended to two-syllable words. Teachers might prefer to hold back teaching the *y* rule until they teach or revise words ending in *y* after a consonant (*fly, reply*). (See page 157 for the suffixing rules shown in a chart format for use as a cue card in class. BDTS sections 1 and 6.)

Long vowels: ī sounds: -y and -ight

Plural and past tense endings *-ies* and *-ied* can be taught here as distinct endings if the teacher does not want to deal with the *-y* suffixing rule at this point. BDTS, section 4.

- Many words don't need to be changed – just join on the suffix (words ending in more than one consonant, words with vowel digraphs or other long-vowel spellings, e.g. *throw*, *stay*)
- In three groups of words the last letter of the root word often has to be changed before the suffix
  1. Words with ONE vowel (usually a SHORT sound) and ONE consonant after it (e.g. *stop*, *run*, *swim*) and words ending in -*r* (e.g. *star*, *stir*)
     DOUBLE the consonant when the suffix begins with a VOWEL: -*ed, -ing, -er, -y, -est* are the main vowel suffixes
     If the suffix begins with a consonant – don't change anything: -*s, -ly, -ful, -ness, -less* are the main consonant suffixes

2. Words ending in -*e* (usually a LONG-vowel sound) (e.g. *make, hope, race, care*)
   DROP the -*e* if the suffix begins with a vowel. (If you drop -*e*, you don't then double the consonant as well!)
   If the suffix begins with a consonant – don't change anything.
   (This rule applies to all words with final -*e*, including irregular words, e.g. *love, give, come*, and to words with vowel digraphs, e.g. *nurse, choose* and many others)
3. Words ending in -*y* after a consonant (e.g. *try, reply, lady, lucky*)
   CHANGE *y* to *i* and add any ending – vowel and consonant – except -*ing*
   If the ending is -*ing*, DON'T change anything

Figure 6.11 A guide to suffixing in one-syllable words.

Extension of long-vowel -e work to the vowel + r words.

All the long vowels are modified by -*r* in different ways, some only slightly. The most distinctly different sound is /are/ as in *care*, *prepare*, *parent* and many other words. This is the main spelling for this sound; *ear* (*bear*) has five examples and *air* about nine common words. These can be taught a bit later, although they should still be kept separate from the vowel digraphs *ea* and *ai* (see BDTS, section 7 and Note 6.2, page 256).

Long vowels: vowel digraphs

The easier vowel digraphs *ee* and *oo* (with its two sounds) can probably be noted quickly (pupils such as Danny and Geoff usually know them); -*ea* (*eat*) should also be taught early because it is such a common spelling of the long *e* sound; -*ee* and -*ea* should be taught on separate occasions because words with these spellings must be memorised –

there is no guiding principle to use. It is impossible to teach them all at one time; it is better to learn them either when they turn up in writing or in batches, linked by 'silly sentences' or themes. (Food words with this vowel sound tend to be spelled with -*ea*; *beef*, *beer* and *cheese* are exceptions.)

Next vowel digraph work

Instead of keeping spellings for the same sounds entirely separate, pupils might be shown immediately how the position in the word can be a guide to the spelling.

Pairs that are alternatives can be taught together. The most common are:

- *ai* and *ay*
- *ou* and *ow* (-*owl*, -*own*)
- *oi* and *oy*
- *oa*; *ow* (-*own*; *owl* – a single word – *bowl*)
- *au* and *aw* (-*awl*, -*awn*).

The second group is less straightforward than the first, because of the -owl, -own patterns, and one or two exceptions such as crowd and foul; -ower and -owel are easier if it is explained that -ow is also a syllable ending.

Similarly, sound can be a guide to the middle and final spellings oa (road) and ow (snow), although these are not, strictly speaking, alternatives. Here again the pattern -own (with long o sound) can be taught; au is a much less frequent spelling than aw but there are a few common words that need to be taught (auto-, audio, author, autumn, sauce/r and Paul) (BDTS, section 2) (aunt, fault and sausage might be included as irregular pronunciations of the same spelling); ew also has its 'middle spelling' eu, but this is so infrequent that it is better to teach ew on its own. In some words it sounds very like oo (crew, grew).

Some vowel digraph spellings are found in fewer words but these include some common words:

- ie, oe, ue (long-vowel -e without the second consonant – pie, toe, cue)
- ea (head, bread, breath, heaven, pleasant)
- ie (field, believe, chief)
- ei and ey (veins, they)
- ei (ceiling, receive, seize, weird).

Note: the rule 'i before e except after c' applies only to words where the vowel sound is /ē/. There are only half-a-dozen common words in this group and two (above) have no c in the spelling. It is not therefore a very useful rule and I usually teach the cei/ei words as a spelling pattern.

The 'w' words: wa- and wo; war- and wor-

The high-frequency words in this group (was, what, want, wash, war, work, word) should be taught as special vocabulary as soon as they are needed. The others can be left until later and dealt with as an irregular but common vowel spelling (see BDTS, section 1).

Other irregular spellings of vowel sounds

- o as in front is the most common irregular short-vowel spelling
- most, kind, old, child: these groups are common words that need attention but do not usually cause problems.
  (See BDTS, section 1.)

Soft c and g and use of k

Pupils should have met this principle first in -e words, such as ice, age and similar words at an earlier stage of the programme. The work should now be extended to the more common words in which i and y soften the consonants. This is particularly important for reading.

- When to use k. This can be explained at the same time. (Briefly, this letter is used when a /k/ sound is needed before the softening vowels e, i and y – see BDTS, section 6.)
- It is useful to help pupils respond automatically to the soft and hard sounds of c, k and g by practising with a pack of cards showing examples of all the combinations – in syllables and whole words, namely:

ca-, co-, cu-; ce-, ci-, cy-; ke-, ki-
ga-, go-, gu-; ge-, gi-, gy-.

(The aim of this exercise is to sound the consonant correctly out of context of any word.) The letter strings may look like open syllables but it is useful to ask the pupil to practise the consonants with a short and a long vowel.

- Point out that *g* can be variable; many common short words with *ge* and *gi* are in fact pronounced with a hard sound. This can be explained by their Germanic origin. The soft /j/ sound of *g* is more often met in longer words.

gu- to preserve the hard sound of g before e, i and y

This follows naturally from the soft -*g* work: *guess*, *guide*, *guitar*, *disguise*, *guy*.

Silent consonants

- *wr*, *kn* and *mb* are the most common
- Consonant digraphs: *ch* /k/ *ph*.

Vowel groups with gh

These include -*ought*, -*aught* and *ough*: about 20 words in all:

- *ought* has five common words that rhyme with it and are spelled like it: *bought*, *brought*, *fought*, *thought*, *nought*(*s*). This is fairly straightforward
- *aught* words: only five common words – *caught*, *taught*, *daughter*, *naughty*, *slaughter*. These should be taught as a separate group. 'Silly sentences' for these groups will help pupils to remember them
- *augh*: *laugh*, *laughter* can be mentioned here – especially useful for reading
- *ough*: there are about 14 *ough* words in common

usage, with six pronunciations; the most useful ones are probably *through*; *rough*, *tough*, *enough*; *though*, *although*; *cough*.

They will have to be learned as special cases.

Stable final syllables: -le, -tion, -sion, -age, -ture and suffixes -ly, -ful,- less, -ous

These are among the most important for pupils at this stage. There are numerous others that can be taught gradually over a period of months, in groups or individually when they are needed.

Making the learning secure and automatic

It is essential that pupils are given frequent opportunities to practise all these spelling points. There are plenty of exercises and games to bring a dimension of interest and fun into the work and teachers can devise their own to suit particular needs. It is even better if these can help to raise interest in vocabulary and language forms.

For using suffixes and prefixes and writing long words the following can be helpful (Figure 6.12):

- 'Word sums' for joining root words and suffixes help pupils to use the different suffixing rules without hesitation.
- 'Word trees' or sprays with whole words or frequently occurring root syllables *port*, -*struct*, -*ject* can be used to explore the way that words can grow or change as different parts are added.

Planning lessons

At any time teachers may want to have two or three topics under way. These need to be selected with care so that the different areas of work complement and do not confuse each other. A

hop + ing	hope + ed
fog + y	ice + y
rage + ed	thin + er
shine + y	mad + ly
slow + er	pup + y
hope + ful	care + less

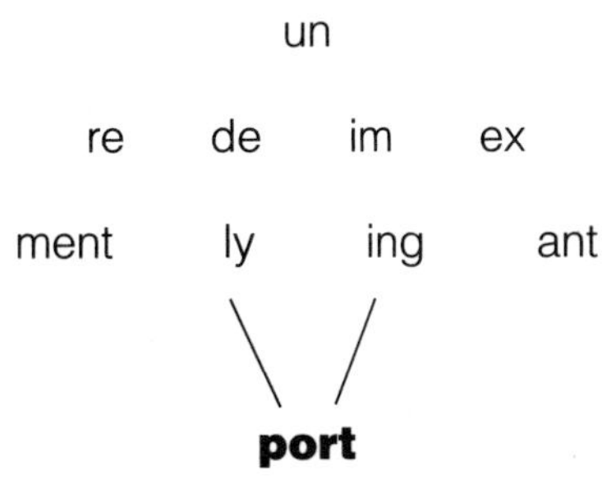

un

re   de   im   ex

ment   ly   ing   ant

port

Figure 6.12 Word sums and word trees.

mixture of exercises and games can help to keep up the momentum and engage the pupil's interest.

Over a couple of terms, work for pupils such as Danny and Geoff could be drawn from the following areas:

1. Vowel work (spelling): after building the early dictionary pages:
   - -e
   - vowel + r: ar, or
   - vowel digraphs: ee, oo, ea (seat); ai/ay, oi/oy, ou/ow, own, owl
   - other vowel + r spellings: ir, ur, er.
2. Plurals and present tense forms:
   - adding s and es; -ies can be noted as the form for words ending in y
   - changing f and fe to ves (e.g. leaf, life).
3. Suffixing:
   - use root words from current vowel work.
4. Syllable work:
   - for long word attack (reading)
   - for spelling.
5. Irregular and difficult words:
   - systematic coverage of essential vocabulary,

and other irregular words as needed
   - teach a multisensory method for learning these words (Figure 6.13).
6. Guided or free writing:
   - to check on the use of recent spelling work
   - to help use of punctuation
   - to encourage self-expression in writing
   - use of frameworks for helping to structure written work (see Chapter 10)
   - to develop strategies for spelling and self-checking (Figure 6.14).
7. Reading:
   - phonic practice related to spelling work
   - on-going book – improvement of accuracy and fluency
   - structured work on syllable division, related to syllable work.
8. Other areas of work:
   - handwriting
   - use of dictionary
   - extension of vocabulary
   - oral expression
   - careful listening.

Preparation: write out word in large letters, preferably in joined writing.

The pupil should:

i. Look at the word carefully and read it
ii. Trace over it, saying the letter names.
   Say the word after each tracing
   Repeat the tracing till he thinks he can remember the letters
iii. Cover the word. Write the word, saying the name of each letter
iv. Check: if right – repeat two or three times
   If wrong – repeat from step 1
v. Test the next day, and the next week

This is a good technique for shortish words.
For longer, polysyllabic words, a letter-by-letter recital can be confusing, and it is better to work in syllables. Comparison of wrong spellings with the correct forms will usually show that only a small part of the incorrect word is actually wrong. This can help to make the task manageable.

i. Identify exactly which syllables or letter strings need to be memorised
ii. Note where they are in the whole word
iii. Learn the tricky bits
iv. Practise writing the whole word. Copy it first to get the tricky bit in the right place, saying the syllables
v. Practise two or three times without copying. Most of the consonant sounds will have regular spelling. Use these and the syllables (say them quietly) as a guide to the whole word
vi. Check that it's right; re-learn any wrong bits. Keep it under review for a few days

Figure 6.13 A multisensory technique for learning words.

* Be logical: follow a known pattern or rule and get as near as possible to a representation of the consonant and vowel sounds
* Listen carefully to the sequence of sounds and syllables in the word you want
* Say it aloud, clearly, or whisper it and listen 'in your head'
* Remember most consonants will be spelled in the regular way
* Make sure you have enough syllables: remember every syllable must have a vowel. (Vowel digraphs count as one; a final -e does not count as an extra vowel)
* Long words: work through them syllable by syllable
* Use knowledge of word parts: roots, suffixes, prefixes

Figure 6.14 Strategy for spelling unknown words.

Danny's reading

Danny chose to read a book about ghosts. It had lively drawings and he thought it was funny. He tried to read with expression, and could manage most of the text, but long words tripped him up and he either substituted others that fitted or missed them out. He did not try to work them out. He said he did not much like reading and comics were difficult because a lot of the words were 'hard'.

He needs encouragement to read so that he will find it a pleasure. Building on his liking for rhymes and 'funny' books, it should be possible to guide him to books that he can read easily, start-ing just below his present reading level (about 8 years).

Michael Rosen's verses and the *Starpol* (Ginn) stories and *Ziggy Zoom* books might start him off. His interest in adventure stories could be used to get him into some of the Barrington Stoke titles which have some funny books as well as 'scary' ones.

All the foregoing spelling work will be helpful for reading and direct connections between the two can be made through word-attack practice and games.

Developing word-attack skills: decoding words

Many children have picked up the idea that 'split-ting up' an unknown word will help them to read it, but they lack efficient ways of doing this. They should be taught some key techniques:

- Look for recognised units, such as whole words or common roots (*-port*, *-struct*, *-ject*), recog-nised syllables (*un-*, *re-*), endings (*-ing*, *-tion*).
- Work on different kinds of syllable, how each can be recognised, and its typical vowel sound (Figure 6.15).
- Look for the pattern of vowels and consonants: code these by colour or by writing C or V above each. Note where there are two or more conso-nants together. This can also be done by pointing to the vowels with stretched-out index and middle fingers, and counting the letters between them.
- On the basis of the techniques above, decide where to divide the syllables; mark them clearly or block them off in turn with a finger, or card.
- Say each syllable separately, then blend them into the whole word.

- closed syllable (short-vowel sound): *sun, fish, strip*
- open syllable (long-vowel sound): *we, no, de-, bi-*. The spelling principle here is that a single vowel coming at the end of a syllable, has a long sound. Understanding of this is particularly use-ful in the writing of polysyllabic words. Contrast the closed syllable, where the consonant 'stops' the vowel sound and keeps it short.
- long-vowel *-e*: *name, spine*
- vowel + *r*: *bird, her, start* (Vowels in vowel + *r* syllables have distinctive sounds; they cannot be categorised as short or long.)
- vowel digraphs: *read, snow, wait* and combined with *r*: *air, our, ear* These have a great variety of spellings. It takes some time to teach them all in detail for spelling; they can be noted as exam-ples of a syllable type. It is important that pupils learn them quickly for reading.
- *-le* syllables (unstressed ending): *bottle, candle*

Figure 6.15 Six kinds of syllables commonly found in English words.

Identifying vowel–consonant patterns

Many English words follow typical vowel–consonant patterns which relate to the different kinds of sylla-ble. Division into syllables can be made easier if examples of the most common types are prac-tised.

- *cvccvc* (*rabbit, trumpet, tripper*): divide between the middle consonants – pupils should be shown how to deal with unstressed final syl-lables such as *er*, which have an ambiguous vowel sound (schwa)
- *cvcvc*: where a single consonant separates the two vowels, the 'rule' is less clear.

The division can be placed either before, or after, the middle consonant. Some experimenting may be needed to find out which is right.

First divide the syllables before the consonant, namely *ba'con*; *ho'tel*. This will give an open syllable with a long vowel sound.

Numerous English words do not follow this pattern, e.g. *robin*, *finish*. If the first division does not produce a recognisable word, try it the other way: *rob'in* (see Note 6.3, page 256).

Base word and suffix

In some words the division into open/closed syllables cuts across the boundaries of base word and suffix (e.g. *gli'der*, *ma'king*). The teacher must decide which should have priority – pronunciation or grammatical structure.

Longer words

In longer words the pattern varies, but observation of the closed and open syllables can help. It is usual to preserve common syllables and endings, and to divide between two adjacent consonants unless these form a consonant blend or digraph. Thus: *re'cep'tion*, *to'mor'row*, *im'port'ant*, *i'den'ti'ty*.

After dividing the syllables the pupil should say each one carefully, watching out for letter sounds such as 'soft -c'. The knowledge of syllable types can help (Figure 6.15).

For pupils who need a lot of practice with this method, guidelines about syllable stress and how this affects the vowel sound will be helpful, e.g.

- If a first syllable is unstressed (e.g. *decide*, *pronounce*) the vowel may have a neutral, or a schwa, sound, even though technically the syllable is open.
- *i* in an open-syllable position before an ending as in *division*, *ignition* and *material* NEVER has the value of long-vowel /ī/ (as in pi'lot). It is pronounced as a short /ĭ/ (vision) or like /ē/ (*ra'di'o*), or even as consonant /y/ (*on'ion*).

Practice with this technique helps to speed up response to polysyllabic words; it also helps pupils to write them.

It is important to look at these different kinds of syllable and syllable patterns in some detail because they occur so frequently in English words. Automatic response in reading can help to develop instant word recognition. Familiarity with the distinctive sound of each one, and knowledge of the spelling pattern, can also be a great help in writing. Spelling and reading work can be drawn together here. As the pupil works through the different forms, systematic practice can be given in reading and spelling examples, both as separate syllables and in a wide range of words. Games are useful here (see Chapter 14) (Note 6.4, page 256).

Nonsense words

When particular word patterns or syllable types have been taught, it can be useful to practise with nonsense words or syllables as well as real words. The nonsense words help to train pupils to apply phonic principles accurately without being able to check for meaning. Pupils often enjoy making up their own nonsense words using the different kinds of syllable and pronouncing them (perhaps inventing meanings or drawing them).

Both kinds of work can help to improve automatic, rapid response to word parts and this helps immediate recognition of whole words (Figure 6.16).

All these approaches to word attack are a means to an end and, having a technique at their disposal, pupils can gain the confidence to try. (For practice materials, see Appendix II.)

When reading, decoding should be a last resort if they fail to guess from context or from immediate phonic cues such as the first letter. If a pupil needs to access more than an occasional word in this way, the text is too difficult and he should be helped to find something nearer his reading level. (This seems too obvious to state but pupils are sometimes expected to struggle with a book that is too hard for them to read independently, in the belief that this will 'stretch' their reading ability.)

Topping up: the poor speller

This section is concerned with those pupils who have become competent enough readers but have persistent difficulties with spelling. They might be

	Syllable 1	Syllable 2	Syllable 3	Whole word
drumstick				
bodnip				
tirnate				
flimmerish				
relation				
jordotion				

1. Mark the vowels and divide the word
2. Write out each syllable and say it
3. Say the whole word

It is important that each step is carried out when pupils first work with this kind of exercise. They often want to skip stages.
(For spelling practice, write out the word again without copying, saying the syllables.)

Figure 6.16 Exercise in dividing syllables.

secure with basic work, being able to write with reasonable fluency and accuracy if they restrict themselves to regular, short words. (They might achieve a 'spelling age' of 9 or 10 on a standardised test.) In practical terms this means that they probably have difficulty with some parts of the basic programme:

- the more tricky vowel combinations
- some common irregular words
- different word endings
- polysyllabic words
- suffixing – especially doubling and the *y* rule – may not be consistent
- learning new vocabulary – such as technical and subject-specific words.

There may also be residual errors in very basic work (e.g. *ck*, *ke*, *tch*, *soft c*.) They may not have been taught (and they will not have picked up) any of the more complex spelling patterns and more advanced principles of spelling such as doubling the final consonant of an unstressed syllable in a two-syllable word.

All this will be a serious handicap as they move through secondary school and may prevent them achieving their potential in curriculum work. Even if actual errors are disregarded, spelling inefficiency tends to interrupt the flow of thought because words cannot be written automatically. If the pupil gets round his poor skills in the mechanics of writing by restricting his vocabulary, the quality of expression will suffer.

At this stage, therefore, the programme of work should have a two-tier characteristic:

- Systematic work: consolidation of early work where necessary and teaching of more advanced work in the phonic programme, so that skills can be improved.
- Direct help with vocabulary for curriculum work.

Exactly what is taught is likely to be shaped by the pupil's needs – immediate as well as long term. He should be helped to state both of these for himself. Nevertheless, if teachers do not direct and shape the programme, and work only from mistakes or immediate demands, there will be a great deal of 'dotting about' which can lead to confusion. It is important to work through the principles and spelling patterns that are likely to crop up, although the exact sequence of the work can be flexible and mistakes in written work can indicate where work is needed.

An example can be seen in the sentence '*My mum is a prashun offiser.*' Rather than merely correcting the words, comparison with the correct spellings will show this pupil that the errors are:

- 'telescoping'
- lack of knowledge of -*tion*
- a missed soft *c*.

Attention to the correct pronunciation of *pro'ba'tion* should take care of the telescoping; -*tion* can be noted for work in the near future; the *c* of *officer* can be linked to *office*, *notice* and *police*. Thus, as well as correcting the two words, links can be made to other vocabulary and some important points can be tackled.

On the other hand, following a predetermined course of work does raise a problem: how does the teacher know what will arise, and is there any point in teaching vocabulary that pupils do not use? The difficulty here is that dyslexic pupils, as has been noted before, tend to restrict themselves to words that they think they can spell correctly. Teachers may be able to give them confidence in their ability to use a wider range of words; this can be done by vocabulary extension work while working through some major topics. (The teacher will need to give practice in the use of such new words and keep them under review.) They should also be taught, and encouraged, to use good learning strategies (see Figures 6.13 and 6.14 and suggestions on page 82).

The 'Spelling Wheel' model (page 97) may help the teacher to respond to the needs of these older pupils. It shows the logical sequence of teaching from the most basic work (the inside circle) and how it expands outwards to more advanced work. It also indicates routes that can be taken where an accelerated pace is needed, by studying particular features and linking them to related points.

As usual, a test should be given to establish a rough spelling level and some written work examined.

David: 13;6

David's work will serve as an example for the 'third stage' pupil. This boy had help between the ages of 10 and 12;6 and had a spelling age of about 10 when lessons stopped. He was a good reader. The work shown in Figure 6.17 dates from just over a year later; this is about a third of the story. He would probably be able to correct many of the spelling mistakes but the work has not gone beyond the first draft. This kind of work presents a problem for the teacher if David was to come for more help. How much of the early work needs to be re-taught?

He has learnt suffixing rules and spelling patterns and can get them right; his difficulty lies in producing them automatically when his major concern is with the development of his story. He needs now to go on to more advanced spellings that he will need for his school subject work: prefixes, different suffixes including compound suffixes, irregular and less common vowel sounds, and subject vocabulary. Along the way, his teacher should be able to create opportunities to revise the suffixing rules, vowel digraphs and other syllable types, and spelling patterns such as -tch and -dge as they occur in root words. He should be given plenty of practice at writing polysyllabic words, aiming at speed of writing.

At the same time he should be helped to develop proofreading techniques, and form the habit of checking and correcting work before handing it in. Eventually, the use of a word processor for much of his written work might help him to become more aware of spelling – either through the error 'beep' or because the words he writes may register with him more fully as they appear in 'printed' form on the screen.

Developing a structured programme for older pupils

The phonic dictionary as a framework for the structured programme

At this stage the phonic dictionary can serve as a brief introduction to the spelling system for a 'first-time' pupil with this kind of need, and as a revision

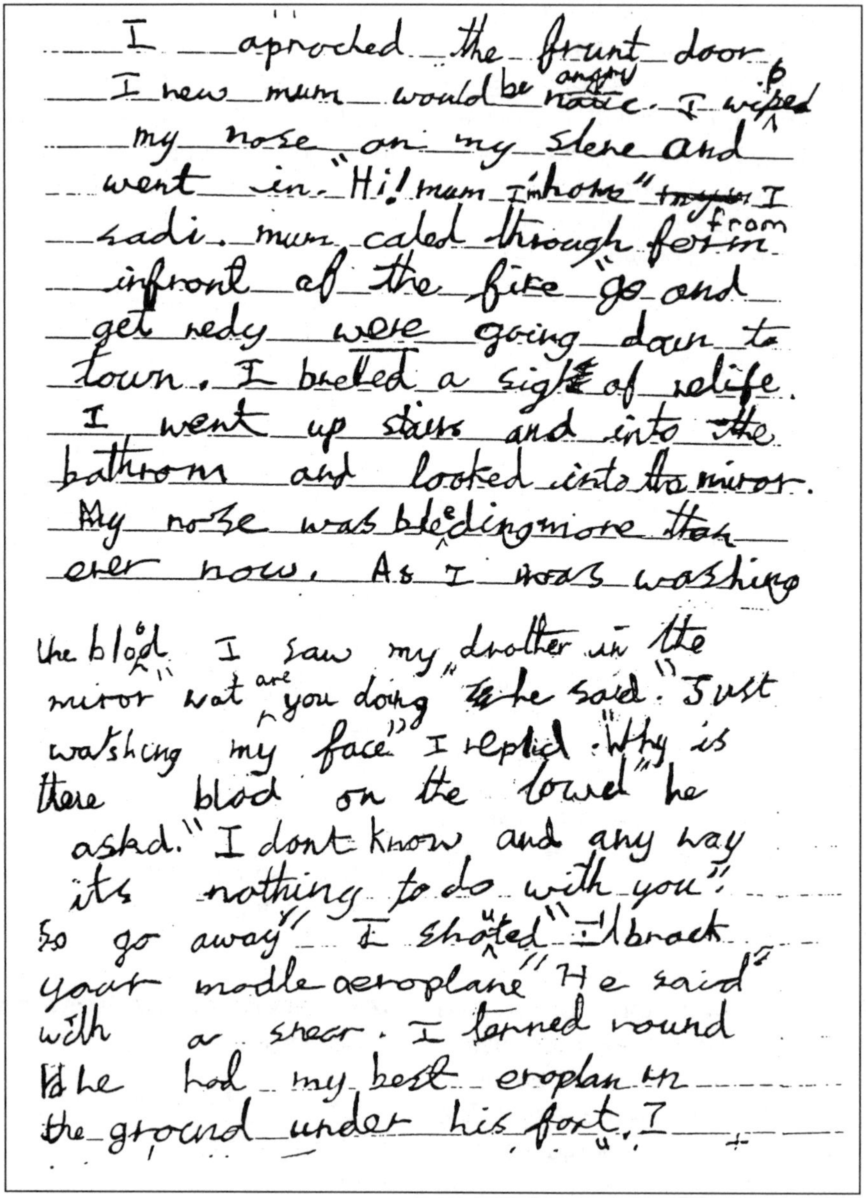

I aproched the frunt door
I new mum would be angry noties. I wiped
my nose on my sleve and
went in. "Hi! mum I'm home" I
sadi. mum caled through for in from
infront of the fire "go and
get redy were going down to
town." I breled a sigh of relife.
I went up stairs and into the
bathrom and looked into the miror.
My nose was bleding more than
ever now. As I was washing
the blod I saw my brother in the
miror "wat are you doing" he said. "Just
washing my face" I replied. "Why is
there blod on the towel" he
askd. "I dont know and any way
its nothing to do with you"
so go away" I shoted" "I brock
your modle aeroplane" He said
with a snear. I terned round
he had my best eroplan on
the ground under his foot. I

Figure 6.17 David's story.

tool for David. For both it can be a handy reference book for basic principles as well as the record of new work. Flexibility of arrangement will now be useful, so a file of some kind will be better than an exercise book or notebook – although this does raise the question of how to make an index. A Filofax with cards, as suggested on page 70, might appeal to the older pupils.

As at the earlier stage, it is important to check right from the start of the phonic programme to ensure that the pupil understands the basic system. This can be done very quickly, and the record can be concise. Although revision work can be condensed, each new topic is best entered on its own page.

Checking and revising earlier work

Some of the points in this section overlap with points in 'Catching up: the strugglers' in this chapter. This shows that, when spelling work is revised with a pupil at a later stage in secondary school, the emphasis will probably change. The way that spellings are explained and the words chosen as examples will be appropriate for an older pupil.

Six kinds of syllable (see Figure 6.15)
Categorising syllables in this way may be a new idea for students who have never had help for spelling. For them, and others like David, it provides a useful way to check on basic knowledge. The amount of detail needed for each syllable type will be determined by the student's needs. The work can be incorporated into the phonic dictionary, either as separate topics or on one page as a summary. In all cases, lists with a few common examples can serve as an anchor for new words as they arise (see BDTS, section 7).

- Short vowels–closed syllables: check and record a selection of common patterns by compiling the phonic dictionary, page 1. Two-syllable words should be included and words with *y* as the short vowel (*myth*, *gym*, *system*) (see BDTS, sections 1 and 6)
- Long vowel -*e*: two-syllable words can be used here too. Words with *y* should be included (*tyre*, *style*).
- Long vowels–open syllables: understanding this principle is essential for reading and writing polysyllabic words. Examples should include two-syllable words so that prefixes can be noted along with real words (*solo*, *pylon*, *pretend*, *direct*).
- Vowel digraphs: many of these will be familiar, but the most common examples should be checked and unusual sounds added. Homophones can be checked and uncertainties noted.
- Vowel + *r*: where this is associated with vowel digraphs, the pronunciation of the digraph is affected and many homophones are found (e.g. *pour*, *poor*; *course*, *coarse*; *pear*, *pair*). New work is often needed on these.
- -*le*: words ending in *able/ible* can be noted as examples here.

The main need with this final sound will probably be to separate -*le*, -*el* and -*al* spellings (see below under 'Choosing among -*le*, -*el* and -*al*').

Alternative spellings for long vowel sounds

At this stage it is important to note the alternative spellings for each vowel. These can be noted in the phonic dictionary as the separate choices for each vowel (Figure 6.18). It is also useful to make a card for use in the classroom showing the main long vowel and vowel-digraph choices. Pupils can often recall a correct spelling if given a cue, or they might try alternative spellings and choose the right one (see BDTS, section 8).

A basic card with the main choices for all the vowels is shown as Figure 10.10 in Chapter 10.

This could be expanded according to need and to what has been taught.

Suffixing
- Check familiarity with the principles, particularly doubling and the -*y* rule.
- Check the use of consonant suffixes with -*e* words (e.g. *safely*).

More advanced spelling work

Doubling after a stressed syllable in two-syllable words: *begin*, *visit*

The consonant is doubled if the stress falls on the second (or third) syllable, but not if the stress is on the first. Contrast *begin–beginning* and *limit–limited*. There is one exception to this principle: a final -*l* is

a – e	-ai-	-ay	$\bar{a}$ open syllable
sale (shop)	sails	say	sta'tion
page	main (road)	rayon	ra'dar
relate	explain	relay	invita'tion
-ei-	-ey	-ea- (3 only)	
veins	grey	break	
neighbours	they	great	
reign	survey	steak (meat)	
(foreign – irregular)			

Figure 6.18 Spelling choices for long /$\bar{a}$/ sound.

always doubled in English spelling, e.g. *travel–travelling*; *compel–compelled* (in American spelling, the reverse applies: *-l* is never doubled) (see BDTS, section 6).

A few words are tricky because they seem to relate to other words where a double consonant would be expected and they may 'look wrong', e.g. *benefit–benefiting*, *focus–focused*, although here usage now accepts *ss*.

Choosing between *-le*, *-el* and *-al*

A useful guideline is as follows:

- *-le* is much more common than *-el*. It is usually found after a consonant with a distinct sound: *table*, *pickle*, *puddle*, *goggle*, *little*, *castle*, *hassle*, *dazzle*. Words with medial *f* also take *-le* (*raffle*, *stifle*), although they might seem to belong to the next group.
- *-el* follows 'softer' sounds, e.g. *satchel*, *pummel*, *tunnel*, *barrel*, *travel*, *vowel*. There are a few exceptions which can be noted (*hostel*, *chapel*, *label*, *rebel*).
- *-al*: it can be helpful to show pupils that *-al* can be a suffix which can denote an adjective (e.g. *fatal*, *tidal*, *loyal*), although sometimes the new word is a noun (*betrayal*). Others, originally adjectives, now function as nouns (*signal*, *pedal*) or can be either (*general*). Some *-al* words are nouns that have no obvious derivation (e.g. *interval*, *metal*, *medal*).

Writing long words – suffixes and prefixes

Suffix and prefix work involves the writing of polysyllabic words. This can also help reading skills and reading fluency, as pupils become more aware of particular syllables, and recognise them more quickly in long words (see BDTS, sections 9 and 10).

Suffixes and endings

 -ous; *-ture*
 -ent/-ant, *-ence/-ance*
 -tion/-sion/-ssion
 -al, *-ful*: the single *l* should be noted – although when *-ly* is added, this becomes *ll*
 It helps spelling if *-ally* and *-fully* are taught as whole units
 Adding *-ly*: to *-le* (*gently*) and to *able/ible* (*probably*, *sensibly*)
 The point should be made that adding *-ly* usually converts an adjective to an adverb.

Prefixes

- Ending with a vowel: *re-*, *de-*, *bi-*, etc.
  Words starting with prefix *a-* (*alone*, *aloud*) should be taught as a special group because they can be confused with words where *a* is followed by a double consonant (*affect*, *allow*). (This is an Anglo-Saxon prefix, not a Latin one like many of the others.)
- Ending with a consonant: *in-*, *ex-*, *dis-*, etc.
  The important point here is the principle of assimilation, where this results in a double consonant, e.g. *attempt*, *connect*. (The prefix, deriving originally from a Latin preposition – *ab*, *ad*, *con*, *dis*, *ex*, *in*, *sub*, etc. – changes its consonant to match the first consonant of the root word – so *ad-fect*, *con-lect* become *affect*, *collect*. Older pupils often find this kind of explanation helpful. The effect is often to produce a first syllable with a short vowel, followed by a double

consonant. Although the sound can be a guide to the spelling, it is inaccurate to teach it as a 'doubling' rule.)

- Suffixes and prefixes can accumulate to make even longer words. Spotting these can make spelling and reading easier and they can be less difficult to write than many short words where decisions have to be made about the vowel spelling (e.g. *contentedly*, *internationally*, *temperamentally*, *inexpensive*, *sensitivity*, *indefinitely*, *unintentionally*, *underestimation*, *unhappiness*, *unmerciful*). It is important to give practice at working through such long words, saying the syllables in turn, and increasing the speed at which they can be written (see BDTS, sections 9 and 10).

More difficult vowels

au; *ei/cei*; *ie* (*field*); *ei* (*vein*); the different sounds of *ou/our* (*youth*, *young*, *court*, *courteous*) (see BDTS, section 8).

Vowel–consonant combinations

- *ough* (seven sounds): *through*, *though*, *cough*, *enough*, *thorough*, *bough*, *ought*.
- *ought*; *-aught* (keep separate) (see BDTS, sections 4 and 8).
- *-eigh*; *eign*.

Soft *c* and *g*

- Longer words and technical vocabulary
- Use of *u* to harden *g* and *c*: *guess*, *guide*, *biscuit*, *circuit* (see BDTS, section 2).

Silent letters and other two-consonant combinations

gn (*gnaw*); -*mn*; *ch* /k/, *wh*, *ph* (see BDTS, section 5).

Use of *i* as a connecting letter between root word and ending

This often sounds like /ē/ or -/y/: *radio*, *curious*, *junior*, *brilliant*. This letter and its particular sound often result from a suffixing change as in *fury* → *furious* (see BDTS, section 10).

Spelling of /sh/ before a word ending as *ti/ci*

This can be related to suffix work because these spellings occur before *ous*, *ent* and *ance*, *al* and *an*, and in *-tion* and *-cion* (see BDTS, section 10).

Many of these combinations – *tial/cial*, *tious/cious*, *tient/cient* – involve choice.

It can be helpful to take them systematically as whole endings, and compile lists of each, noting related words. The pupil can then see:

- the relative frequency of each spelling
- where there is a related spelling that makes the spelling easier to remember, e.g. *ambition* → *ambitious*; *race* → *racial* (but note the oddity of *space* → *spatial*!); *music* → *musician* (this pattern for words ending in *ic* + -*an* has no exceptions)
- he can also mark for special attention the words that he is likely to use in writing.

Known 'death traps'

For example, *successfully*, *necessary*, *professor*, *immediate*, *definite* and the pupil's own examples.

Some sentence writing, with carefully graded words, will help pupils to practise all these tricky patterns and principles.

Multisensory approaches for older pupils

It is often felt that teenagers cannot be expected to use such techniques in case they are seen as babyish, and put the pupil off, but teachers should not assume that they will be rejected out of hand. If they are rationalised, and the teacher talks about learning methods and recall in a slightly theoretical way, many students will at least try them out. Using the technical terms for the senses may also help to give this work a more adult appeal. Pupils and students who play a sport, ride a bike or drive a car will understand explanations about the need for automatic performance and complex tasks.

They can be encouraged to develop their own ways of combining the different senses and applying these techniques to other curriculum learning tasks.

Kinaesthetic or motor modality

- Finger trace for learning tricky spellings and for correcting badly formed letters. Write words with eyes closed.
- Increase speed of writing words.

Auditory/oral modality

- Use alphabetic oral spelling (AOS) – say and listen – for learning spellings
- Segment syllables, saying them emphatically as a cue to spelling
- Repeat syllables, sounds or letter names using a strong rhythm when meeting and learning new vocabulary.

Visual modality

- Add writing to AOS to add a visual factor and more reinforcement
- Cut-up words on cards, to emphasise separate syllables
- Use the cut-up syllables to explore possible words, re-build words in a timed exercise.

This can help the pupil to become accustomed to the syllables as chunks, e.g.

Prefixes: *pro-*, *con-*, *de-*, *re-*
Word roots: *-mote*, *-struct*, *-vise*, *-port*
Suffixes: *-sion*, *-tion*, *-ing*, *-ive*.

Read or say letters, words and syllables aloud to get multisensory input and feedback. When words are studied and processed in this way, they are learned for spelling and word recognition at the same time.

Curriculum work

A regular look at written work can identify the areas where work is needed, along with particular words that are proving difficult. Help is likely to be needed with the words of most frequent occurrence, and important subject words and technical expressions. These can be cross-referenced into the phonic work if time permits and if it is likely to help.

It is useful to obtain a list of words for each subject; these can be arranged into spelling groups for easier learning, and in a glossary by alphabetic order for easy reference. It is pointless to force-feed pupils with large numbers of difficult words. They do not have time to learn them and will probably not remember them. It is more useful to ensure that they have this subject vocabulary available, and form the habit of checking important terms before handing work in.

Where such lists are kept is for the pupil to decide, but some discussion about it may help him to think about how he will use such a study aid. The options are:

- in the phonic notebook
- in the subject file – in a marked section
- in a pocket notebook that he can carry around easily and always has handy.

It might then form part of a pack which includes Eileen Stirling's *Spelling Checklist* and a guide card to basic principles of spelling and vowel sounds.

Strategies for self-help

It is most important to train pupils in methods of helping themselves to learn. Sooner or later, they will have to be self-reliant.

1. Change attitude. Do not allow the pupil to adopt the label 'poor speller'; get him to think more positively of himself as an 'improving speller'.
2. In general, encourage him to use the word he wants to use: if unsure, he should pencil mark it for checking later. (If it is marked, it can be tracked down easily.)
3. Keep a checklist of words that are most often wrong, and try to learn them. Use mnemonics

for odd or difficult words if it helps. Although personal ones are probably best, familiar tags such as *Ed on the edge* for *-dge* and deliberate mispronunciations (*Wed-nes-day*, *pe-o-ple*, *fri-end*, *k-now*) often work well.

4. Know probabilities: for instance, *le* is nine times more common than *-el*; *-tion* more common than *-sion*, etc.
5. Know the different priorities for written work:
   - communication: others need to read it; use logical spelling as much as possible (for *crane*, *crain* is better than *cran*; *habbit* would just be acceptable, *rabit* would not)
   - dictation, or note taking for own use: the priority is speed, legibility, and readability; use abbreviations and short forms of long words – either standard forms, (e.g. *i.e.* [*that is*], etc. [often written and pronounced *ect*], ∴ for 'therefore', 19C, E1 for Elizabeth the First) or work out personal ones (e.g. *immy/immediately*, *necy/necessary*, *parlt/parliament*, *govt/government*)
   - handed-in course work; formal letters; writing on forms; any kind of application: correct spelling is necessary. Work from a draft and proofread carefully before the final version is prepared.
6. Proofreading – look out for some key points:
   - long words: make sure every syllable is there
   - known rules, e.g. long-vowel *-e* words; dropped suffixes – past tenses and plurals; suffixing rules; 'double consonants' with prefixes
   - 'un-English' spelling such as *-cke*; words ending in *-v*; *ul* instead of *le/el*; *shul* and *shun* for *ti/ci* spellings; *uns* for *ence/ance'*

- personal 'death traps'; keep a checklist of these and use it.
7. Use guide charts for vowel spellings; if in doubt, use the most common spelling (see Figure 10.10).
8. Punctuation: read work aloud (pen in hand) and mark where the pauses come.
9. Spelling of long and difficult words. 'Navigate' through these by syllables, not letter by letter; it is much easier to keep track that way. This also has the advantage of splitting the syllables into prefix–root–suffix parts, or into open and closed syllables. Individual syllables can be tackled letter by letter if necessary.
10. Correcting mistakes. Be positive about mistakes; use them as guides to where the learning is needed. Comparison of right and wrong versions will probably show that only a small part of the word is wrong. The most common mistakes occur over vowels and in unstressed syllables, either medial or final (*genral*, *libry*, *seperate*, *definate*). Sometimes, more careful pronunciation can help – most people gloss over the medial syllables. All such words must be learned.
11. Use good learning techniques (see Figure 6.13).
12. Use the phonic file and other reference books and charts regularly.

Reading: developing word-attack skills

As pupils move through secondary school, increasing demands will be made on their reading skills and even good readers may run into difficulties. Texts will be more complex and there will be pressure to read quickly as well as accurately. Many may still need help with the 'mechanical' aspects of word recognition if they are to cope with more difficult vocabulary. At the very least, hesitancy and inaccuracy over long words will slow down their reading; more seriously, it may affect comprehension.

- Systematic decoding of polysyllabic words can help immediate recognition of word parts, endings such as *-tion* and *-sion*, and more difficult syllables with *-ti-* and *-ci-* such as *-tious* and *-cial*.
- Practise recognition of most common suffixes. Long words with compound suffixes (such as *mechanically*, *deficiency*, *regularisation*) can create the feeling of panic in a dyslexic reader – yet they are not difficult once the boundaries of root and suffix can be seen.
- Use knowledge of the different kinds of syllable to mark syllable divisions. The most useful syllables for this kind of word attack are open, closed and vowel + *r* syllables. Note that, when prefixes that are open syllables are unstressed (*return*, *describe*, *protect*), the vowel then loses its long sound and becomes indefinite, like a schwa.
- Working through a number of similar words can show how the place of a syllable in a word affects the accent and stress pattern, e.g. in a word ending in *-tion* – or any of the *ti/ci* syllables – the stress always falls on the vowel preceding the *-tion* syllable (e.g. *exception/exceptionally*). Often, the position of the stressed syllable moves as different syllables are added. This can affect the spelling too (e.g. *refer*, *referred*, but *reference*).
- Knowledge of word roots and derivations helps both word reading and comprehension, and can be a guide to spelling too. Lists of common elements such as *soc-* (*social*, *society*, *associate*), *-cess* (*success*, *access*, *necessary*), *sign*

(*design*, *signature*, *signify*) and associated words – *machine*, *mechanical*; *debt*, *debit* – can draw some of the problem words together. Saying them aloud emphasises the connections.

- After decoding words by these methods, make sure the pupil writes a few. This gives further emphasis to the syllable structure, and it highlights unstressed syllables that cause trouble in spelling (*general*, *library*, *secretary*).

This kind of work can be useful in helping older pupils to cope with the increasing vocabulary demands of their curriculum work. It trains them to work through words in chunks, to spot base words, endings and common syllables and to recognise and pronounce words quickly. If this kind of work is presented as word play, and used as a challenge, most pupils find these exercises quite acceptable – especially if they help.

Reading and spelling support each other in the word-attack and multisensory work, particularly in the word exercises. Exercises similar to those described in the 'Catching up' section (see Figure 6.16) can be adapted for these longer words.

Strategies for improving comprehension are discussed in Chapter 8.

The English spelling wheel: a model for a teaching programme

The wheel model in Figure 6.19 presents a programme for teaching spelling, and suggests how a teacher might construct a sequence of work to fit the particular needs of an older pupil or student. The programme itself is arranged according to the phonology of English and the phonic and linguistic structure of written English words. The diagram shows the main topics to be taught and the general sequence that might be followed, but the details can be varied according to need without losing the overall structure. Further examples and topics of the programme are included in the Key below.

Any model of spelling is an artificial way to describe the orthography of written language, and the phonic structure is, of course, imposed upon it. This model, with its circles and spokes, and talk about travelling along routes, is a fanciful invention. It is deliberately informal in order to help the pupil understand how words are constructed; it may also help the teacher to show how spellings can connect with each other. It allows a 'top-down', or global, view of English spelling at the same time as a 'bottom-up' approach to teaching it.

Structure of the model

The programme is arranged around a central hub in concentric circles. The most basic, or core, work is at the centre. Work of gradually increasing difficulty is shown on the circles as they move away from the hub. Observing the sequence of work as it moves outwards should help to ensure a programme that moves in a structured way from easier to more difficult work. The circles are cut through by a number of spokes. These show more general principles underlying spelling such as suffixing 'rules' and soft *c* and *g*, and other aspects of work such as grammar and handwriting. The spokes link the topics in the circles and offer the teacher a route from one to the other. Teachers working with older pupils can take different routes through the spelling topics while still keeping to a coherent structure of work.

The basic material shown here is the same as that shown on the linear chart on page 9 but extended

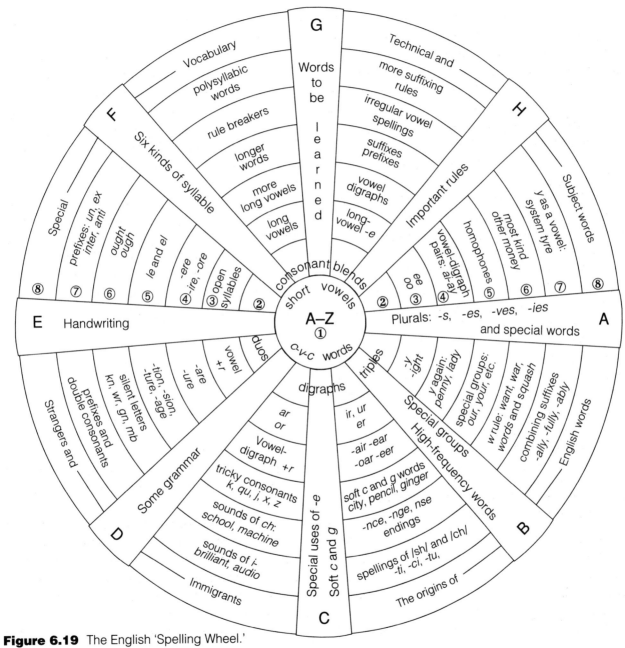

Figure 6.19 The English 'Spelling Wheel.'
(Permission to copy)

to include more advanced work. (For younger pupils, teachers will probably wish to follow the earlier linear chart.) The suggestions about the development of the spelling work with David, in the previous section of this chapter, could be fitted into the wheel.

If taught 'straight through', the programme would take 2 or 3 years to complete. It is more likely that teachers will want to vary what they include, and how fast they go through it, according to the age and needs of the student. The model provides a way to start a programme with an older student (especially one who already has a basic competence) by explaining the most regular phonic structures of English spelling, then accelerating immediately to more advanced work.

The teacher could also use the model to demonstrate the sequence of work that is being followed; the student could himself keep track of where they are in the programme and see how the topics link together. It may help to show that English spelling – in spite of its diversity and oddities – has a basic regularity and logic.

The circles of the wheel show topics and phonic groups with some keywords and other examples. The main groups in each circle are stated in the segments between spokes F and H at the top of the wheel.

The key gives a more detailed view of these topics. It also explains how the routes along the spokes may be used to link a number of different spelling points and how points can be linked in different ways. More detailed lists of phonic spelling work may be found in some of the programmes listed in Appendix II.

Key

The circles

Circle 1:	the hub of the wheel letter sounds and names short vowels	Alphabet *cvc* words with short vowels: *hat, pen, pig, dog, cup.*
Circle 2:	consonant digraphs, blends and other clusters	consonant digraphs, blends, 'duos' and triples (*sh, ch, th,* etc.; *bl, tr, st,* etc.; *ll, ss, ff, ck; tch, dge, squ, str, thr,* etc.) consonant blends in final position (*ng, nd, mp,* etc.) Although all the digraphs would be located in this circle, most teachers would not introduce them all at the same time. Work on digraphs would begin with *sh, ch, th* and perhaps *wh.* It could be re-visited for *tch* and *dge,* and again later for *ph* and *gh.*
Circle 3:	first long vowels single vowel + *r*	long-vowel -e, ee, oo; open syllable words (*me, no*), -*y* (*my*), -*ie;* -*ight* vowel + *r* (*car, for, her, turn, bird*)

Circle 4:	more long vowels vowel digraph + -*r*	vowel digraphs – pairs (*ai/ay, ou/ow, au/aw*, etc.) and others (*ew, ie/ei, ei* , /ā/, etc.) vowel + *re* (*pure, care*) vowel digraphs + *r* (*near, cheer, pair, bear, pour, poor*) unstressed *y* ending (*penny, lady, lucky*)
Circle 5:	writing longer words suffixes and prefixes with 'rules' for adding them	two-syllable words *le* and *el;* words to be learned, including homophones heads and tails (different prefixes and suffixes) and other 'add-ons' (*age, tion/sion, ture*) soft *c* and *g* words tricky consonants (*k, qu, j, v, x, z*)
Circle 6:	irregular vowels and rule breakers; oddities and special endings	*most, kind, old, wild;* o spelling /ŭ/ (*other, money*) the '*w* rule' (*want, war, word, squash*) *robin, habit* words different sounds of *ch* (*school, chef, machine*) silent consonants; silent *u* (*guess, build*) *ought; laugh; through* and other *-ough* words *-nce, nge; nse* (*change, pence; sense*)
Circle 7:	polysyllables: more difficult suffixing rules	combining suffixes; spellings of /sh/, /ch/ and other consonant–vowel combinations *ti/ci, tu* (*ture*) *du* (*dual*) *i* sounding like / ē/ or /y/ (*media, junior, brilliant*) prefixes with and without double consonants (*unreal, extend; difficult, success*) suffixes and syllable stress (*limited, preferred, travelling*)
Circle 8:	special words	technical, maths, science and other curriculum words; strangers and immigrants (*ski, chef, spaghetti*)

The spokes

There is no prescribed order in which the routes from circle to circle should be followed. (The circles are now abbreviated to C.)

So, for instance, the teacher could go along a route from the hub to different parts of the wheel via different routes – or just move outwards – depending on what kind of approach she wishes to adopt:

- To C2 – blends and digraphs – as that is the next logical step.
- Along the plurals route to investigate simple adding of -s and back to C2
- With a student who is secure with the spellings in the hub and C2, the next move could be along spoke H to C5 to start suffixing work.

These routes can be followed and revisited at any stage of the phonic programme. Some more examples of sequences for teaching are given later.

Spoke A: plurals	this will probably be the first route to be explored because it follows immediately from *cvc* words. It has its own rules: *es* – hissing plurals; changing *f* to *ves*; changing *y* to *ies* irregular plurals could be included
Spoke B: special groups	irregular groups to be taught early (*you, your, our; some, come, gone, done*, etc.) The *w* rule could be included here in the early part of the programme and again under rule breakers (C6). This route will be re-visited many times
Spoke C: special effects of -e	soft *c* and *g* and the different uses of -e at the end of words (*note, house, freeze, live, ice/age*)
Spoke D: some grammar	parts of speech (linked with suffixes -y and -ly) tenses (linked with suffixes -ed and -ing) phrases and sentences; capital letters; punctuation
Spoke E: handwriting matters	points where poor letter formation might affect spelling (e.g. *b/d, o/a* mistakes) joining strokes; word spacing
Spoke F: six kinds of syllable	a route for teaching syllables for systematic word attack or for revision. The route would be: C1: closed syllable C3: open syllable C3: long-vowel -e,

C3: vowel + *r*
C4: vowel digraphs
C5: *-le* (and possibly extend to *-tion*)

Spoke G: words to be learned

high-frequency irregular words (*they, said, are, friend*) numbers, days and months; commonly misspelt words (*necessary, business*)

Spoke H: important rules

adding suffixes – beginning with a vowel/beginning with a consonant; prefixes and assimilating consonants
soft *c* and *g*

The teacher is in control, not the programme. If the student needs to have a point taught, that need has to be met. However, if a point, or spelling is dealt with as a one-off, not linked into other work, it is helpful to make this explicit.

Some examples of programme sequence

After each diversion along a spoke route, the teacher could return to the circle from which it was made, or go to another linked point.

- Long-vowel *-e* (C3), followed by soft *c* and *g* (spoke C), then on to C6 to pick up *pence* and *change*, or other *soft c* and *g* words (for word recognition rather than spelling).
- After teaching long-vowel *-e* (C3) follow spoke H (Important Rules) to C5 to teach suffixing work with the rules for 'dropping *-e*' and 'doubling'. Next go back to C4, vowel + *re* and vowel digraphs.
- Teach *-y* (*try*) (C3) and *-y* again (*penny*) (C5), then follow Important Rules (spoke H) to teach the *y* rule for adding suffixes to *y* after a consonant.
- For an older pupil, needing spelling help for curriculum work: start in C1 and move outward – rapidly – along spoke F (Six Kinds of Syllable), stopping briefly at each point to check knowledge. Many pupils do not understand the structure of syllables and therefore cannot make use of it in their reading and spelling. Teaching closed, open and vowel-*r* syllables can facilitate the reading and writing of many long words. Stop at C5 for a check on knowledge of basic suffixing rules and common word endings (*-age, tion, sion*).
  Move next to C7 – prefixes (*untie, television, connect, difficult*), multiple suffixes (*lingeringly, temperamental, wonderfully*) and with both affixes (*internationally, unsuccessfully, dismissive*).

Keeping track of the work

The work taught in the Spelling Wheel can be recorded in the phonic dictionary/phonic file because this too is a flexible system. It may also be convenient to use a new chart for each pupil and highlight the points as they are taught. It could be enlarged to A3 size for extra points to be added as required. It is for teachers to use as they wish.

The chart may be photocopied.

Chapter 7

What goes into a lesson?

Wherever special provision is made for dyslexic pupils, local factors will affect the time available for lessons and the way that these are organised within school timetables.

The length and frequency of lessons are a question of major concern. If provision is limited, pupils may have only 1 hour a week. Is it enough? At the other extreme, pupils may be given half an hour or an hour every day. Can teachers make good use of this? The main concern for teachers must be to use the time available to the best advantage.

A 1-hour lesson will be too long for the youngest pupils: two half-hour periods, or three of 20 minutes, would be better, both for attentional reasons and to create more frequent opportunities for reminder and practice. Naturally, the range of activities will be divided between the lessons, although the week's work may be planned as a whole. However, a lesson of less than 20 minutes may not be very productive. It is important to have sufficient time for a profitable range of work on each occasion: to make firm links between reading and sounds work, to go through linkages work, with some listening, some reading, and possibly another activity. This division of time should not be confused with daily 5- or 10-minute slots for sounds work, or hearing of reading; these are not 'short lessons' but valuable on-going practice sessions.

By the age of 8, most pupils should be able to work individually for at least 45 minutes, extending to an hour as soon as possible. The longer lesson time has great advantages, not least being the training in habits of sustained work and concentration that it affords – even though work on any single topic should usually not exceed 15 minutes.

At the other extreme – the daily lesson of half to one hour – the problem of content might arise. Dyslexic children cannot be force-fed: they need time to digest and assimilate their learning. Such frequent lessons could include curriculum work and the teacher may consider different ways of working. It might be profitable, for instance, to spend some of the time in the classroom acting as support teacher. (One might also question whether the good pupil–teacher relationship that is so often a valuable feature of the one-to-one lesson could survive such contact hours!)

Just as dyslexic pupils' needs will differ, the content of lessons is bound to vary and the detailed planning can be done only by the teacher. However, general guidelines on lesson content and organisation can be given that will apply to most pupils and most situations and these are the focus of this chapter.

Lesson content

Each 1 hour of lesson time (however divided) should include the following work:

- Testing and revision to ensure that the last lesson's work has been remembered and understood.
- New work: every lesson should contain some new work – even if only one word; the pupil should feel he is moving on.
- Reinforcement of previous work and of new work, either separately or in the same context; this would include linkages drill and writing sentences to dictation.
- Reading aloud by the pupil.
- Use of language: oral expression; written work such as sentence work or free writing.
- Special points depending on the pupil's need and school year: handwriting; help for speech difficulties; specific problems, e.g. *b*/*d*; learning of months and days; telling the time; alphabet work; dictionary work; laterality.

- Homework: checking work brought back, setting next work.

A game, puzzle or drawing should be included in lessons and/or some reading by the teacher with younger pupils. Older pupils appreciate some relaxation too – perhaps a crossword or lighter reading (jokes and funny stories!), books of cartoons, etc.

Lessons with older pupils may differ from this pattern in that the work will often hinge on writing, study skills and curriculum-related work. Overall, however, the range of work done will probably be similar.

Division of time

In general terms:

- New work should usually be covered in the first part, after revision, while the pupil is still fresh.
- Concentrated sounds work should also be done in 'prime time'.
- Reading by the pupil should not be left to the very end.
- Fifteen minutes is ample for any one 'block' of work, and that might include approaching the same topic from more than one angle.
- 'Special point' work can be interspersed with more concentrated work to give the pupil a chance to relax.
- Throughout, the pupil should be kept busy with purposeful work; he should also be given a chance to talk – but not allowed to capture the lesson!
- A coherent theme – running through a single lesson or through the week's work – gives the

teacher a chance to introduce the same material in different ways. There needs to be a balance, however: lessons that are very restricted in their topics can become boring whereas too much variety can overload the pupil.

- Although each lesson will be planned in detail beforehand, the teacher needs to be ready to change course if necessary. Opportunities may arise for making a relevant point, or something might not go according to plan.
- There will be occasions too when the pupil does not respond for some reason. Teachers might prepare for such days by having an extra game available, or a new book to read to him.

Sample lessons

The following plans are examples of typical lessons, one to illustrate each phase of the work as described in Chapter 6. (They are all actual lessons, with comments on how each worked out.)

Lesson 1: Jon (8 years 6 months), eighth lesson

Jon knew about half of the letter–sound correspondences, including *a* and *o*. At our first meeting he could not read any words, and wrote '*i am* 8'. He is an amiable, easy-going boy. He has two lessons a week of 45 minutes each.

1. Linkages practice with sounds flashcards: *c, h, f, d, m, p, t, l, a, b, g, v, r, s, o*.
2. Teach *j, k, w*. Multisensory work.
3. Read words written last lesson *pot, got, mop, hop*.
4. Words work:
   - word build with letters: *jot, pop, jam, ram*
   - look for rhyming words; think of some orally
   - write words without help
   - write sentence: *I am not hot*. Draw picture.
5. Handwriting: multisensory work – *h, l, p*: emphasise that letters start at the top.
6. Read *Mac and Tab. Book 1* of Primary Phonics.
7. *the* for reading and spelling: multisensory tracing and response to flashcard. Explain: two letters together make a special sound: */th/* and every word needs a vowel so we put *-e*, which doesn't speak.
8. Game – matching letter names to pictures: *h c f m p t l a*.
9. Classwork and homework: worksheet – Domain Phonics pack (Oliver and Boyd), recognition of initial consonants.

Comments

1. All the linkages letter to sounds work correct; *p* not automatic – he had to think of the picture cue (*pipe*) first. Multisensory work on *p*.
2. New letters taught: although his name is Jon he does not reliably recognise lower case *j*. Decided to leave *w* till next time.
3. Word work OK, although rhymes not immediate. Sentence OK. Had to think quite hard about vowel change *a* to *o*. Drew a man in a vest under an umbrella for 'I am not hot'!
4. Reading: he recognises very few words as wholes; wants to sound out most of them; blends them easily but needs to think of each letter sound separately. Frequently stuck on *the*. Use 'slider card' next time to practise generalising sounds over five or six words.

5. Writing: practised two examples of each letter: finger traced on wall with full arm movement, then written on paper over four lines. (Have not started on joined writing by agreement with class teacher; Jon reluctant anyway.)

6. Enjoyed *Mac and Tab*; making good attempt at words though most of them sounded out.

7. Time spent on oral work for *the* instead of game. He had to listen and count how many times I said *the* in different sentences; matched to *the* in written form. He thought this was very funny!

Lesson 2: Jon – 18 months later

Jon learnt the separate letter–sound correspondences very quickly, but had great difficulty learning to read whole words.

His memory for sight words has been very poor. I abandoned strictly phonic readers in order to make him look at and remember whole words and used the *Oxford Reading Tree Magic Key* books, which helped him break through this problem. He still needs a lot of practice with new words, however.

He remains very reluctant to write: he has to think very hard about which letters to use and where they come in the word. He also has great difficulty organising his thoughts. As he has two lessons a week, I do a certain amount of curriculum work with him, helping him to write. We also use the computer for spelling and word-recognition practice and for writing – but this, and the last in particular, takes a lot of time. He works hard in the lessons but does very little follow-up work between, and very little writing.

I leave a worksheet to follow each lesson's work or for more general revision.

1. Check classwork – wordsearch exercise about Bonfire Night.

2. Revise endings -*er*, -*ing*, -*ed*. Read examples in *Read, Write and Spell Workbook 2*.

3. Revise magic -*e*:
   - read and write *like, smoke, flame, invite, brave*
   - use cards to show how suffix is added to -*e* words by covering up final '-e' of root word
   - discuss different ways of saying -*ed* ending
   - assemble some words.

4. Months: work on July–November order. Finish making Months card: he can cut it out (see Figure 12.5, page 181).

5. Write date: November. Count syllables and say carefully.

6. Write words and sentences with -*ed* examples. Oral work to identify -*ed* words first: *I liked those chips. Mum hoped to go to Chester. Richard invited me to his party.*

7. Read: *Trog and the Fire.*

8. Study skills (Charles Cuff): *The Garden Spider*. Look at pictures to collect information; to continue in class.

Comments

1. Had enjoyed wordsearch: make another.

2. Suffixes: no difficulty at any stage.

3. Sentences: had to be reminded about capital letters and full stops. Preliminary oral work helped.

4. Place names: surprised himself by writing *Chester* easily. I decided to do some polysyllable practice with place names instead of Study Skills work and to emphasise use of capital letter. *Manchester, Liverpool, Birmingham* – gave

ir and said very carefully. Very pleased with himself.

5. Order of months July onwards still troublesome.

6. Now using joined writing quite confidently, but beginning to squash letters together instead of making distinct linking stroke; *tt, ll, pa*. Needs some separate practice, possibly do some patterns.

7. Reading more fluently although still not reliable on recalling new words from one occurrence to the next. Works them out each time.

8. Classwork: Read, Write and Spell exercise, adding endings.

Lesson 3: Ben (age 13)

Ben has one 45-minute lesson each week. He needs practice in writing longer words to enlarge his written vocabulary. His reading is fluent but he stops at the occasional long word and laborious decoding interrupts the flow. He needs to recognise patterns more quickly.

1. Reading: we had read a number of pieces about Hurricanes. We did regular work on English exercises to combine reading comprehension and writing. Check homework: comprehension questions.

2. Spelling: check – *their/there*
test/revise – *ought; rough*.

3. Word attack, reading and spelling. Long words, *-tion* endings. Write words (about five – Ben to choose) in phonic lists; two sentences:

   The expedition set off at midnight.

   There was a celebration when the men got to their destination.

4. Read: Hurricane passage – the Boys and the Mules – from *Those Happy Golden Years* (L. Ingels Wilder).

5. Make notes of facts as preparation for written homework: two paragraphs re-telling incident as for news-story; invent headline.

Comments

1. Homework: had answered three questions adequately; needs to work on using all available information.

2. Spelling:
   • *their/there* known: he just puts the wrong one!
   • *ought* words OK. Re-do *rough* group.
   • *-tion* sentences OK. Enjoyed the decoding exercise.

3. Hurricane: points selected well. Headline – *Boys and Mules in Hurricane Terror*.

Chapter 8   Reading

This chapter is concerned with reading work at successive stages, hearing pupils read and the development of reading skills. Building the basic skills of decoding, blending and word attack are discussed in Chapter 3.

When a non-reading dyslexic pupil starts on an intervention programme, the immediate need is to be taught word-attack and word-recognition skills. For children whose phonological aptitudes are poorly developed, acquiring these basic skills can be very hard work. As with most activities, reading improves and develops with practice. The dilemma here is that children cannot start becoming successful readers until they have developed a measure of proficiency, and some of the skills are normally promoted by the very activity that they find so difficult. It can be assumed that many dyslexic pupils will have tried to read and either failed, or not advanced very far; others, although they have acquired a basic ability, will not be sufficiently fluent and will need help to improve. Many of them, even those who have made a start, are likely to have negative attitudes towards books.

How do readers read?

Reading as a cognitive process has been investigated in many research studies in the past 20 years. It is generally agreed that access to the meaning of written words can be via two routes:

1. The lexical route: words are recognised immediately and automatically, and their meaning processed, without explicit reference to the sounds (a 'top-down' process).
2. The phonological route: words are processed by phonological/phonic decoding and blending (re-coded) before they are recognised and matched to a word in the memory (a 'bottom-up' process).

Skilled readers probably use the first route, and respond straight to meaning. Experienced readers read most of the individual words on the page – unless they are deliberately skimming the text. As word recognition is automatic and immediate for them, there is no reason not to process each word. They do not depend on prediction for word reading or comprehension, even though they are able to predict when necessary. In addition, the 'bottom-up' route is always available when needed, e.g. to deal with an unfamiliar word. For a skilled reader, the re-coding and matching process will be fast and automatic. In fact, the two routes are probably working in synchrony all the time.

On the other hand, poor readers cannot rely on instant word recognition because their skills are inadequate. They therefore use context to help themselves through the text, and guess at many words. However, guessing from context itself depends on a minimum level of word-attack and word-recognition skills. If words can only be read by decoding and blending, the process will be so slow that meaningful reading will not be possible (Note 8.1, page 257).

Teaching the essential early skills is best approached as part of a programme that teaches the elements of the writing system as a whole, in which words are approached through spelling. (This is discussed in detail in earlier chapters of this book.)

Starting off: the pupil's reading level

It is standard practice for teachers to start by carrying out some kind of test to find out what a pupil can (or cannot) do and to get some idea of his reading age, or level. He needs to be given a book with which he can succeed and it is useful to find what books he has already tried. A trial-and-error method of arriving at the right level is not satisfactory; children who have failed to make progress need to be given a taste of success right from the start.

A test that uses continuous passages (such as the *Neale Reading Analysis* or the *Macmillan Individual Reading Analysis*) or a sentence completion test will give more information about how a pupil reads than a word-recognition test, although the Reading Age score provided by the latter can be a guide to finding a book to start him off. A more detailed test of phonic knowledge can provide useful information, but it will probably not help to find a suitable reading book. The books being used as reading material for the Literacy Hour by the pupil's class group could also indicate the approximate level at which to begin – but the possibility that he gets support from other children must be kept in mind. It is necessary to know the reading levels of the available books. The National Association for Special Educational Needs (NASEN) publish a useful guide with information about reading levels of many series. (See Appendix II for details of this and of test material.)

Careful study of responses to the tests should reveal the level at which the problems lie:

- Word level: word recognition may be so poor that many words have to be decoded and blended. Poor phonological skills may hinder the child here. Letter–sound conversion may be slow and blending may be difficult (possibly due to problems holding the sounds sequentially in working memory).
- Sentence level: most words may be recognised but they are not integrated across the whole sentence, so that punctuation is ignored and fluency

suffers. There may be partial comprehension.

- Orthographic level: the less regular spellings or more advanced word patterns may not be known, leading to guessing and inaccuracy. Fluency may be interrupted. This and the inaccurate guessing prevent full comprehension.

With such information the teacher should be able to decide the instructional level at which the reading work should be set (Note 8.2, page 257).

Finding the right books

Early stages: phonic reading books

Dyslexic pupils should have a reading book as soon as possible. Until they do, they can hardly begin to think of themselves as readers. In the earliest stages the work of building basic skills is best approached as part of the phonic programme in which reading and spelling go hand in hand (see Chapter 4). The most suitable books for a non-reader are, therefore, those that complement the early phonic work and use a structured vocabulary similar to that of the spelling programme. Here the child will meet words that have been thoroughly prepared in the word-building work, so he should be able to read them without undue difficulty.

Plenty of practice at each stage is important for pupils with the most severe difficulties; they need a great deal of help with remembering letter–sound correspondences and blending sounds into words, and much repetition of simple words to improve their capacity to read words as wholes. Words should be regular and easy to read, and the style simple, so that the pupil will be better able to achieve fluency over a sentence.

Comprehension is necessary, however simple the story, so that even at this most basic level a pupil can be encouraged to think about what he is reading, and use this understanding to help word recognition and decoding. Good use of picture cues can help too.

Many of the popular reading schemes have a separate phonic unit intended for those progressing at a slower rate than others, but this often moves on too fast and does not have enough material at each level. *New Way Readers* have a structured phonic approach, as do the two series most often used for children with learning difficulties – *Bangers and Mash* and *Fuzz Buzz*. The *Sound Start Readers* (Nelson Thornes) series offers a carefully controlled phonic progression. However, in making an entirely fresh start, it may be preferable to avoid books that are in use in the pupil's school. Two other series, written specifically for dyslexic children, *Primary Phonics* and *More Primary Phonics* (an American publication), and *The Zed Project* are useful in the very early stages. (See Appendix II for further details of these and other reading materials.)

Both these series have very short books (12–20 pages) with limited text and simple line drawings that can easily be read in a lesson. (A page from *The Zed Project* is illustrated in Chapter 4.) Admittedly, some do not look as attractive as most present-day children's books, but the stories are lively and the experience of reading straight through a very simple book can give a tremendous boost to a child who has previously failed. Getting right to the end of a book can set up a momentum of reading, with the child feeling that he wants to start another one, and moving through a series can be very satisfying.

Spelling and reading

As pupils advance through the spelling work it is important that it is accompanied if possible by readers which follow the same phonic sequence, because reading and spelling support each other in these early stages. (A probable sequence would be from short vowels in words with single consonants, consonant digraphs and blends, followed by the long vowels *ee* and *oo*, long-vowel *-e*, *-y* and then the vowel digraphs.)

Of course such material has limitations! Severely restricted vocabulary, with few irregular words, cannot produce interesting writing, and occasionally it may be artificial. Even so, it should be remembered that these texts are used for a specific purpose: that of presenting the pupil with vocabulary that has very regular sound–spelling patterns. Such words will be easy to decode, so he can begin to build skills of word attack and word recognition.

Recognising the words

For the pupil to move successfully from this very structured phonic material, he must be able to read a basic core of common irregular words – *are*, *you*, *my*, *said*, *some*, *have*, *give*, *your*, *could*, etc. These can be found in the Literacy Hour material or teachers may have other lists such as the J. McNally and W. Murray or Dolch lists of high-frequency words.

Many of the words in these lists are regular and will be included in the phonic spelling programme, but children must be able to read words such as *on*, *in*, *and* (and many others) by immediate response. They may need to be taught and practised with flashcards, or through probe exercises. Irregular words will probably need more intensive work. This can be achieved by teaching reading and spelling together, using a simultaneous oral spelling approach and emphasising saying the word. Practice with flashcards can follow.

The problem with remembering and recognising these function words – including those with regular spelling – is that many in the first 50 most frequent words are short and even look alike (e.g. *on*, *in*, *an*, *and*, *is*, *it*, *the*, *they*, *her*, *here*, *where*, *there*). What makes them even more difficult to remember is that there is no pictorial quality to give a strong hook into meaning. This has therefore to be invented and emphasised. One way that has been found successful is for the child to write the word, put it in a sentence and draw the picture (e.g. *I got on the table*. *The cat sat in her milk*) (Note 8.3, page 257).

Moving to other graded readers

At some point, and as early as possible, the very structured phonic material must give way to ordinary readers. Careful selection is important. Schemes differ in the way their vocabulary is controlled and in the number and variety of books at each level. Although it is important that struggling readers get experience of different genres – stories, poems, information – the schemes that have a set of characters, or a story line that runs through a number of levels, are more suitable than those that have variety as part of their general rationale. Most dyslexic pupils will benefit from readers with restricted vocabulary that is carefully expanded, and a high level of word repetition. Schemes that have accompanying workbooks are a help, especially where the basic approach is that of a 'keywords' principle: pupils have plenty of opportunity to become familiar with the keywords before or while attempting each book.

This move may be particularly helpful (and should perhaps be considered sooner) for a pupil who gets stuck on sounding out words, seemingly unable to make the step to saying words as wholes. A scheme that uses keywords – few enough to learn and remember – can help to make this transition. It will be possible for the pupil to bring his new phonic understanding into action to help get into the words, but not to use it to decode them by sounding out. (I should emphasise that this is not an argument for approaching reading through whole words taught by a look-and-say method. Dyslexic pupils simply do not remember words taught by visual strategies alone. They need the grounding in phonic strategies.)

A change of schemes is advisable after a while. This will introduce a new 'set' of vocabulary and a new style of writing. Even a change of print style and general design is useful for making clear the point that words do not change if they are printed differently. In any sideways move of this kind, it is as well to drop back by half a year in reading level.

The method of grading across a number of books – reading schemes and others, such as colour-coded grading – which is used in many classrooms, can be useful for helping children who do not have reading difficulties to develop their skills in a progressive way. For dyslexic children, more control is needed in the early stages. Books that are highly regular, predictable and very familiar will help to give children a sense of security and they are more likely to succeed at every attempt. This in turn will help their self-confidence to grow. Until this point is reached, the child should not be encouraged to risk failure by attempting a book that is too difficult.

It is important to stay with graded reading material until pupils have sufficiently well-developed skills of word recognition, and have built up a substantial lexicon of words that they recognise and say automatically, and sufficient confidence to be reasonably fluent. An occasional hesitation or pause to decode a new word is significant only if it impairs comprehension.

A distinction is sometimes made between 'readers' and 'real books', with 'readers' being seen as inferior. This is demeaning to children for whom learning to read requires a huge effort. We need to enhance the pupil's self-esteem and should acknowledge that any book a child reads successfully is a 'real' book to that child.

Books on computers

Many books in reading series and other individual titles are now available in computerised form, and children can use them alongside the printed versions. These are a valuable contribution to resources, particularly as they enable children to get into the stories that their peers can read. They can give the repetition that is essential to word recognition while keeping the child's interest, but the teacher must ensure that the program is being used productively if it is part of the teaching strategy. Are skills being learned that will transfer to reading the printed book, or to reading the same words in other formats? Is the child looking at the words as they are spoken by the program? (Even if he is, the speech rhythm may be too fast for the words to be read with close attention.) If the child is attempting the reading, does the program offer the right kind of help and is he using it? Teachers will be familiar with pupils who can parrot a book – helped by the pictures – after hearing another child reading (see Chapter 13 for further discussion on IT).

The transition to independent reading

Plenty of practice and gradually increasing difficulty are important for the development of reading. Often the problem is how to persuade a pupil to keep trying when the immediate rewards are small and he may not value them anyway. This stage is perhaps the most critical because it is here that pupils can begin to think differently about themselves and what they might be able to do. Success must be guaranteed because it will create a momentum that can carry them along, and it has to be sustained for the idea that they can read independently to grow (Figure 8.1). (To guarantee positive enjoyment at this stage might be more difficult!)

Vocabulary and style are among the crucial factors. If vocabulary is too difficult, and sentences are long and complex, the unskilled reader may not be able to make connections between the words as he reads each one, so that he produces a string of unconnected words. In consequence, the meaning does not unfold as he proceeds through each sentence; he will forget what has gone before and comprehension will be correspondingly reduced. It is as if the child has

When choosing material to bridge the gap between structured text and standard children's books look at:

vocabulary level
sentence length
the writer's style
length of sections or chapters
title and chapter titles
complexity of plot
familiarity of key points, e.g. names, theme, etc.
pace and development of story
attraction quality:
    length of book
    size of print
    paper colour and quality
    cover
    illustrations – quality and number
    exciting 'blurb'

Figure 8.1 Choosing bridging material for reading.

not enough space in his thinking capacity (sometimes called 'resources of attention') to tackle both aspects of reading at once. Something much simpler is required. (I sometimes say to a pupil who fails to understand, 'You've used up all your "think" sorting the words out'.) Yet if the same passage is read aloud to him it is understood perfectly well.

On the other hand, style that is simplistic can be surprisingly difficult to understand. Many short words – particularly the 50 most frequently used words – carry very little meaning.

Stories that over-use this kind of simple vocabulary, combined with short sentences and a lot of dialogue, can be difficult to follow. Reading age analysis is not always a reliable guide to text readability because it is based only on the ratio of number of syllables to number of words in a short passage of text, and cannot take other stylistic features into account.

Several publishers have materials that aim to develop reading skills in a progressive way, especially for rather older pupils. Books with reading level of 7 to 8 years, but interest levels of 10 and over, are not difficult to find. Some are interest focused, but there is a wide choice of other themes: sci-fi, romance, mystery, 'true-life' stories, etc. Although not exactly 'graded readers', such books serve the same purpose and can be used sequentially to build skills, fluency, confidence and (one hopes) willingness to read.

The same kind of developmental material for younger pupils can be found in the *Trog* stories, the *Oxford Reading Tree* middle and later books (*Magpies*, *Robins* and *Treetops*), *Starpol* and *Ziggy Zoom* books (Ginn). These would all be appreciated by readers aged 9 or 10.

Information books can be a help and appeal to some readers more than stories do. The design of such books can make reading easier. Text is more likely to be set out in short paragraphs and sections than in story books, with colourful illustrations to help explain difficult principles and technical words. This helps to show pupils that every part of the book can be used to gain understanding. They can also be read in short segments – unlike stories, where a minimum number of pages usually have to be read to get the story along.

Again, careful selection is necessary. In some books the font is small, illustrations and text are too crowded together, and the whole page looks busy and confusing.

A word about colour

Many publishers use coloured pages to give variety and enhance the appeal of books. Children (especially those affected by Meares–Irlen syndrome) can have difficulty with glossy white pages, so colour could be helpful, but, as they have different colour preferences, this will be a hit-and-miss matter. It is not unusual for children to have strong aversion to some colours (e.g. purple or violet shades) and if the colour is too strong the print clarity can suffer.

Poems

Right from the start poems can be a good source of reading matter and children usually enjoy them. All the characteristics of poems appeal to youngsters: rhyme, rhythm, the short lines and concise expression that puts an idea in a pithy, often funny, way. They are often very short – four lines is still a whole poem – and can be finished easily. They can also have a predictability that carries the reader along.

All these are valuable aids to those who are struggling. For the dyslexic pupil who has difficulties with rhyme, a simple poem can be a good way to sharpen up his perception of sounds. Repetition that is not favoured in prose (the 'Run Red, run, run, run' of old-fashioned readers!) is permitted in a poem, so allowing many 'goes' at the same words and phrases without artificiality. *Beginner Books* (*Dr Seuss*) such as *The Cat in the Hat* and *A Fly Went By* make effective use of all these features. Poems often have titles that invite the reader into the book: 'Smelly Jelly, Smelly Fish', 'Green Eggs and Ham'. Many reading series have a poetry section, *Oxford Reading Tree* among them. Teachers can read the more difficult ones aloud as a treat.

It is best to start with verse that has relatively direct language such as some of Spike Milligan. More classic children's poetry found in the standard anthologies can come later.

Two-tier reading

While the pupil's reading experience is gradually extended, the phonic approach should not be abandoned altogether; each new step in the spelling programme should be backed up by structured reading of some kind. This helps to secure the knowledge of new vowel spellings and more difficult word patterns, and can help with word attack and word recognition. (The *Oxford Reading Tree Woodpecker* branch is useful here.) After the earliest stages, when pupils are moving on, it is more difficult to find acceptable material in 'book' form. There are specially written short passages and poems that supply the need (see Appendix II), and it is possible to make games that use structured phrases and sentences as part of the activity. 'Real' reading can go ahead separately and phonic reading now becomes an exercise in the lesson, but it does not disappear.

Going on to ordinary books

It is a big step from the reading material described above to ordinary children's books. The numerous short, brightly illustrated paperbacks are ideal for this bridging purpose; books such as *Burglar Bill* and *Six Dinner Sid* are great fun and stories such as those of *Frog and Toad* (Arnold Lobel) may help to convince pupils that reading can be a pleasure. Even pupils who might be considered rather 'old' for these titles usually accept them (although they might prefer to read them in private – or those with younger siblings may find these books around at home and might be encouraged to read them 'casually'). Comics can provide the same 'nutritional boost' for literacy. Anything that a child feels inclined to read repeatedly has its own kind of value. As they have missed the stimulus that the experience of reading provides at the 'normal' time, they have a lot of catching up to do.

For the next step – into books with fewer pictures and more print – it is even more important to get the right book for the child. At present, many publishers have a 'young' or 'first read alone' category; it is worth skimming through a number of individual titles to vet them for story content (often excellent), level of language, length of sentence, difficult names, etc.

Most have largish print, well spaced out on the pages, with careful line breaks that help to preserve related words (such as pronoun and verb) and do not cut across meaning. In some series the story is told at two levels – in continuous text and directly in speech bubbles. This offers a chance to share the reading, but children need to understand that the words in the bubble usually condense and comment on the action, not add to it. Any book should be short enough to be finished in three or four 'goes'.

For those becoming more proficient, Banana Books and Jets are among the suitable series, and children like them. Barrington Stoke Publishers target this specific group with titles for teenagers as well as for younger readers. Their books are carefully edited so that vocabulary and style are at an appropriate level; colour of paper (a light cream) and font have also been selected for ease of reading. Classics such as Ted Hughes' fable *How the Whale Became* are simple yet sophisticated and children might at first need a little help. Most of all they want to be able to read Roald Dahl books for the sheer fun and impossible stories. *The Magic Finger* is probably the most accessible at this transitional stage. With the longer books, teacher or parent will probably need to help by reading a few pages to get through the story in a reasonable time.

'Choose Your Own Adventure Books' were popular a few years ago but seem now to be out of fashion. They hand over control of the story to the reader and, as these books are constructed of short episodes that are often tediously similar, there is no pressure to finish. Interest wanes long before the story is finished – which is not a recommendation for reading.

In a different genre, diaries are also written in short sections, but are more like real life. Teenagers often enjoy *Adrian Mole's Diaries*, and can perhaps get more involved with this character than the artificial 'heroes' of fantasy adventures.

Books based on television series, particularly those with animal themes, appeal to some children. Familiarity with the characters and plots make the books less daunting, and they are usually short and fairly simple, with several substories.

At a rather later stage the 'horror and mystery' genre is popular with young readers and some of these, such as the Goosebumps books, may be accessible to dyslexic readers. *Famous Five* and the other Enid Blyton books also offer a route that many dyslexic children will accept.

There are also dozens of 'pony' stories, and stories about clubs and secret gangs; they may appeal more to girls than to boys. Again it is necessary to look at the format; a child's tentative approach to particular stories might be ruined by small print.

A bigger hurdle at this stage is that many dyslexic children do not like reading longer stories even when they have become more competent with word recognition and are reasonably fluent; they say they cannot see the point. This might literally be true. Reading a story entails sophisticated understanding: remembering the characters, keeping hold of the developing action, ploughing through long sentences, putting information together for complete understanding, meeting new (sometimes 'literary') vocabulary and writing styles. Along with these textual demands, stories require the readers to bring their own experience of the world to the book so that the author does not have to state everything explicitly. Inexperienced dyslexic readers may find all these demands far too much. So it is a steep step up to more literary works such as the *Narnia* books – which relatives buy them for Christmas! In the simpler books, the action moves along quickly, something is always happening, much of it conveyed in direct dialogue form. *Narnia* makes many more demands on the reader. Description of characters and places, the literary style, the need for understanding of family situations and relationships: these require an advanced level of reading skill. Beyond that, it is yet another jump to a text like *The Secret Garden*, which is 'very boring – pages and pages where nothing happens'. (Quote from a bright 12-year-old.)

The 'popular' books are valuable for their very simplicity: they can help to improve and secure basic reading facility, so that at the right time children can begin to develop more advanced comprehension skills. But they often need a nudge to get them to move on.

Harry Potter books cut across these categories. They probably fit in between Enid Blyton and the classics such as *Narnia*. The language is not very difficult, the style is immediate and the stories are packed with action. Children want to read them. Some of the names can be awkward (not least because some characters have more than one) and the overall plots are quite complex, so they will need help to keep hold of the larger picture. If 'read to' or helped the first time through, many dyslexic children will be able to tackle these books on their own.

For a child who wants to get into books but cannot quite manage to sustain a long book, hearing it read on tape is a lifeline. The advantage of a 'live' reader is that difficulties of understanding can be sorted out. Knowing what happens, the dyslexic reader may be tempted to read the book again – or browse through for the favourite parts. (This is apart from the value of taped books for pleasure and experience of stories.)

Information books may be more attractive than fiction at all levels of development. The Horrible and Terrible series – *Horrible History* (separate titles for different periods), *Geography* (e.g. *Volcanoes*, *The Weather*), *Science* and numerous others are aimed at making the curriculum popular for readers of between 10 and 14. The text is organised in short sections and they are fast paced, factual and funny. Illustrated books are plentiful but careful choice is needed because print size can again be the critical factor, however attractive the pictorial material.

Personal interest can also be a powerful motivator. Here again, however, some caution is needed. If the pupil's interest seems to demand reading matter that is far too difficult, it is better to look for a compromise. The interest may not survive if the struggle to read is too great.

Much depends on the individual pupil. Sometimes a keen footballer will be interested in the newspaper sports pages. Older pupils might tackle the Highway Code if they are bicycle riders or saving up for a motor bike. (This is available on tape too.) (See Appendix III for a note on finding the reading level of books.)

Reading to children

This is, of course, an immensely important part of a child's whole development, not simply part of learning to read. Children who become readers in the 'normal' way can get a lot from having stories and books read to them, although they are not dependent on it. For children who cannot get into books for themselves, listening to stories read aloud, whether 'live' or on audio-tape, is the only way to experience not only the events of the story, but everything that goes into it: imaginative language, a wide range of vocabulary, different ways of saying the same thing, humour, contact with fictional people, etc. Television can provide some of this, but the medium is very different; listening without an accompanying visual stimulus requires another kind of concentration.

Sometimes parents worry that if they read to a child he might become lazy, and that they should try to get the child to make the effort for himself. Books with 'extended' stories can fill the need here, enabling parents to read to a child and listen while the child reads at his own level. However, teachers who hear such fears should reassure parents that their worries are unnecessary; parents can make a tremendous contribution to the development of literacy just by reading aloud.

Reading instruction: helping pupils to develop their skills

Hearing pupils read

In the one-to-one lesson hearing reading is a very different activity from the standard classroom practice where there are few opportunities for giving undivided attention to an individual for more than a very short time. Most of the detailed attention to reading will be done in the group work session of the Literacy Hour.

It is generally recognised that dyslexic children find reading aloud in a class a distressing task and even a group situation can be daunting. If a pupil wants to try out his reading in this way, of course he should be supported in his attempt. There may be opportunities to gain experience in activities such as play reading. Although teachers may encourage, the first move should come from the pupil.

Much of the reading work in the ordinary course of the child's day is done silently, or subvocally. Reading aloud in the individual lesson is a very different matter and should be a regular part of lessons until he has become proficient. There is no better way to check on how reading skills are developing.

Unlike paired reading (see below) – or sharing a book – this is an instructional activity and it should be done by the specialist teacher. If the class teacher hears the pupil reading as well (or parents or someone else working with the child), this is a great advantage, but the reading work should never be left entirely to someone else. The specialist teacher must have first-hand knowledge of how her pupil is getting on. Verbal or written reports – no matter how detailed – will not convey the whole picture. The reading activity will lead to further work in the development of his reading skill; it is more than just helping him to get access to books.

Starting off

Before starting a book, a little time should be spent in talking over what it might be about; the pupil should get what clues he can from the cover picture and title, the chapter headings, and the 'blurb' if there is one. The pictures are important too, not only to anticipate what might happen, but also to whet the pupil's appetite for the story. It is also good training in using every part of the book to get information. It is surprising how often pupils do not bother to pick up clues, for instance by reading chapter headings. If the beginning of a book is difficult, or the story is slow to develop in the first pages, it is useful to read it to the pupil. This sets the scene, and helps to establish the tone and style of the story.

Putting a new part of the book into context is important: can the pupil remember what has happened so far? Look through the pictures on earlier pages to remind yourselves – the teacher is in this too! – or perhaps read a paragraph from just before the taking-off point. Discussion of what has happened is important for more than cueing into the story. Dyslexic children often do not get full meaning from their reading; they are apt to be surface readers, getting the immediate information and obvious facts but missing underlying meanings (Note 8.4, page 257). They do not build up information to make deductions – about characters, or about why things happen – or make predictions. Recalling what has gone before is one way to make such discussion entirely natural.

It also emphasises that it is important to remember what has been read. Reading is not just knowing what the words say and making sense of them for that occasion only. It includes carrying the meaning forward, not only to understand what comes next, but for use at some time in the future – tomorrow, next week or even next year.

If the instructional level is right, there will be something in the reading that needs preparatory work. It may be a long or irregular word, a name or perhaps punctuation such as an exclamation mark that will affect the expression. The pupil's attention should be drawn to anything he might stumble over and preparation done in whatever way is appropriate. (Of course, he may still forget when he gets to the tricky point – but long explanations should not interrupt the reading work.)

The comfort factor

A reader may be able to see the book more comfortably if is placed at a sloping angle, not flat on the table. The position of the light needs to be considered too; an overhead fluorescent light often produces a glare on a shiny page which can be quite disturbing to vision. A coloured overlay might help. If the pupil reports dazzle, or print distortion, try different colours. (Many pupils find the blue tints most helpful.) Some children (and dyslexic adults) find that visual effects make reading difficult: they report that print is unclear, or moves around, or word boundaries merge; that 'white rivers' down the page distract from the text and that overhead light creates glare on the page. Whatever the reason for these effects, they should be taken seriously. If the overlays are helpful, screening by an optometrist for possible use of tinted glasses might be considered (Note 8.5, page 257).

Helping the pupil along

Pupils should place their book so that a line guide can be used, or a finger run along under the words – whichever he finds most useful. (If the teacher does the pointing, a pencil moved above the words can be easier because it doesn't get in the way.) The line guide should be moved before the pupil gets to the end of each line, so that the beginning of the next one is not obscured and the fluency broken.

Beginning readers often separate words as they read, finding it hard to get speech rhythm, or they read in a very flat voice. Ways to help are suggested in Figure 8.2.

As far as possible, give cues and let the pupil do the work, rather than rush in with the troublesome word:

- give hints about syllable division
- remind him to use his phonic knowledge, e.g. 'What does the vowel say?'
- remind him of helping strategies if *b*/*d* trips him up

- Move a pencil, keeping the movement steady, although matched to the pupil's pace, and draw him along
- After a short sentence cover it up and say: 'Tell me the words you have just read.' Almost always the sentence (or a paraphrase of it) will be repeated in natural speech rhythm. Point out that it can be read that way too
- Point out the significance of commas and full stops, and help the child to keep the reading going from one punctuation mark to the next
- Modelling: read a sentence and ask the pupil to read it in the same way, copying your version. This can help to teach inflection and put in some expression
- At an obvious point, make the link between the story and real life: 'Do you think he really said "No" just like that? Wasn't he cross?' (or whatever is appropriate). Make sure the pupil understands how to respond to exclamation marks, or words printed in another style, such as italics
- Use a tape recorder: ask the pupil to record a short passage and play it back while he follows. Then run it again while the pupil re-reads the passage, trying to beat his previous performance. This can provide some fun in the lesson; many children (but not all) enjoy using a tape recorder, and hearing their own voices – but it must be done carefully and needs trust in the working relationship between teacher and pupil. You need to be sure, before doing this, that he will succeed

Figure 8.2 Helping the development of fluent reading.

- draw attention to context to make an informed guess
- watch the punctuation.

But too much struggling over a word can increase the confusion and reduce understanding; the teacher should provide it and perhaps add the next two or three to get the pupil going again.

If mistakes crop up, but the reading is going along fluently and making sense, it is best not to interrupt too often. The wrong word can be taken up later. If the pupil makes a lot of word substitutions, or omissions, it can be instructive to copy his reading afterwards, getting him to check by watching the text. This can sometimes misfire – he may simply not notice – but that in itself is revealing.

The practice of making a running record while listening to reading enables the teacher to spot the weak points and plan work to cover these. If much detailed work on subskills is needed, this should be done as a separate activity and not in the 'reading-the-book' part of the lesson. (See Chapter 3 for discussion of work on the subskills of reading.)

Sharing the reading can be valuable. It helps to get through the story and it gives the pupil a rest. More than that, it models good reading style. If he is asked to follow the words (which is itself good practice at following a text) and to put in the next word when the teacher stops, it is surprising to see how often a difficult word can be recognised that would have caused a problem had he been doing all the work himself. This shows, as mentioned earlier, that a reader who is having to work too hard at word reading or decoding has little attention to spare for comprehension and use of context.

Pupils should be given reading to do at home with parents (or anyone who will listen) or they should be encouraged to attend the school's 'reading club' if there is one (Note 8.6, page 257). The importance of frequent practice cannot be stressed too strongly. There is a snowball effect in reading development: it grows by being rolled along.

Paired reading

This technique can be a good way of making books accessible and is particularly appropriate for parents to do. The method allows the child to take control of the reading, but to read only as much as he feels able to. The parent does not correct; instead, she or he takes over if a mistake is made and carries on until the child feels able to resume. (They agree on a signal for this before starting.) The choice of book is entirely up to the child – and he may select one that is too difficult. In that case, the parent will do much of the reading. As a dyslexic child gets most of his experience of books from being read to, this might be acceptable. However, paired reading – supposedly a joint activity – should be distinguished from 'hearing Johnny read' and 'being read to'.

More advanced reading skills: adolescent readers

It is not always easy to recognise reading difficulties, or the reasons for them, among older pupils – and especially difficult for subject teachers in secondary school. Problems can be hidden because pupils have reached (or it is assumed that they have) what is considered an adequate reading age for GCSE and A-Level examinations (10 and 12 years respectively). Some reasons for reading difficulties among older pupils and students are set out in Figure 8.3.

Hearing older pupils read

Adolescents often dislike reading aloud to a teacher. They will say they can read better silently and in some respects this may be true. Removing the need to pronounce words takes out one part of the task – possibly a laborious part if there are many long or technical words. But it is necessary to check on how a pupil's reading is developing for all the reasons suggested in Figure 8.3 and this can be done quickly by listening to them read. It may be sensible to choose curriculum material where reading will be seen to be relevant, e.g. material such as science texts can be used to draw attention to the importance of factual accuracy. Examination papers – both questions and instructions – are useful and so are forms that ask for information and have directions for completing.

Skimming and scanning

It is important that pupils are taught different kinds of reading process, and understand when each one should be used: when it is essential to be accurate; when it may be more useful to scan a text to pick up specific information quickly, or to skim a passage for a general idea, followed by a closer, more detailed reading. A pupil may know what the terms mean, and even when to use each one. However, it is not easy to persuade a reader who has struggled with words to let his eye move faster over the page and not to read every one. It is again a matter of graded practice. Setting some questions and giving a time limit can help. A high-

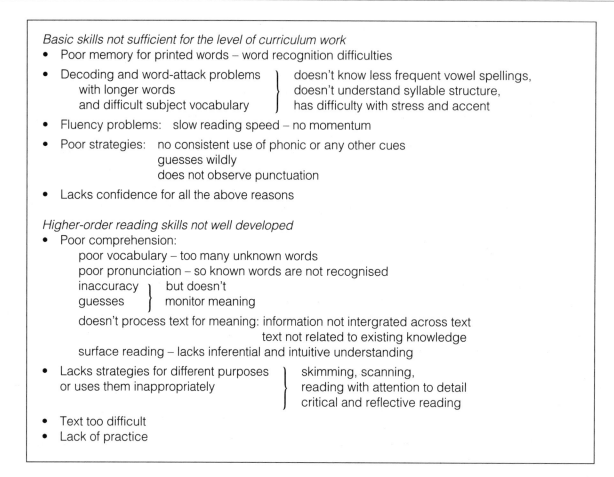

Figure 8.3 Reading difficulties among older pupils and students.

lighter can be used to select important and relevant words and phrases.

Silent reading

This is the usual way we read and has its own kinds of skill. It can be at least twice as fast as oral reading and the pupil who is becoming a practised reader has to develop the skill of reading quickly.

When we read to ourselves (above all when it is for enjoyment) we do not need to read every word – skimming and scanning make use of this – and we may read to some degree inaccurately. In exams, of course, silent reading must be done with maximum attention to accuracy. The teacher may want to check on this by asking questions about passages that have been read silently.

Reading comprehension

Reading work with older pupils can focus on the development of comprehension skills. Right across the curriculum, they have to be able to extract information from printed sources and present it in good written language for which they need complete understanding.

Adolescent readers whose skills are still developing often fall short of this point especially with the more complex material – especially the English syllabus – of the Key Stage 4 curriculum. Fast, but accurate, reading and immediate understanding can be crucial to success in an examination. Integrating the text can be the main cause of difficulty, because either word recognition is still not fully automatic, or the pupil does not fully process each part of it. 'Barking at print' can be found at every level (including among skilled readers if they are in a hurry or tired).

One of the difficulties for unskilled readers is that they do not know how to check on their comprehension. They may not be able to ask themselves useful questions, or realise how much they need to bring in their implicit knowledge or other background information.

Teachers who work with secondary school pupils can make use of 'comprehension' exercises of all kinds to help with these study skills:

1. Cloze exercises can be a good test of fluent reading and immediate comprehension especially if the exercise is timed. The gaps must be filled with sensible words, or the right one chosen from options. Reading and comprehension are inseparable in cloze-type work. (It is more difficult to guess nouns and verbs than to find syntax words – prepositions, articles, conjunctions, etc.)

2. Direct questions (on any text) that require written answers are all-round tests of full comprehension and writing ability.

3. Multiple choice answers are by no means 'soft options', because they demand the ability to read with full understanding and make inferences.

4. Exercises in which students read and answer questions can make explicit the importance of continual checking for meaning and show them how to do this. The technique is that of frequent questions and reviewing at intervals, with conscious effort to carry the meaning forward. It is important that they should understand that they are learning a skill that they can transfer to any reading activity (Figure 8.4, page 125).

5. Understanding the different purposes for reading will be a guide to how the text should be read and what needs to be understood and remembered:
    - narrative fiction – characters, details of the story
    - information: general outline; key details
    - discussion: the general theme/s; the main arguments with supporting details or facts
    - curriculum subjects: overview of the topic: key facts and some detail.

    For some kinds of text, preparation by a quick overview and skim-reading can be helpful.

6. If they have not understood what they have just read, they should try to assess the reason: have they missed or misread some words; have they forgotten information from previous

sections of the text; have they read it too quickly, or missed punctuation? Perhaps their background knowledge of the subject matter is poor and they should ask for help.

7. Ask pupils to prepare questions for the teacher to answer about something they are reading. (A very short time is allowed for the teacher to read the section indicated.) The real objective is to improve their questioning skills, but pupils enjoy trying to catch the teacher out – or test her reading speed. This is a good exercise for younger pupils too.

8. Reading aloud is a good way to check on, and improve, comprehension. Hearing the words can alert the reader to parts of the text that may have been read without attention; it also slows the reading, which may make the meaning more accessible.

9. Study different kinds of text – narrative, dialogue, information, discussion – including the way it is laid out on the page, so that the right mental set is brought to the reading. Make sure that all the information is surveyed, including title and headings – which dyslexic pupils often ignore.

10. Help the student to understand the way that different kinds of writing are structured, e.g. in an informative text, there is probably a summary sentence at the beginning, and possibly at the end, of each paragraph. Details supporting or amplifying this will be found in the paragraph. Using highlighter or coloured pen, the paragraph can be mapped out to show the structure. This method can help memory and comprehension and is especially important in timed situations such as examinations.

11. The value of note making should be stressed. If a student knows that his short-term memory is poor a Mind Map, or flow chart, with single words, short phrases or drawings, should be made as the reading goes on. This may also help to carry the meaning along. It is a tough discipline – but it is necessary for study purposes and exam revision. It can come as a surprise to pupils that teachers too have to work at understanding and remembering some texts; we all need to make notes if we are reading for study purposes.

These are just some of the techniques that can improve reading accuracy and comprehension. In the long term, if the processes can become automatic, they may also help to speed up reading. They can show that reading is always for meaning, not just a matter of saying the words correctly. They also stress that a reader must remember what he has read, and that he should make sense of it as he goes along. If a pupil's comprehension remains poor it may be that basic word recognition still requires too much effort, so that memory is not available for the sentence as it develops. It might be useful to check on his listening comprehension: can he understand and answer questions if a similar passage is read aloud? If so, attention to word-attack skills might help, along with plenty of reading practice at the right level.

Simple versions of such activities are also useful for pupils who are at an earlier stage of reading. They would also benefit from the writing frame approach to questioning and for making written notes. (See Chapter 10, and Appendix II for suggestions about teaching materials.)

1. Prepare passages of text of different kinds: narrative, discussion, informative, etc.
   Make frequent breaks (every four to five lines at first) for questions of different kinds:
   simple re-telling
   information – getting the facts
   inference – reading between the lines, surmising
   reflection – commenting, making wider connections
   prediction – looking ahead
   integration – making sense of the whole passage
   critical – language factors, vocabulary, style
   overview – summary
   Make explicit the different kind of response that each question needs.

   The breaks can be placed further apart and the questions can be more searching as the pupil gets used to the method.
2. The pupil should devise his own questions at the prepared breaks.
   It is important to help pupils to ask themselves useful questions. What is happening here? Who is this character? are useful starters, going on to more open questions such as How does this bit take the action forward? or How does this character fit into the story? What does she think about the others?
3. The pupil should decide how often he needs to break off and review his reading.
   This will be determined by the kind of text being read and the purpose of the reading.

Figure 8.4 Activities for training comprehension skills.

Perhaps we should remind ourselves, after all the serious purposes for reading and why students should 'work at it', that there is still a place in lessons for reading for its own sake, for sharing a book for the enjoyment, to help pupils grow in their appreciation of good writing, and for fun.

Chapter 9

Numeracy and mathematics

This chapter is intended for teachers working on a literacy programme with pupils who also struggle with maths. Teachers who do not have expertise in maths (or those who usually avoid it altogether!) may be able to provide a little help at a basic level, especially as the same kind of approaches can be used, and the child's difficulties may overlap with his reading and spelling problems. For more fundamental problems and work at a higher level teachers should refer to one of the titles in the references (Appendix II).

What kind of difficulties?

Nearly all dyslexic children have some kind of difficulty with aspects of maths. Thinking about the different points of weakness and why they might occur can be a first step to seeing how they might be tackled.

The problem may arise from the reading difficulty; children may not be able to read the explanations and questions on worksheets and in their books. It may be a problem of memory – basic number learning, number facts, tables, mental arithmetic, terminology, ways of 'doing sums' and names of symbols. Or it may be at a more fundamental level, such as failure to understand basic concepts – what numbers mean and the number system itself. Sometimes specific difficulties with the language of maths, and with the 'writing system' of numbers, can be the reason for trouble.

It can be puzzling when children have their own ways of calculating numbers. It is sometimes impossible for the teacher to see how they arrived at the answer without watching them work and asking them to talk through what they are doing – if they can. These roundabout methods of working are inefficient and take too much time but the pupil may be reluctant to let go and learn a 'better way'.

Often, the chief difficulties are at a 'surface' level – with the way that numbers are written and the literacy content of maths. When these are tackled, the way is open for progress, especially if the learner is taught helpful ways of learning and remembering. Some may then even go on to do well at a higher level where work is of a more conceptual kind.

The Mathematics National Curriculum and the Numeracy Hour

The nature of the National Curriculum for Mathematics can itself be a cause of difficulty, with its four distinct strands and the many different topics within each one. Maths learning is sequential: every step is dependent on mastery of the one before it, and on generalisation of basic understanding and numerical skills. Dyslexic pupils work more slowly than many other pupils so they can miss steps or important points. They need time to take in new information. They often do not make connections for themselves. Teachers cannot assume that learning will be generalised from one topic to another and each one may need to be re-started at a basic level.

The Mathematics National Curriculum is taught in schools in the Numeracy Hour – a daily lesson of 45–60 minutes, depending on the age of the children. The strategy gives a central role to direct teaching and stresses that this 'gives [pupils] instruction and demonstrates, explains and illustrates mathematics, setting the work in different contexts and linking it to previous work'. It includes teaching to the whole class and to smaller groups, where there will be differentiated work and the teacher will be able to 'interact' with children. It is expected that, for most children, the pace will be brisk and they will move on rapidly.

The Numeracy Strategy stresses that children at primary school should (Note 9.1, page 258):

- have a sense of the size of a number and where it fits into the number system
- know by heart number facts such as number bonds, multiplication tables, division facts, doubles and halves
- use what they know by heart to figure out answers mentally
- calculate accurately and efficiently, both mentally and on paper, drawing on a range of calculation strategies

It is expected that most dyslexic children will receive all their maths education within this structure. Many will find it difficult to keep up with the group – particularly in the early years. They may need more experience with early concrete work than other children or to work longer with representations of number, such as dots set out as on dominoes, before being presented with symbols or digits. It is likely that they will need more time to consolidate one step, or one piece of learning, before moving on to the next. Sometimes the difficulties will be more closely related to problems with learning literacy rather than a problem with numeracy. All these will need a different response from the teacher. Particular areas of difficulty are shown in Figure 9.1.

Other factors – learning style and emotional responses – often compound the problem.

Learning style

There can be a mismatch between the way that maths is taught and the learning style of an individual pupil. When people work in mathematics they can fall into one of two distinct groups – sometimes referred to as inchworms and grasshoppers.

Aspects of maths that most frequently cause problems for dyslexic learners include:

Many of these are interacting	language – verbal and written
	basic number concepts
	linking concrete, real-world experience to abstract thinking
	learning and interpreting the symbol system
	money
	memory: working memory limitations
	remembering sequences – of names, facts or instructions
	learning and recalling number facts, e.g. number bonds
	carrying out steps in a predetermined order
	orientation and direction
	telling the time
	using a calendar
	setting out work and general presentation
	organisation of work

Figure 9.1 Dyslexic learners' difficulties with mathematics.

Inchworms go through a sum carefully, number by number, attending to the details. Grasshoppers prefer to work in a more visual way; they are more likely to proceed by making links between numbers, seeing patterns and estimating. (Teachers may also not be aware of their own learning style – they have never needed to worry about how they 'think'.)

Dyslexic learners often prefer to work in a 'top-down' way, starting with a view of the whole before they can cope with the details. They may take a 'grasshopper' approach to arithmetic. Others – possibly the less confident children – try to keep hold of the detail but their approach is hindered by their poor memory for number facts and the algorithms of computation. Whichever is preferred – and maybe a mixture of styles is being used – the teacher needs to find out how the pupil is working and adapt the teaching to suit him.

There will be also occasions when one strategy is more effective than the other. If pupils themselves understand the different way of working, they can choose the better strategy or be aware of the pitfalls of over-reliance on one.

Emotional factors

Fear, panic and 'shut-down' can affect any of us in situations where we feel threatened. These are primitive responses, and they can block learning. They also get in the way of others' attempts to help. A sensitive approach is needed from the teacher if work is to be possible. Games, fun activities and IT (Information Technology) may help the pupil to relax and lower the drawbridge. Parents and class teachers can help by not putting pressure on the child – any suggestion that he is 'not trying' or 'dense' has to be avoided. Progress in literacy can suffer for the same reasons, but they seem to be intensified in maths.

Some guiding principles for helping are comparable to those used in literacy work: some of these are shown in Figure 9.2.

Language

Maths is heavily dependent on oral language and literacy:

- vocabulary – learning terms and using them
- reading the words
- interpreting and understanding the written language.

There is often a mismatch between the reading level of individual learners and their understanding of the maths itself. Difficulties of comprehension that may appear to be poor maths may actually be related to incomplete understanding of the written language in which it is expressed. At primary

---

Give attention to specific areas of difficulty
Start at the point where understanding has broken down
Use concrete materials before going on to work with symbols/digits
Give time for learning and opportunities for practice before moving on
When teaching principles and rules explain them clearly with practical demonstrations
Reduce load on memory
Use multisensory approaches for teaching and learning
Give prompts and cue cards that pupils can use on their own

Figure 9.2 Some guiding principles for action.

school, class teachers will know how well their pupils are reading and may be able to provide appropriate support. In secondary school specialist maths teachers may not be so well informed.

Maths vocabulary

Most of us are dependent on words when we do maths, but maths talk can be problematic for children with a language difficulty. The maths vocabulary of the National Curriculum and the Numeracy Hour, contains hundreds of words. Children are expected to understand, to read and sometimes also to write them. They can be difficult because:

- many are difficult to read or to say – e.g. isosceles, parallel, protractor, quadrilateral
- common terms are not understood – fraction, decimal, equation
- there are many synonyms for the +, −, ×, ÷ and = signs and they are used interchangeably, e.g. minus, subtract, take away, take off, less than, reduce, from, difference, decrease
- some words have other everyday meanings: take-away, carry, table, scale, degree, power, etc.
- words can also stand for different values, and numbers may have different names according to the numerical context, e.g. in place value: 5 is not the same as 0.5 (which also means half) and changes its name in 15 and 50
- instructions have their own conventions and idioms which may not be understood.

Success can be related to how quickly the words are understood, or recalled.

Numbers and symbols

The reading and writing of numeracy is a specialised language with its own symbol system. Digits and mathematical symbols have to be learned and named, and their meaning understood. The task of learning the symbol-to-word correspondence is similar to that of learning alphabetic linkages, except that letters represent phonemes only; digits carry conceptual information and mathematical symbols have a functional purpose.

To add to the problem, the use of letters as symbols in algebra and geometry can be confusing for a child who has struggled to learn them for reading and writing, and finds that the significance has changed.

Reading and naming numbers

Being slow to find the name or getting the name wrong can result in an incorrect answer. One hundred per cent accuracy is usually essential. In literacy, errors in reading and spelling need not be serious because context can help with the meaning.

If a child cannot learn or remember the number names, arithmetic is almost impossible. ('How could I do it when I didn't know what they were called?' This was said to me by an adult, when she finally sorted out the names for numbers as they related to place value.) Eleven and twelve can be difficult; they have two digits like the other teen numbers, but have special names. If the child cannot say the name of a number without counting from one, the working process may be so slow that it breaks down.

There is also a problem of misreading a number: if a child cannot recognise and name 15, or reads it as 51, it can be difficult to separate the problem from failure to understand place value or from a specific difficulty with direction.

Reading and naming the numbers also need a lot of words: a seven-digit number (e.g. 1,876,824) may take as many as 13 words to name. The naming cannot be separated from understanding of place value but, if the digits are not named immediately, confusion can follow.

Symbols and notation

Some of the maths symbols are particularly difficult for dyslexic children because:

- they depend (like *b*, *d* and *p*) on correct orientation, e.g. +/×, </>
- the 'four rules' and equals have so many different names
- they have strange, arbitrary shapes (*ratio* is:) and odd names such as '*pi*'
- the significance of the decimal point or brackets may not be understood because they resemble punctuation marks in writing.

Conventions

The maths way of 'doing things' is sometimes similar to literacy, sometimes different from it and a convention can change within the field of maths itself. For instance:

- beginners learn to recognise × as multiply, e.g. 2×, 4×
- later, in algebra any letter placed immediately after a number signifies multiply. So 2x, 2y, 2a all mean multiply 'something' by 2
- x and y can represent different numbers in different sums – they change identity.

This is all different from the literacy alphabet where the letter names are known and consistent.

Memory

It is useful to distinguish between:

(a) retrieval or recall from long-term memory of information previously learned, and
(b) immediate working memory which is involved in:
- processing of numbers in mental arithmetic
- working out sums on paper
- the learning process itself, learning of multiplication tables, arithmetic methods, etc.

Thus, (a) may be helped by frequent opportunities for recall of the information and practice with methods of computation, and (b) can be helped by:

- clear explanations, ensuring understanding at each step so that the child is able to work from known principles if memory fails
- multisensory approaches
- cue cards and a 'ways-of-working' book.

Efficient working of both kinds of memory is essential for success in maths, especially for mental arithmetic. If memory is poor, compensatory methods need to be developed. Giving extra time and taking the pressure off can be the first steps in giving help.

Learning and recalling sequences and number facts

- The names of the numbers, multiplication tables, days of the week, months of the year

- Number facts: learned through tables and as separate facts, e.g. 3 + 7, 9 − 5
- Sequence of steps – algorithms for sums (dyslexic learners sometimes use bizarre methods of working, using relationships and patterns based on the facts they know). These must be all recalled immediately if performance is to be efficient.

Direction of working

The way we read numbers and how we make computations change according to what is being done. In the earliest sums, numbers are set out horizontally and worked from left to right as in reading and writing. Then, not much later, they are set out vertically and the method of working changes direction and goes from right to left:

$$3 + 4 = \qquad \begin{array}{r} 6 \\ +2 \\ \hline \end{array} \qquad \begin{array}{r} 16 \\ +28 \\ \hline \end{array}$$

For division (usually taught after the other three rules), left-to-right working returns. (A dyslexic learner has been observed working division sums from right to left rather than change the direction. By observing place value he still got it right.)

In algebra, the left–right sequence of working is subject to different factors, e.g. brackets, where the numbers in the bracket are calculated first, and equations, where the work is carried out on both sides simultaneously.

Geometry calls for understanding of spatial relationships. The dyslexic pupil may be able to succeed here, although failing with the arithmetic.

Setting it out on paper

Dyslexic children may have additional difficulties of motor coordination and poor visuospatial skills.

They will probably have difficulty writing the numbers and setting the sums out neatly on paper with the degree of precision that enables a sum to be calculated correctly. (Presenting the maths work tidily on the page can also be a problem for children who do not have a specific difficulty.) This can lead to confusion even if the child understands the arithmetic. Numbers may also be wrongly lined up if place value is not understood, which again will affect the calculation.

They need to have particular help with this kind of organisation and to understand why neatness is so important.

Calculators

A calculator can be a boon to a dyslexic child if:

- he has a poor memory for number facts
- his pace of working is slow,
- he has problems with direction.

Some children do not find them easy to use and there may be particular problems:

- They may punch in wrong numbers or symbols, e.g. 6 instead of 9 or + instead of ×.
- It is still necessary to remember what to do, the order in which to enter numbers, which keys to press and how to proceed through the calculation.
- If they cannot estimate the range in which the answer is likely to be – whether hundreds or thousands – they may not be able to check whether the answer is about right.
- They may not read off the answer correctly, e.g. may not notice a decimal point.

A talking calculator gets round some of these difficulties and a version for IT is especially user friendly (see Chapter 13).

Some suggestions for helping

Language: verbal and written

The teacher should ask the child to read aloud the maths worksheets, textbooks, or old test and exam papers. This can show the kind of difficulty that is involved. Is it part of the general reading problem or difficulty with specific words? If the reading is competent, the problem might come from failure to understand what maths tasks are being set.

Vocabulary – difficulties with words

Maths words can be long and difficult, often obscure and with odd spellings, e.g. isosceles, prism, parallelogram, rhombus. Recognising them, decoding and pronouncing them, and comprehending them can all be a problem:

- Attention to word-attack skills can be generalised to the literacy work and the same kind of approach can be used: attention to vowel sounds, syllable structure and recognition of common syllables.
- The maths words can be included in the phonic dictionary as examples, e.g. pence, circle, circular, cylinder, angle/triangle/rectangle, parallel, fraction, multiplication, temperature are all useful words for phonic spelling and reading topics.
- 'Chunking' into syllables can help with pronunciation. Meanings can be discussed at the same time.

- Use maths and number words in word-recognition activities – flashcard practice, precision-reading exercises and games (Bingo, Memory, board games).
- If the difficulty is one of word comprehension, exercises and games in matching word to meaning could be helpful.
- Inclusion of maths words and number concepts, in literacy work (fewer than, greater than, how long – hours as well as metres). Taking them out of !!MATHS!! may help to de-sensitise them.
- General progress in reading skills will help the child to access all parts of the curriculum.

If the standard vocabulary can be read more easily, the child can give more attention to the specific requirements of the subject.

The materials suggested for literacy work in Appendix II, and some of the games, can be adapted for helping with maths words.

Sentence reading

The style of maths questions varies between the informal stories that accompany problems to the condensed style of questions at Key Stage 3 (KS3) and KS4 maths work. Practice with oral reading – or silent reading – followed by discussion may help to conquer the panic reaction 'I can't read it/don't understand it':

- Sentences in maths carry very particular information which must be read with complete accuracy, and remembered and understood. Hesitations over words can disrupt comprehension and guessing from context is not, in this case, an appropriate strategy.

- 'Problem stories' can be tricky. Attempts by the writers to locate the maths in ordinary life can involve names that may be unfamiliar as written words and non-English terms (such as foreign currency, e.g. *drachma*). It is difficult to anticipate when this kind of difficulty will crop up. If children are preparing for exams and SATS, a look through different maths texts may help the teacher to see where help can be directed. Practice at reading a variety of sentences can then be given.
- Questions in arithmetic are often expressed in very terse language, with words used in unexpected ways, e.g. from a question about the cost of posting a package: 'Between what limits must its weight lie?' Or a geometry question: 'Rotate the triangle P by 90 degrees clockwise about the point labelled O.' The pupil needs to be taught to read the question in two stages: What is the question telling you? What do you have to do?
- Problems that need to be worked out logically may be difficult because the order in which to calculate the information has to be worked out: 'Ann has 8 sweets, Jack has 2 more than Ann. Jim has 3 less than Jack. How many do the children have altogether?'

It is useful to think about what is needed to find out 'more than', 'less than' and to show how to decide where to start.

Spelling

Some questions ask for answers in the form of written words or sentences. Pupils must therefore learn to spell the maths terms:

- Use a multisensory or memory technique as for literacy work (see page 82).
- If spelling is a general problem, include the words in the regular spelling work.
- Select a minimum of essential words and teach those.
- If pupils are very poor at spelling, encourage them to write the words they need accurately enough to be understood – without spending time on them.
  The maths must take priority.

Digits and symbols

If the child cannot recognise digits, does he understand the number concept itself? If not, there is probably a need for specific help in mathematics, but the language teacher might help with simple counting skills and the reinforcement of digits knowledge.

Written numbers and number names crop up in all kinds of reading so recognition and understanding is important for literacy work too.

- Use concrete aids and materials e.g. objects, an abacus or pictures, wherever possible when working on number.
- Take opportunities when they occur in the phonic work to include sorting and counting exercises, e.g. how many objects/pictures beginning with /f/? Find four animals with a /s/ sound in their name.
- To help with simple counting and to reinforce the one-to-one correspondence, use a number line with dots, before adding the digits.
- Saying the 'number line' from memory: most dyslexic pupils will be able to say the numbers

from 1 to 100 and beyond, but a few may need help with the names for the teens, twenty, thirty, etc.

- Counting backwards is a necessary skill for which they will need practice.
- Use multisensory work to make the link between numeral, name and concept. Make digits with Plasticine, glitter glue on card, etc.; talk through the shapes.
- Include 0 with both its names – nought, zero. We often call 0 by the name of alphabet letter O, especially when saying telephone numbers or car numbers. Be explicit about the difference and encourage the use of the maths word.
- Don't let the pupil associate 0 with 'nothing'! This can have serious consequences in maths: 10 is not 1 and nothing; 200 does not mean 2 and 2 nothings; 705 is not 75.
- Use plastic or wooden digits in the same way as letters, and simultaneous oral/auditory work to help the learning of names and forms.
- Drill with flashcards to practise the digits/names link (as in the phonic linkages drill).
- Make sure that the child can confidently associate the plastic or written digits with the right number of objects before teaching him to write it.
- Use a multisensory approach when teaching the writing of numbers. Start with large forms and talk through the shape; orientation of the digits can be troublesome.
- Teach the recognition and spelling of number words.
- When number words occur in reading or spelling (ten, six, three, nine are phonically regular and might occur early) make sure the child really understands what they mean.

Symbols

- Knowledge and recognition of symbols: these will benefit from the same multisensory approach as numbers.
- The symbols are different from number names, as each has many associated words. Associating names and symbol can also be a focus for reading work.

Numeracy in literacy games

Many games can be used for counting practice and number recognition at the same time as the literacy work. (Many literacy games do not include numbers so these may need to be added.)

- Counting on: some children cannot add one by counting on. They may not be able to read particular numbers (e.g. 7 and 8) without counting from 1. Play a game that moves by single steps (reading single words perhaps) and show that, for instance, a move of 1 from 4 brings you to 5. That also means 5 words have been read. Use short games numbered 1 to 10 at first. Reading the numbers is not necessary to a board game, of course, so make a point of asking: what number are you on now? When these are secure, the same practice can be given in games with higher numbers.
- Dice: these can have digits or dots. Use whichever suits the child's numeracy needs. Blank dice can be customised for the individual pupil.
- Recognition of pattern with dice: in board games a three-way association – pattern/name/ digit – can be made which will help instant recognition; there is also motivation – and reward – to remember and get it right.
- Include verbal explanations while practising numbers – talk through any shaky point.
- Simple number bonds can be practised: if the player is on 3 and throws a 4, ask where he will land (if the answer is right without counting, give a bonus point). Use of two dice extends the number-bond practice and may help in understanding of double numbers and doubling.
- Early games that follow a single linear or circular path may be preferable to games with a square format, where the direction changes from row to row. With these games it will be important to explain that this is for board games only: reading is different, and maths has its own rules for working from right and left.

Basic number concepts

If this is a serious problem it will need specialist help and dedicated time, but the pupil may be afraid of maths and not able to approach it. In the literacy lesson the teacher may be able to include a little basic help without emphasising that it is MATHS. At first it can just be conversational. Use of digits should be postponed until the child has a grasp of some simple principles about number: it is how we talk about how many and how much (quantity).

Start with the child's own experience, e.g. How many brothers and sisters do you have? Do you get pocket money — how much? What do these numbers mean?

- Include maths words casually in the talk.
- Use whatever objects are around to talk about numbers.

- Help with counting through games.
- Use multicubes, multilinks, cubes and rods of different sizes (e.g. Cuisenaire) to explore counting and number size with words that express number concepts – more/less, bigger/smaller, longer/shorter, odd/even, square.
- Make up stories that relate numbers and number concepts to real life, e.g. 'odd' and 'even' can be explained by reference to wildlife:

  - 1 bird is on its own – odd
  - 2 birds build a nest – even
  - 3 birds – one is the odd-one out
    needs a mate to be even
  - 4 birds – are even and so on

  This can also show how adding 1 changes odd to even and vice versa.

- Trading games can help the child to understand place value: rods and cubes of Cuisenaire are useful here. Penny and tenpence coins can be used to work in tens, but this will not show the size of the relationship between the numbers.
- Different coins can help work on simple number facts about addition.

Money

- Teach the money symbols £ and p and what they stand for.
- Raise awareness of different coin and note denominations. Plastic money can be used but real coinage has more meaning. Use coins as counters in games.
- Reading the money numbers often needs explanation and practice. The £ symbol is written first, yet we say it after the number (e.g. £3 is 'three pounds'), unlike the p sign which is written after the digit (e.g. 5p is five pence).
- The literacy teacher's main contribution may be to talk about what money amounts mean. What exactly is a pound? How do money amounts relate to each other; which is more expensive – something costing £4.30 or something costing £3.99p? Which sum is more? Some children could think that £3.99 is more because 99 is the higher than the other numbers. Help them to understand which number gives the clue.
- Ways of adding prices and checking change is a necessary everyday skill: the child will need practice to become familiar with the methods. Estimating – working to the nearest 10 – can give a rough idea to begin with. (Use a number line to see each number in relation to 10.)
- Working out change by counting on is simpler than counting backwards, but pupils need to be shown how to do it. The example in Figure 9.3 shows the kind of detail that some children need for an understanding of arithmetic.

Memory

Although it is not possible to expand working memory itself, it is possible to learn strategies to remember more efficiently. Helpful ways of learning and being able to recall number facts, number relationships and the ways of making calculations, may be found:

- Group the facts to be learned.
- Present a few at a time. It is important in such piecemeal learning that the pupil should be

> Q: You buy an ice-cream for 44p. How much change do you get from £1?
>
> Count **up** from 44 to the next 10. That is 50. Note down the answer: 6.
>
> Now count in 10s to 100 (£1) starting from the **next** 10 along (60).
>
> Keep a check on paper, or on your fingers of how many 10s there are:
>
> 60 – 70 – 80 – 90 – 100. There are 5. 5 x 10 = 50. Add the first number you noted down: 6.
>
> The answer is 56p change.
>
> This can also be demonstrated on the number line.
>
> (Make sure they understand that they do not count the first 10 they get to)

Figure 9.3 Counting change by adding on.

helped to understand what the learning is about, so show how each part relates to the whole (e.g. tables, or number bonds within 10).

- Work with the pupil's preferred way of memorising: vocal rehearsal, visualising, building up the facts from first principles so he can see relationships and patterns.
- Give practice at vocal repetition, written repetition and finally recall. Use the facts in arithmetic examples.
- Provide support cues to fall back on, e.g. number facts on cards; worked examples of sums. Keep them handy but encourage a pupil to try to remember before using the cards. Build up confidence – if memory fails he can still do the task by referring to the cue.
- Make a 'how to do it' book. If pupils have a working maths book, they can look up methods when they need to and follow the pattern of the

procedure, e.g. how to do 'impossible subtractions' by decomposing the number; long multiplication and division. The teacher can use the book for revision. (What is there has been taught. Compare the 'phonic dictionary' with its spelling lists.)

Number facts

Help the pupil to understand that addition and multiplication facts (number bonds) are commutative, i.e. the order in which the numbers are presented does not matter (e.g. 6 + 8 = 14; 8 + 6 = 14). Two facts are being learned as one. Show this with pictures, cubes or on a grid. This will take an immediate load off the memory. (Make sure he does not extend this to subtraction and division.)

Addition facts

Practice with dice and simple games can give the repeated practice that is needed. Use the literacy board games and convert the tasks to number facts responses.

Multiplication tables

There are many strategies for learning tables (see Appendix II, page 233). Many of them rely on over-learning by frequent practice, and some children are able to learn them with song or rap tapes.

If this is quite impossible, other ways of learning the number bonds need to be found:

- Emphasise the commulative nature of the number order. This immediately reduces the number of facts to be learned in tables 2 to 9 from 72 to 36 which is a more manageable task.
- If each fact can be learned separately, saying

the table is not important, unless the school insists, but it must be the complete fact of course, namely 4 × 6 = 24. Encourage the pupil to learn a few each week – both ways, i.e. 7 × 8 = 56; 8 × 7 = 56. Use magnetic numbers (on the fridge!). Change them each day and keep a success chart (bright colours). 'Look how many I know; how many still to go?'

- Does the pupil realise which part of the tables task is difficult? Often, it is keeping the place in the recitation, rather than not knowing the answer. A suggestion that helps to guide the way through the recitation can be seen in Figure 9.4.

Mental arithmetic

Oral and mental calculation from the earliest school years is stressed in the Numeracy Strategy which emphasises that children should be able to make mental calculations, although it also expects that they will record facts and answers on paper as part

of the process. Children (and their parents) get very worried by the memory and mental calculation aspects of maths, although the acceptance of note making may reduce some of the fear. In fact, some dyslexic pupils are good at mental number work; it is the writing part that they find difficult.

Suggestions

Show short cuts:

- Working with 10s. How to spot and work around 'round numbers'.
- Adding and taking away 9. Pupils need to be careful, when they round up to 10, that they adjust the first answer in the right way, by then taking away one for addition of 9 and adding one for subtraction of 9.
- Counting in 5s: 5× is one of the times tables that they all know because the numbers end alternately with 5 and 0. This can be shown with a pattern on the table square.

Show that there are three parts to the recitation of a table but there is only one set of facts that has to be learned and remembered.

(a) Number in the sequence 1 → 10
(b) Number of the table being learned (the multiplicand)
(c) Answer.

(a) is a matter of keeping the place;
can be done with fingers if necessary

(b) does not change during the table;
place a large digit where you can see it so you don't forget which table you are on
(c) has to be learned and remembered in the right order;
can be learned as a sequence of numbers if necessary and practised separately.

Now put them all together. Say it with a rhythm and keep it going, but not too fast.

Practise two or three numbers at a time. It's good practice to be able to start in the middle.

Figure 9.4 Learning the tables.

- Learn double-numbers facts, up to 20 if possible, and look for ways to work with these. This helps to reduce dependence on knowing other number bonds.
- Explore ways of noting answers in the working process and using them to get the final answer.
- Use grids and number squares to discover other short-cuts and important number facts.
- Knowing the 5× table (including being able to say it backwards from 30) is important for telling the time as well as for general calculations.

Presentation of maths work

Help the pupil to understand why it is important to set out work neatly. Use squared paper. The standard 1-cm squares may be too small for children whose handwriting is poor, and who have difficulty with spatial organisation. If possible, find – or make – a grid with larger squares.

Give some supervised practice. Remind him of the reasons for being tidy.

Using materials and equipment

Using rulers, addition and multiplication squares, calculators, compass

All these can be explored in a few minutes' work:

- Ruler: simple measurement can be incorporated into written work, e.g. creating a border around a piece of writing. The child can be shown that a ruler can be used as a short number line, useful for addition and subtraction up to 30 (centimetres).

- Addition and multiplication squares: these allow the pupil to see and to explore patterns in a way that calculators cannot – and in that way they are more valuable as learning tools.
- It is important to talk through the correct procedure when using a calculator and check that the right key has been pressed.
- The compass can be used to make drawings for talking about the vocabulary of circles – arc, segment, diagonal, radius, circumference – all useful for practising spelling principles and word-attack techniques. Children with difficulties in fine motor skills may find a compass difficult to use. Give them a chance to practise.

Time and calendar

(See Chapter 12 for suggestions about learning to tell the time and read the calendar.) Practise working out sums about length of time, both clock time and date time. Refer to clock and calendar. Use different calendar layouts.

Digital time

Some pupils prefer this because they do not have to worry about 'past' and 'to' and clockwise direction. But they still have to understand what is meant by the numbers. For instance 8.37 is meaningless unless the time reader knows the relationship of 8 to 12 and 37 to 60.

Even if he works out that he has 23 minutes to get to school or college – what does that mean in terms of time left? (Dyslexic pupils and students have a poor reputation for time keeping. This is not inevitably the result of poor calculation skills, but more of not understanding how long 23 minutes is in real time.)

It may be helpful to use the quarter and half-hour numbers and work around them. Use the clockface to demonstrate the point – but reassure the pupil that you are not suggesting that they change to it, although at some time they might have to know how to read it.

24-hour clock

This is important for timetables and dyslexic pupils will need extra practice in working it out, especially converting one time to another.

Work on the relationships between digital 'afternoon' time and the 12-hour clock. These can be tricky, especially 17:00 and 19:00 which catch many people out, especially when they are in a hurry. It will be useful to work on the number facts between 12 and 24.

They may need to work on number lines to 12, 24 and 60 in order to keep their place in the hour.

Chapter 10   Into the classroom

The first section of this chapter looks at different ways in which the pupil can be helped to transfer skills to the general work of the classroom. The second looks in more detail at some approaches for helping pupils to become independent writers and at other aspects of curriculum work. The third summarises some of the National Curriculum English targets.

The transfer of skills from the individual lesson to curriculum work

Dyslexic pupils who have one-to-one help of the kind described in earlier chapters must be able to apply their new skills to their work right across the curriculum. This is often not easy for them, as there is a vast difference between the learning environment of the classroom and that of the individual lesson.

The specialist teacher structures the learning for her pupils, and supports them while they learn. In the classroom the language part of the work is not so structured (or not in the same detailed way) and the class teacher can provide very little direct help for individual pupils. It is assumed that they will be able to carry over and use their new skills, even though there may still be a big gap between these and the demands made by the curriculum. If they are to cope, they will need help from both sides.

Many dyslexic pupils have difficulties with some aspects of work in the classroom, particularly time pressures or situations where they may feel 'shown up' in front of others. They can become quite distressed about being unable to keep up, or if they never seem able to satisfy their class teacher's expectations (Figure 10.1). It may be possible for the specialist teacher to discuss adjustments for particular children, e.g. the amount of work that is expected or how much time they have to complete it.

Where transfer of skills is concerned, the specialist teacher may be able to give direct help, especially if she is familiar with the content of the

- Reading aloud in the class or group
- Completing work, particularly written work, within the same time as other pupils; reading also takes longer
- Copying from the board and other displays
- Reading hand-outs of notes, or worksheets if these are closely printed (or faint photocopies or duplicated sheets)
- Keeping up with the teacher when taking notes or dictation
- Taking in, and responding to, complex instructions
- Maintaining concentration when there are distractions
- Relationships within the peer group might be troublesome

Figure 10.1 Points of difficulty that dyslexic pupils may meet in the classroom.

curriculum and knows what is expected of her pupils.

- How to use new skills in a wider context needs to be addressed 'head on' and she has detailed knowledge of what the pupil can do.
- She can teach him how to use support frameworks.
- The higher level skills required for secondary school curriculum work benefit from explicit individual attention.

Regular consultation between tutor and teachers is essential if work is to be transferred effectively. Other teachers also need to know how far each child has progressed in the spelling and reading programme with the individual tutor, so that they can mark work appropriately. It is also important to get general agreement about what can reasonably be expected of dyslexic pupils; if expectations are realistic they are more likely to succeed. Figure 10.2 shows the kind of exchange that is useful.

Discussion about the current curriculum work is also important and about the levels at which both pupil and class are working in the National Curriculum and the Literacy Hour and Numeracy Hour. This can be a guide to what the pupil's next general needs are likely to be and can also identify where more work should be done on areas already covered, e.g. if someone is still not coping with written work in class, is it because the spelling work has not been assimilated or because he is still inhibited about writing? Some kind of drill or concentrated practice might be needed to help spelling automaticity; on the other hand, reluctance to write may be helped by taking the spotlight off spelling for a while and focusing instead on what he wants to say.

Observing the pupil in class

It can be helpful for the specialist teacher to spend time with the pupil in class occasionally. She can then observe directly what the pattern of classwork involves and how he copes with it. Sometimes, children tend to 'pigeonhole' their work: 'spelling' is done with Mrs X on a Monday in the staffroom – it does not occur to them that it is relevant also to classwork. If Mrs X sits with her pupil in class and helps him to apply what she has taught, perhaps in some science work, it makes the point directly.

It can be useful to look at other factors too, such as where he sits. Can he see the board easily? (Classroom layout can result in children sitting at

From class / subject teacher ⟷ from dyslexia tutor

```
From class / subject teacher  ←——————→   from dyslexia tutor

pupil's NC level / group / band          particular difficulties

curriculum work                          skills level : reading &
                                                         spelling
                    ⎧ texts
mode of study       ⎨ worksheets         objectives : short term
                    ⎩ projects                         medium & long term

performance /   ⎧ in written work        programme of work
attainment      ⎨ practical work
                ⎩ oral expression        what point has been reached
                                         in programme
policy on homework
                                         progress anticipated
particular difficulties
                                         general attitude - confidence
general attitude - confidence

                    points to watch for
                    suggestions for help
                    expectations
                    recommendations
```

Figure 10.2 How useful information can be exchanged with class teachers and the SENCO.

tables at an angle to the board.) Is it possible for the teacher to keep an eye on what he is doing? Are the chair and desk a comfortable size?

Discussions and good understanding between teachers are clearly important if practices of this kind are to be developed. If the pupil has help from support assistants working in the classroom, it is essential that they join in such exchanges.

Transfer of skills at different stages

Knowledge of basic phonics and language work

In schools in England the Literacy Hour curriculum introduces the teaching of sounds and letters during the Reception Year; by the end of Year 2, pupils will have had direct teaching of all the main vowel spellings of English. By that time, it is expected that they will be independent readers at their age level, and able to write using full stops, commas and capital letters. Their reading and writing will include material from different genres and they will be expected to be able to work independently and in groups.

Language terms are also taught, with an emphasis on using exact words to refer to letters and sounds (e.g. phoneme, grapheme, digraph, onset and rime) as well as grammatical terms – parts of speech, tenses, punctuation, etc. (See Appendix V for information on the terms and vocabulary taught in the Literacy Hour.)

Children referred for individual help even as early as 7 may already be a long way behind their peer group in all these areas of literacy. They, and older pupils, may be placed in groups receiving additional help to master the early part of this curriculum. It is important that a teacher working one-to-one is aware of arrangements for the child in the Literacy Hour. It may be possible to coordinate follow-up work so the child can have regular sound practice and linkages drill, and work on simple word patterns alongside other children. Use of materials such as the worksheets of the Phonological Awareness Training (PAT) programme could be helpful to other children too (see Note 10.1, page 258).

The most useful way to help pupils apply their basic skills work is to persuade them to write. Direct attention to the structures of writing is given in the Literacy Hour. A dyslexic pupil will be able to work at his own level in the group section, where he will work independently or with other children. He should be able to make use of supportive materials, such as writing frames, for English and other subject work.

In individual sessions extra attention can be given to basic skills such as good sentence production. The teacher can make sure that a pupil understands what a 'verb' is, and the difference between complete and incomplete verb forms; the term 'working verb' is useful here. Children can be shown how to write longer sentences by using a variety of joining words (not just *and* and *then*) and how to make sentences more interesting by adding details. Punctuation can be explained – and reminders to use it given.

They will probably also need to sort out and revise much of the language terminology that has been introduced, especially in the earlier years.

Some children need to prepare written work by verbalising ideas, expressing themselves clearly and using words accurately. This can be easier for them in an individual situation than in a group. It will also help with the Speaking and Listening part of the curriculum.

When individual help is available for pupils in secondary schools, 'English' work – essay and comprehension – is quite properly within the province of the specialist teacher. Dyslexic pupils benefit from explicit help of this kind. When attention is given to such work in a group or class, they often do not absorb or apply it; they need direct instruction in techniques, help with the different ways of using them and opportunities for supported practice. Work on these higher level skills should, at the same time, provide a format for the practice of spelling work and for developing competence in reading (Note 10.2, page 258).

This kind of interaction between the different learning situations should help to ensure that skills are carried across from one to the other, at whatever level the pupil is working.

Mesh curriculum work with individual tuition

The work of the individual programme can be meshed directly with classwork if subject matter from the curriculum is used as the starting point for spelling and sentence work and for written expression. Technical and other subject vocabulary can be studied, and this should be slotted into the phonic work where possible. Material for development of reading and comprehension skills can be drawn from the curriculum in a similar way. Such to and fro movement of work between classroom and individual lesson should help pupils to see how the two are connected. There should also be regular follow-up to see if they are using their knowledge and spelling strategies in other written work.

The strongest links can be made in the development of different kinds of writing and this is where the main area of need may be. The teacher must judge when the pupil is ready for work to broaden out in this way; it will also depend on the amount of lesson time available.

Developing skills for written work and reading

The writing task

If pupils are to cope with the curriculum, they must be able to write freely and for many different purposes. Writing is a complex task, needing organisation of thought for written expression and selection of an appropriate form even before syntax, spelling, punctuation and legible handwriting are called for. So often, these different demands all compete for attention, leaving the dyslexic pupil unable to attend to more than one or two of them. (It is worth repeating here the statement of the 12-year-old girl, quoted in Chapter 3: 'When I write, I can write; when I spell, I can spell; but I can't do both together.')

A teacher working individually can show pupils how to take the task apart, and work separately on each aspect. If this is done in the context of curriculum, they may have a better chance of transferring their new skills into more general use.

Using learned spellings in written work

In the individual or small group situation, spelling work is regularly practised in a structured context. At each step the new vocabulary is practised in dictated sentences so that it approximates to the 'real' writing task, where there is a context and meaning. Irregular words are introduced gradually and the progression of difficulty can be carefully graded so that the pupil will not make mistakes:

1. Simple sentences with spelling patterns and 'rules' restricted to those currently taught.
2. More complex sentences with greater variety of spellings. This is a useful way to keep work under review for a time.
3. Directed writing: the pupil uses the words he has been taught in his own sentences. He is expected to get these words right and to have a good try at spelling others. The teacher should help by prompting and reminding him of strategies, but only give spellings if he is totally stuck. The whole sentence should be thought out and said aloud before writing begins, then written as quickly as possible.

Curriculum vocabulary should be part of the spelling work.

Getting into writing: structures for support

In any piece of composition, two major demands coincide – the content and the mechanics. Sometimes extreme responses to the writing task can be seen. X has lots of ideas and is not worried about spelling mistakes or poor handwriting. He writes enthusiastically but his work is impossible to understand. Y has trouble with spelling and is inhibited either because she does not like making mistakes or because she has no strategy for getting into words. Z may not know what to say; or he may have ideas – even some spelling skill – but he does not know how to begin.

- X may need to have the writing done for him (possibly by a support assistant) until he has acquired some skill with the mechanics. Alternative ways of working are needed; he may like to provide drawings to support his writing, and to help others to understand it. Working on the computer with a word grid might help (see Chapter 13). He might use a tape-recorder.
- Y needs to be reassured that mistakes are not crimes: reward her efforts without worrying her about spelling until she has learned some routes into words and built up some confidence. (This will need the cooperation of class teacher and parents.)
- Z needs to be supported by structures of different kinds so he can get ideas together and put them in order.

In fact the step-by-step strategy for Z is one that many pupils need to learn and most need to be shown how to think first about the content. Then, when they are ready to start writing, they are able to give more attention to expression, vocabulary and punctuation – and perhaps even to spelling and handwriting. Different ways to handle the 'thinking stage' need to be shown and practised before they can be used independently.

Pupils may also discover that they prefer one approach to another. Different kinds of structure for writing are shown in Figure 10.3. They can all be drawn up to fit any part of the curriculum.

Another advantage of working from a structure is that it offers an overview of the task from the start. The structure shows how much information is needed, and where it belongs. This can be reassuring to the inexperienced writer and the dyslexic student who cannot organise the information – especially if there is a mass of facts to sort out. In the structures shown in Figure 10.3, the first three present this kind of chart. Mind Maps work in a rather different way, and this is explained below.

When pupils are shown how to use a structure, the teacher should first model the process, making explicit the way that she is working. The pupil should then do a similar exercise with the teacher, making explicit what he is doing. This exchange may need to be repeated before he works on his own.

Discussion with the child's teachers will be needed to find out what kind of work is being done with the class or group. Writing Frames and Mind Maps are among the approaches recommended for routine use in the Literacy Hour so he may have met them already, but individual attention to consolidate work previously introduced in class can make a lot of difference to how a pupil carries it out. Suitably adapted, all these methods for approaching written work can be used with children right across the age range. Some, e.g. Mind Maps, may be more appropriate than others for older pupils.

At the writing stage the sequential arrangement of material collected in a Mind Map might be helped by a flow chart or a framework showing the structure for an essay (see Figure 10.8). Examples of all these models can be provided for use in class.

Sentence starts

Dyslexic pupils (along with many others) often have difficulty in thinking what to say when they

- Guided sentences:
    - sentence starts and word banks provide ideas and formats for pupils who need help to start writing

- Flow charts:
    - provide a linear, sequential structure to guide writing
    - are useful for chronological writing, stories or reports
    - can ask questions or indicate steps in appropriate places
    - ideas can be organised and put into order stage by stage
    - permit drafting of work from the outset

- Writing frames:
    - generate thoughts or ideas by questions, statements or sentence starts
    - permit immediate expression – drafting
    - guide sequence of ideas and information
    - ask questions as a guide to subject matter
    - can be used as a framework to collect information from different sources

- Mind Maps:
    - act as expandable nets for collecting ideas or facts
    - are non-linear
    - encourage drawings or diagrams as well as words
    - can be a highly visual medium
    - break down task into stages:

        - collect material
        - decide on structure and order
        - write

Figure 10.3 Structures to support writing of different kinds.

are presented with a topic, or title for writing. A support structure for the least confident writers gives sentence starts and possibly also keywords that the pupil has suggested.

Example: Write about how you made a den.

To make it we got _____
We built it in _____
First we _____
Then _____
After that _____
It looked _____

It is also helpful to show how much is expected. The page can be mapped out to show exactly what has to be done. It could be divided into sections (using the page in 'landscape' format, i.e. with the longer side horizontal), with room in each for a drawing and some writing; in addition, the drawing could be done first. In this way an unconfident pupil can be helped to fill a whole page – which is a great morale booster.

Later the sentence starts should be replaced with general headings: topic; materials; method – suggested number of sentences; finish.

This kind of writing fits in with National Curriculum writing targets from levels 2–4.

Flow charts

Another way to start the flow of ideas is to ask questions about the title word – for instance, the *wh/how* question words (Note 10.3, page 258).

For a piece of writing on 'Making a den' a few simple questions might be presented on a flow chart and this could lead to more extended work (Figure 10.4). Children should be shown two ways of using the flow chart:

- Write answers to the questions in order, thinking out each sentence before writing it down.
- Make brief notes in answer to the questions in order; then go back and write the sentences.

The first might be best for younger children. The second might be a good way to show how to make one-word notes which act as the peg for ideas.

The flow-chart method can be adapted for different kinds of writing, but it is most suitable for structuring a chronological, or linear, account – a story, or a report, e.g. on an experiment or a process. For a story

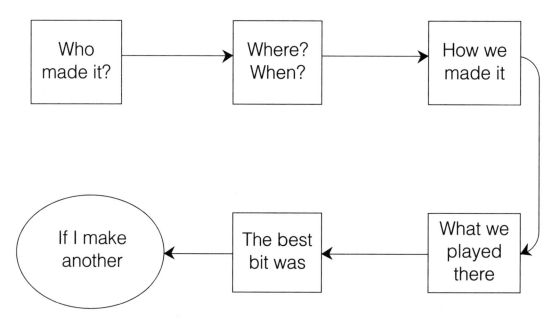

Figure 10.4 Flow chart: How we made a den.

chart some of the frames might suggest particular points of action, such as a jagged edged frame for the crisis or high point, and a circle for the resolution.

It provides a series of checkpoints which can ensure that the pupil takes the topic point by point, gets every point in the right order and leaves nothing out. Specific questions and guide-words are appropriate to the content of the work.

This model is useful for the pupils who cannot start because they do not know how to, and for others whose ideas tumble out in random order. For older pupils it would have more appeal than sentence starts. These pupils might also be able to make their own flow charts using examples that they have worked on as models, either with numbered boxes or using the *wh/how* question words as prompts. In this way they are able to exercise control over the way their work develops.

Organising writing and using drafts to improve and develop writing fit in with National Curriculum writing targets from Level 3 up.

Writing frames

Guided writing with frames offers a route into many different kinds of work, including composition, collecting information and responding in writing to different subject topics. They usually employ a mixture of sentence starts and questions, and steer the pupil through the different stages of the work with appropriate language.

In the English curriculum they can help pupils to structure writing of different kinds – narrative or descriptive composition, discussions or presenting an argument.

They often begin with a statement followed by sentence starts that guide the organisation of

ideas. The example shown in Figure 10.5 shows how to approach a discussion. It opens with a topic sentence then guides the pupil to present different viewpoints in a balanced way, and round off by stating her own opinion.

Frames are often set out on the page allowing room for the response to each 'start'. Those linked to subject areas might ask direct questions about a topic that has just been taught. For more general purposes, they can be provided on cards as open formats from which a pupil could select whichever best suited his purpose, e.g. a report, a letter or discussion. Used in this way, they can be a tool that trains the pupil to use appropriate forms for writing and helps to develop independence.

Reading can also be supported by frames that show children how to ask questions about the text. These can be linked directly to the collecting of information for writing about specific topics. A series of points that children should look for is set

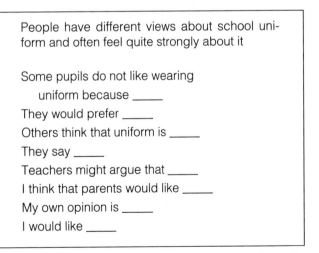

People have different views about school uniform and often feel quite strongly about it

Some pupils do not like wearing
    uniform because _____
They would prefer _____
Others think that uniform is _____
They say _____
Teachers might argue that _____
I think that parents would like _____
My own opinion is _____
I would like _____

Figure 10.5 Writing frame. Should school pupils have to wear uniform?

out as a sheet on which they write what they discover. In this way the frame guides them to find the information they need, restricts the amount of detail they copy and teaches good 'research' methods by asking for the source of the information (text and page number) (Figure 10.6).

If they make their own frame, pupils should be shown how to start by thinking about what information they want to find out and set themselves some specific questions before starting to read. This helps to avoid copying chunks of material that they do not need.

The last stage is to present the information they have collected in continuous writing and at this point sentence starts or the sentence/paragraph model (Figure 10.7) can be used as a guide (Note 10.4, page 258). This fits in with the National Curriculum writing targets Levels 3 and 4.

Mind Maps (Figure 10.8)

Many dyslexic students like to use this method of getting information and ideas together because of its highly visual approach. The emphasis is on drawings, icons, diagram and much use of colour: writing should be kept to one-word notes. (Sentences are against the 'rules'.) The first stage is to brainstorm ideas, then link these together by arrows and joining lines. Each group of ideas is given a keyword which shows the general point.

In stage 2, everything is brought together on a new sheet. The points are set out around the keywords along branching lines and new ideas can be added. Finally, the ideas are put into order for writing. It is not until this point is reached that linear structure has to be considered – description or narrative, organisation of two sides in a discussion, or any other subject matter.

The main ideas and detailed points have been sorted out already in the preparation stage. The work may still go through several drafts in which the student can give his main attention to the expression and language. He may then be able to think also about the mechanics of writing (Note 10.5, page 258).

Question	Answer	Detail	Source
When did they live?	A long time ago	In the Ice Age Died out 3000BC	Life in the Ice Age p 42
How do we know about them?	Remains dug up, cave paintings	Bones, skin, fur Drawn in caves by hunters	Our ancestors p 37
What were they like?	Big, fierce, elephants	Long curved tusks Lots of hair	Our ancestors p 38

Figure 10.6 Mammoths: a framework for collecting information.

The writing stage: paragraph and essay

This fits well into a simple formula (see Figure 10.7). The guide starts with a reminder about sentences because dyslexic pupils so often need a nudge about basic points. After that, it shows that a paragraph and an essay have similar structures. The different sections of a flow chart, or the 'bags' of ideas in a Mind Map, might each correspond to a paragraph. The ideas can be written about, and expanded, in an organised way. (The guide could be put on card and clipped into a work file.)

When the writing stage is reached, the pupil should be encouraged to use the first attempt as a draft version which can be altered and corrected (National Curriculum writing targets Levels 4, 5 and beyond).

Sentence
A sentence is a statement or question that is complete and makes sense
It has a working verb
It starts with a capital letter and ends with a full stop or question mark

_____

_____

Paragraph
First sentence introduces topic
Three or more sentences to give information, develop ideas
Summing up sentence to end

_____

_____

Essay
Opens with paragraph introducing subject
Three or more paragraphs to give information and develop ideas
Winding up paragraph to end

Figure 10.7 Guide card for written work: sentence, paragraph, essay.

Working on the work

Many children have to be persuaded to work on their writing and teachers are sometimes reluctant to insist. Producing any written work is already an achievement and it is feared they might be 'put off' further efforts. If pupils are resistant it might help to explain that writing and speaking are like cooking and eating. Although speaking and eating are natural processes, writing and cooking are not. Words and food ingredients are raw materials for writing and meals. Although we could eat most of our food raw, most people like to cook at least some of it. Our everyday speech is 'raw' and when we write we have to 'cook' the words in different ways. To produce good written sentences, paragraphs, etc. we have to assemble the ideas and the words, weigh them and stir them around. The Sahara Desert sentence on page 153 went through several drafts; the ideas were reduced and swapped around and different linking words tried. It is for the 'cook' to decide when the writing is properly 'done'.

Writing concise sentences

Pupils often fail at an early stage in their writing because they lack skill at composing sentences.

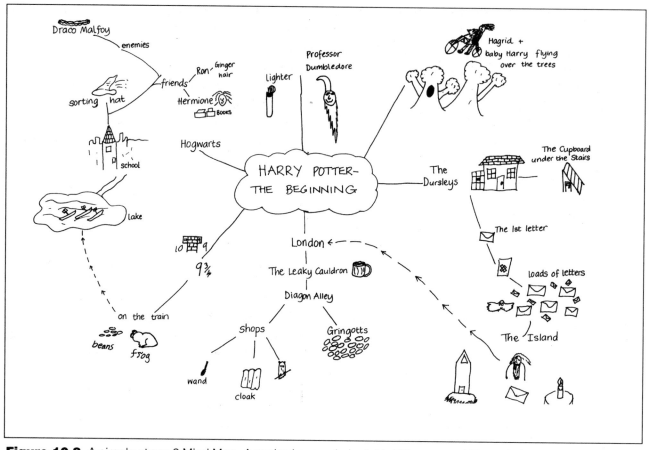

Figure 10.8 A simple stage 2 Mind Map. A worked example by L.H. (10 years and 7 months) and his teacher.

These are unfocused and loosely put together – in a conversational manner.

The technique of writing 'point sentences' can help to tighten up the construction so that a good deal of information can be concisely expressed. This is an appropriate way to start off a piece of work – a paragraph or an essay. Each point in the sentence – there might be three or even four – will be the focus around which ideas can be developed.

The sentence will contain information or ideas carefully linked together; good use of joining words is a key part of the technique. The ideas themselves might already be collected in a Mind Map, or writing frame. A mini-diagram for the sentence is useful:

• Write the topic word in the middle of a horizontal line and cross it with a vertical. This provides four point positions.

- A keyword or phrase important to the topic word is attached to three or four of the points.
- The next step is to see how these can be connected. (If a satisfactory sentence cannot be made, another set of ideas must be tried.)
- Good joining words need to be found: they might link the points, or compare or contrast them. Different possibilities can be tried out before the sentence is finally completed.
- The result should be a complex sentence with three – or even four – linked ideas that carry a summary of the paragraph or essay which will follow.

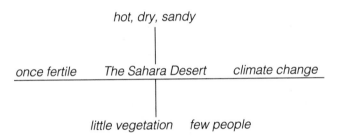

The Sahara Desert was once a fertile region but because of climate changes it is now hot, dry and sandy with little vegetation, which means that very few people can live there.

Discovering structure

It can be useful to show how a piece of writing is constructed by taking an example apart (carefully selected) and showing explicitly that writers use standard formats. By marking the main topic statements with a highlighter pen, the pupil will be able to see that these are usually at the beginning of the paragraph, and that a summary, or linking sentence, rounds it off. A different colour can be used to show the keywords for the details in between, and to find out how many sentences are used to express each idea. (A book page can be used if a transparent plastic file cover is slipped over it; the highlighter marks stay on the plastic and can be wiped off afterwards.)

This kind of exercise helps reading too, because it directs the pupil to look in the right places to get a summary or an overview of the information in a text. Related points can be tracked through a paragraph with the highlighter.

The general objective underlying all these models must be to give pupils strategies for organising their own work. If a process is made explicit as it goes along, it is more likely that the pupil will be able to learn the underlying skills.

1. Demonstration: the teacher does the work, discussing the process.
2. Step 1 is repeated with the pupil's verbal contributions.
3. The process is repeated with the pupil doing more of the work – including writing.
4. In the final stage the pupil takes over and explains the process to the teacher.

(The approach is similar to the 'scaffolding' method, Note 10.6, page 258.)

Computers

Computers can be used to follow up and develop in the classroom the work done in one-to-one tuition. Use of software for spelling practice, and structures to help writing in the ways described above, can all help to promote the transfer of learning. Again, discussion with other teachers is important so that work can be coordinated.

The use of computers is discussed in Chapter 13.

The reading task

Teachers can encourage pupils to extend their reading skills by using many different kinds of reading matter in lessons, including attractive story books that other children can read, and information books that reflect pupils' own interests or which they are using for topic work. In this way, the teacher can help them to understand the different purposes for reading – and that there are different approaches to the reading task.

Pupils need to be taught how to use books and other written material effectively:

- how to use the index, chapter titles and headings
- to read captions under pictures
- to use the pictures themselves for information and as a guide to context
- how to get an overview of the text by skimming
- how to scan text for specific information
- where to look for the information in any part of the text.

They should be taught to start any reading assignment by taking a look at the whole of the text they are about to read: flick through the pages to find out how long it is; look at the kind of content – pictures, graphs, diagrams – and the captions; are there subheadings and sections, or is it divided into unlabelled paragraphs? With this kind of overview an estimate could be made of how much time the work will take.

This kind of skill in picking up cues and guides to the content of reading matter is especially important for dyslexic pupils. It is particularly important for

exams, and here the overview must take in the whole of the paper. Highlighters are essential tools. One colour could be used to mark the key information words about the number of questions to be answered and how many in each section. This must be done before separate questions are tackled; the specific keywords for each question should be marked before it is started. (National Curriculum targets include the overview skills as early as Level 2, and up to Level 5 and beyond for the more advanced skills of skimming and scanning.)

Silent reading

Silent reading can by-pass certain skills that are needed for reading aloud, although phonology and knowledge of word pronunciation do have a role in silent reading (Note 10.7, page 259). In the individual lesson it is the skill of reading aloud that is almost exclusively taught. Yet the classroom environment demands that pupils read to themselves. They will probably be slower than others – but how much do they get through and how much do they understand? It may not be easy for class teachers to check on how well pupils are coping.

The process of reading silently needs to be made explicit to the pupil in the one-to-one lesson and its development should be monitored. This is particularly important for older pupils. A slow reading speed can affect a pupil's results in Selective Assessment Tests (SATS) at Key Stages 2 and 3 as well as at GCSE. Extra time may be justified, or even a reader, especially if there is a discrepancy between reading and listening comprehension.

How can you listen to a pupil reading silently? As soon as pupils can read simple text with reasonable ease (perhaps at an 8-year reading level), it is useful to check that they can read equivalent passages silently to themselves with equal fluency and accuracy. This can be checked by timing the reading, by asking the child to recount what he has read and by direct questions. The class or subject teacher will be glad to have feedback.

Reading and writing: 'comprehension' work

In English language 'comprehensions', reading (in this case, silent reading) and written work come together in one exercise. This is another area where the individual teacher can help the pupil to apply his skills to general work; in fact, this is where his skills apply most widely because being able to read with understanding, abstract information, and write it down efficiently is essential right across the curriculum. Dyslexic pupils often remark that they 'know the answer but can't write it down properly'. It is important that pupils understand the kind of demands made by different subject areas.

English curriculum 'comprehension' questions tend to follow a particular pattern: they move from questions asking for factual information to more searching questions which require more reflective responses, comparing and contrasting, bringing in the reader's own opinions and feelings, and summarising content. (Factual answers carry fewer marks than the others.) Although dyslexic students can usually answer the information questions quite well, they have difficulty with those where they need to make inferences, and make use of more general understanding. They often also lack the written language skills to answer the more complex, searching questions.

It is useful to separate the task of answering a comprehension question into different stages, so that pupils can approach it in a structured, logical manner (Figure 10.9). This looks a lengthy procedure, but failure to carry out each step is one reason why pupils who do understand what they have been reading still get poor marks in written exercises of this kind. Other factors in skilful handling of 'comprehension' include:

- complete understanding of the questions
- providing the right amount of information in the answer
- summarising information from the passage in good English
- writing the answer in the same language register as that of the question.

Teachers of dyslexic pupils in the years leading up to public examinations at 16+ can profitably spend time on this kind of work, making explicit these more advanced requirements and giving support while pupils practise the needed skills. It is a matter of developing more advanced reading techniques and deeper understanding, as well as learning to use good, concise, written language. However, the steps in Figure 10.9 are the essential starting point and can be begun quite early. Oral practice, stopping short of writing, is useful preliminary work and can help to establish good habits of reading for meaning.

Aids for use in the classroom

Teachers should discuss with pupils the kind of aids that would be useful – and how they would use them. Discreet cue cards can be helpful:

This method can be used for any work where written answers based on text are needed

1   Reading stage: read and understand passage/material
- Overview of all material – title, text and headings, graphics, pictures, etc.
- Skim-read passage
- Read questions quickly
- Read text more slowly

It may be better to read questions first, instead of skim reading – especially if time is limited – as the questions can give clues to what the text is about.

2   Answering questions: preparation stage
- Read question carefully. Check form and words of question
  Look for 'keywords' – *how*, *why*, *who*; *show*, *explain*, *comment*; highlight or mark them

- Read passage carefully and select material – relevant, enough to answer fully
  Make notes if necessary – or highlight

- Think out answer. Check against question: 'Am I giving what's wanted?'

(It is best to tackle questions in numerical order)

3   Answering questions: writing stage
- Use short sentences
- Use more than one sentence if necessary
- Make sure the answer is numbered correctly

4   Checking stage
- Have I written down what I intended to say?
- Have I answered the question? All of it?
- Have I copied correctly the important words (for example, names and technical terms), dates, numbers. Check against passage and question
- Punctuation: capital letters – including names – and full stops

Figure 10.9 Comprehension: a four stage strategy for reading and responding in writing.

ā	ē	ī	ō	ū
name	seed	ride	bone	tube
sail	seat	tie	boat	new
day	(these)	light	bow	
	lady	by	toe	

Vowel digraphs

au/aw	oa/ow	oi/oy	oo	ou/ow
Paul	road	boil	book	shout
paw	snow	boy	spoon	now
				town owl

Figure 10.10 Chart: vowel choices.

Study word pattern	e.g.	Action Vowel suffix	ed, er ing, y, etc.	Action Consonant suffix	ful, ly less, etc.
End: 2 cons. - w y after vowel	fish tank slow play	**No change**	fished playing	**No change**	slowly
vowel digraph	sleep		sleepy		sleepless
Short vowel: 1 vowel and 1 consonant at end	sad swim	**Double**	saddest swimmer	**No change**	sadly
'r' word	star		starry		starless
Long vowel: ends -e	wide hope	**Drop -e**	widest hoping	**No change**	widely hopeful
ends: y after consonant	try carry heavy	**Change y to i**		**All suffixes** } **except for ing**	tried carried heavily - - - - - - - - carrying

Figure 10.11 Chart: suffixing rules.

1. Spelling cards:
   - individual words
   - helpful hints, rules and mnemonics
   - charts: vowel choices (Figure 10.10)
               suffixing rules (Figure 10.11)

   Keep these where they can be easily seen or reached, such as clipped inside an exercise book, or in a plastic wallet.
2. Models for writing in the form of diagrams or 'skeletons' on card:
   - sentence, paragraph, essay (see Figure 10.7)
   - flow charts
   - general purpose writing frames or reminders for mind mapping.

   These can be kept in the relevant book or file. Use them with pupils first. If possible, get pupils to add their own strategies, and work on the layouts and design so that the models are personalised.
3. Subject glossaries: keep in the back of relevant exercise book.
4. Spelling dictionary – with person additions.

It is best if these aids are kept under review. They can be up-dated and modified, and any not being used can be looked at again. Is it just forgotten, no longer needed or not useful? The pupil can decide whether to revive, revise or discard it.

The National Curriculum for English

Programmes of Study and Attainment Targets

The National Curriculum for English is set out in three sections: Speaking and Listening, Reading, and Writing. It is emphasised that, although each of these has its distinctive elements, language development depends on their interrelationship. The detailed Programmes of Study and the Attainment Targets for each field are arranged under two headings: Knowledge, Skills and Understanding, and Breadth of Study. The first specifies what must be taught at each Key Stage; the second indicates the 'context, activities and range of experiences' through which this content will be taught.

It is expected that there will be a great deal of interchange between the different aspects of the English curriculum (Note 10.8, page 259).

Attainment Targets for all the NC programmes of study are divided into 10 levels; these summarise the expected attainments of pupils as they move through their school years. Arrangements for pupils with particular needs, including learning difficulties (such as dyslexia, although separate difficulties are not identified), are stated in a section headed 'Inclusion: providing effective learning opportunities for all pupils'. This states that teachers 'should teach . . . in ways that suit their pupils' abilities. This may mean choosing knowledge, skills and understanding from earlier or later key stages so that pupils can make progress and show what they can achieve.' In the section headed 'Pupils with special educational needs' the need for 'greater differentiation of tasks and materials' is stated. These sections do not mention specific learning difficulties of any kind. Section 3 states:

Teachers should take specific action to provide access to learning . . . [by] providing for pupils who need help with communications, language and literacy.

Dyslexic learners will be included in this group.

The most relevant suggestions (non-statutory i.e. not obligatory) about how this access to learning might be achieved are:

- using texts that pupils can read and understand, and
- using ICT, other technological aids and taped materials.

This does not mean that dyslexic learners have any 'entitlement' to ICT, although access to a computer or audio-tape could be crucial to the success of individuals in the group. It is left to the discretion of teachers, and – presumably – to the availability of the technology.

The profiles of dyslexic pupils are typically uneven across the range of Attainment Targets and there will be many Levels, particularly in Literacy, which they will not reach at the same time as others in their age group. However, the majority of dyslexic learners are in mainstream classes. It is expected that they will follow the whole curriculum, although it is recognised that some will need to work at the level of earlier stages. Some may be in small groups for literacy and possibly for mathematics. They will still be expected to take the Statutory Assessment Tests/Tasks (SATS) at the end of each Key Stage along with others in their peer group. (Those still working at earlier levels at KS3 SATS may take additional tests that are targeted at a level more appropriate for them.)

The National Curriculum should mean that (in theory) a pupil with dyslexia cannot go unnoticed and that he or she should be able to achieve in the areas where their skills are not dependent on literacy performance.

- It highlights the fact that they cannot achieve at the 'norm' in the basic skills of literacy and possibly numeracy.
- It provides a means of identifying and reporting on other skills and abilities, such as verbal ability, grasp of subject information and abilities (often of high level) in subjects with more practical content.

However, the expectation that dyslexic learners will 'fit in' to the requirements of the National Curriculum underlines how important special help might be. It also highlights the importance of regular communication among specialist teachers, class teachers and subject specialists.

Literacy Attainment Targets

Individual dyslexic pupils – like many other children – will be working across several levels in many subject areas; this will be greatest in the Literacy Targets of Reading and Writing.

The teaching of phonics and the subskills of decoding, sound blending and other basic skills for literacy with which dyslexic pupils need explicit, detailed help are part of the National Literacy Strategy (1997) and are taught to children at school in England in the Literacy Hour during Key Stage 1. Reading and spelling work is carried out at word, sentence and text level, and the links between spelling and reading are made explicit. However, the syllabus of the literacy programme and the pace at which it is delivered are aimed at children of average attainment who are learning in the normal way. Children with dyslexia and similar learning difficulties are often not able to keep up with the group and need more opportunities to learn and consolidate the work. Additional materials are provided for work in the Literacy Hour in Years 2, 3 and 4 for the teacher to revisit and re-teach the phonic work of KS1 – but these may be delivered by teaching assistants.

Writing in KS1 and KS2

Writing is taken as a single Attainment Target, grouping together the skills of composition, spelling and handwriting. This means that these skills cannot be graded separately and a dyslexic pupil's attainment may be assessed at the level of his weakest area.

In Writing, e.g. at Level 2 (average age 7), it is expected that the child should be able to produce writing (both story and informative) using 'a sequence of sentences, sometimes demarcated with capital letters and full stops' with 'simple monosyllabic words usually spelled correctly' and where there are errors these should be 'phonetically plausible alternatives'.

Many dyslexic children – much older than 7 – may be able to write stories with good ideas, expressed in vivid language, long before they can write in correctly punctuated sentences or get much of the spelling correct. They need to be encouraged to try to write even if the mechanics are faulty. It is important that results in SATS should not give pupils (and their parents) the impression that they have 'failed' the tests.

At 7, however, if they have individual help most dyslexic children should be able to achieve the Level 1 Target of Writing: 'communicates meaning through simple words and phrases'. They should know the alphabet letters and their sounds and be able to write simple regular words and some common irregular words by the end of Year 2 of school.

The Targets from Levels 2 to 4 specify that pupils should be able to write for different purposes, to write sentences that are usually grammatically correct with simple correct punctuation and accurate spelling of common polysyllabic words.

By Level 4 (School Year 6), it is expected that the majority of children will be writing in a lively, thoughtful way, appropriate for the purpose and the reader. They should be using grammatically complex sentences with a range of punctuation and organising their work into paragraphs. Vocabulary should be used for effect.

By the same time – if they are to cope at secondary school – dyslexic children should be able to communicate in writing in a number of different forms; they should be able to spell short regular words correctly, using simple suffixes, and use different strategies (phonic analogy, visual) to spell unknown words. They should be able to work independently and to make use of spelling aids, writing frames and other aids in class.

Targets for Handwriting state that children should develop legible handwriting and be able to use different forms of handwriting for different purposes. The expectation of joined writing comes at Level 3 (ages 7 to 9 for most children), with the objective of achieving a fluent joined style by age 11. These are reasonable targets for many dyslexic children too.

Reading

At Level 2 it is expected that 'pupils' reading of simple texts shows understanding and is generally accurate'. They are expected to use a range of strategies to read unfamiliar words and understand what they are reading; it is expected that they will be able to express opinions about what they have read.

By Level 3 (age around 9) they should be able to read 'a range of texts fluently and accurately' and to read independently.

The aim for the dyslexic pupil should be competence by age 9 at the Level 2 Target: 'Read a range of material with some independence, fluency, accuracy and understanding'. By the time he goes to secondary school he will need to achieve Level 3 and be moving towards Level 4, particularly 'show understanding of significant ideas, themes, events and characters, beginning to use inference and deduction', '. . . locate and use ideas and information'. In many cases, this will be possible only if he has help from the age of 7 or shortly after.

The Programmes of Study at all Key Stages state that ICT should be used where appropriate 'to plan draft and improve their work' and to check spellings and word meanings. These are of particular importance to dyslexic children; the wording 'where appropriate' should be noted.

The Speaking and Listening Attainment Target is probably the area in which the dyslexic pupil is most likely to succeed at the 'average' age, although even here he may need help to fulfil some of the detailed provisions such as the requirement at Level 3 to 'adapt what they say to the needs of the listener, varying the use of vocabulary and the level of detail'. It is important that he should have constant encouragement to improve oral and listening skills (see the section on Oral work in Chapter 12). Such pupils may need help to express themselves clearly. Many teachers notice that they can have difficulty finding the right words, especially when asked to explain a meaning or process. Dyslexic students are often worried if they have to report on projects to their peer group, so even their verbal skills can let them down. In individual situations they can be as articulate and expressive as anyone else.

Children take SATS in English (or, in Wales, Welsh), Maths and Science before the end of Key Stage 1 (School Year 2). Most children are expected to attain at least Level 2.

By the end of KS2 at the age of 11, it is expected that children's attainment levels will range between Levels 2 and 5 – and this would include those with dyslexia.

Key Stage 3

In secondary school, the National Curriculum has, in some ways, become something of a nightmare for dyslexic children; the 'entitlement' to follow the whole curriculum can seem like a cage from which there is no escape. It can be difficult to fit a period for specialist help with literacy skills into the school timetable, even though proficiency in reading and writing is essential to success throughout the curriculum. Educational psychologists are often unwilling to recommend exemptions from the curriculum for dyslexic children who have provision of individual help, even though the full range of subjects (including a foreign language) is a heavy load for dyslexic pupils to carry.

A direct link might be made between the specialist help and the curriculum if subject materials are used as the basic matter for the literacy work, as suggested earlier in this chapter. If a pupil is withdrawn, say, from geography, he might bring his classwork for the teacher to use for some of the reading, writing and spelling work. This would assume means of regular liaison between dyslexia teacher and subject specialists – which often has practical difficulties. It should be easier to achieve where the teacher, even if not full time, spends at least part of the week in the pupil's school.

A further possibility may be to move the one-to-one work into the classroom, where the teacher can give direct curriculum support. However, this should not normally be considered until the pupil can function independently as a reader and has achieved a 'spelling age' of between 9 and 10 years. (By that time, help may have been withdrawn.) Until then, the main focus should continue to be on the improvement of basic skills and the work needs to be carried out in a withdrawal situation.

Summary of some of the main Attainment Targets for Levels 2–6

Reading

Level 2

- Reading of simple text shows understanding and is generally accurate.
- They express opinions about major events or ideas in stories, poems and non-fiction.
- They use more than one strategy . . . in reading unfamiliar words and establishing meaning.

Level 3

- Pupils read a range of texts fluently and accurately. They read independently . . . show understanding of the main points and express preferences.
- They use their knowledge of the alphabet to locate books and find information.

Level 4

Responding to a wide range of texts, pupils show understanding of significant ideas, themes, events and characters, beginning to use inference and deduction. They refer to the text when explaining their views. They locate and use ideas and information.

Level 5

- . . . responding to a range of texts, select essential points, use inference and deduction.
- Identify key features, themes and characters and select sentences . . . and relevant information to support their views.
- They retrieve and collate information from a range of sources.

Level 6

- . . . identify different layers of meaning and comment on their significance and effect.
- . . . give personal responses to literary texts.
- . . . summarise a range of information from different sources.

Writing

Level 2

- . . . communicates meaning in both narrative and non-narrative forms, using appropriate and interesting vocabulary. Ideas are developed in a sequence of sentences sometimes demarcated by capital letters and full stops. Simple monosyllabic words are usually spelt correctly – [errors are] phonetically plausible alternatives.

- Letters are accurately formed and consistent in size.

Level 3

- Writing is often organised, imaginative and clear.
- . . . words are chosen for variety and interest. The basic grammatical structure of sentences is usually correct. Spelling is usually accurate, including that of common polysyllabic words.
- . . . capital letters, full stops and question marks . . . used accurately. Handwriting is joined and legible.

Level 4

- Writing in a range of forms is lively and thoughtful with ideas developed in interesting ways . . . using grammatically complex sentences within paragraphs.
- Spelling including . . . [regularly formed] polysyllabic words is generally accurate . . . beginning to use punctuation within the sentence including inverted commas.
- Handwriting style is fluent, joined and legible.

Level 6

- Pupils' writing often engages and sustains the reader's interest, showing some adaptation of style and register to different forms . . . they use a range of sentence structures and vocabulary to create effect.
- Spelling is generally accurate, including that of irregular words . . . a range of punctuation is usually used correctly to clarify meaning – ideas are organised into paragraphs.

Speaking and listening

Level 2

Show confidence in talking and listening; on occasion show awareness of the needs of the listener, speak clearly and use growing vocabulary when explaining ideas. Beginning to be aware – on occasion – of need for more formal vocabulary and tone of voice.

Level 4

. . . . talk adapted to the purpose in a range of contexts. Describe events and convey opinions clearly. Listen carefully – are responsive to others' ideas and views. Appropriate use of some features of standard English and grammar.

Level 6

Talk engages interest of listener through variety of content and expression. Use vocabulary precisely and organise talk to communicate clearly. Make significant contribution in discussion – evaluating others' ideas and varying their participation.

Chapter 11   Handwriting

It is nearly always necessary to work on handwriting when teaching dyslexic individuals. This is a complex task involving fine finger movements, larger wrist and arm movements, visual observation, coordination of visual and spatial skills, and visual and muscular memory. (This is leaving aside knowledge about spelling and other aspects of the language that is being written.) It requires much practice to become wholly automatic. When assessing how much work needs to be done, the teacher should watch pupils as they write, noting the pen-hold, posture, the general attitude and the speed at which the writing flows, as well as looking at samples of their handwriting.

Many pupils, particularly the younger ones, often have poor mastery of the letter forms and their details; even if they are recognisable by their general shapes, these may be tentative or distorted, showing uncertainty about orientation, where to start and the direction of movement. They do not know the position of the letters on the line and their relative sizes. In these cases, all the letters should be revised or re-taught. Punctuation marks can also be a problem.

If pupils of 9 and over are still printing the letters, they will probably benefit from starting on joined writing; where necessary the basic letter shapes can be re-trained as part of the process. Where someone is already attempting joined writing, but hesitantly or with untidy results, being shown the correct way to make the linking strokes should produce improvement.

Perhaps the most difficult task is to help adolescent pupils to improve their handwriting. It then becomes a re-training exercise. Teacher and pupil together will need to determine what are reasonable objectives, taking into account factors such as constraints of school work and years of habit.

It is a good idea to use a separate book for handwriting, in which large forms, patterns and pictures can be made; this can be decorative and colourful. Children may also need a book with specially marked lines for their first practice of relative letter sizes and the position of letters on the line.

Physical factors: motor and visual difficulties

The handwriting task requires a combination of mental and physical concentration which creates considerable tension in some children. Performance may be affected also by the physique of the child. Even mild difficulties can hamper a task that requires motor and visuospatial functions to be integrated. 'Clumsy' children call attention to themselves by frequently knocking against things or falling over, but mild difficulties of other kinds may be overlooked unless a teacher knows what the tell-tale signs might be.

If a child is making great efforts with handwriting, but without success, there may be an underlying, undiagnosed difficulty. Habits of posture or behaviour in other school tasks – or in the playground – should be looked at too. The teacher should check if there have been earlier problems with motor development, and if the child's eyesight has been checked by more than the school's routine eye test.

Motor development

- Difficulties of muscular or reflex development can result in poor posture or problems with balance, or the child may not be able to sit still comfortably. Children who are loosely jointed, or have poor 'muscle tone', are almost certain to experience difficulties. They may develop strategies to compensate which are unhelpful in other ways. They may feel more comfortably balanced if, for instance, they hold the side of the chair or desk; if they have poor muscular development they may clutch the pen very tightly or keep a rigid forearm, or lean over and support their head on their hand.
- A child may have a poor sense of spatial organisation relative to his own body, which makes it difficult for him to control the regularity of his writing. He may have difficulty 'crossing the midline', i.e. reaching across his body, so that reaching across the paper to start at the left margin might not be easy.

In both cases, the school's PE specialist will be able to comment on the child's performance in PE and games, and may be able to set up some exercises that would help. If the problem is causing great difficulty the child may need to be referred for specialist assessment by an occupational therapist. (See Appendix II for suggestions about sources of specialist advice for motor and visual difficulties.)

Optical/visual difficulties

- If the writer gets very close to the paper or leans over to one side, visual anomalies might be suspected, e.g. short sight or uncertainty about the reference eye. (This could also result in tracking difficulties when reading.) Long-sightedness may be less easy for the teacher (or the routine eye test) to spot, because the child will be able to see the board and the vision chart, but may not be able to alter his focus easily for the close work of writing.
- A child with visual discomfort (complaining of itchy or sore eyes, rubbing his eyes, blinking frequently) may be reacting to the glare of white

paper, especially under fluorescent light. A pastel shade of paper might help and he may have a colour preference.

(The child could be given a coloured plastic overlay for the reading book. An assortment of coloured acetates or plastic file covers could be tried, but this is a very temporary measure because it is important to find the exact colour for the individual – and of course it cannot be used for writing work.)

Ways that the teacher can help

Even without physical difficulties children develop poor habits of grip and posture. Attention is often needed to correct a poor pencil hold and to help pupils to relax their grip and develop more free wrist and arm movements. Left-handed children sometimes develop a rigidly hooked angle of the wrist as they try to prevent the pen hiding what they are writing.

- Grip: a plastic grip, triangular or moulded, or a specially shaped pen or pencil can help to correct the grip. Pupils will vary in what they can use with comfort.
- A writing implement must be found that fits the child's hand and one that flows well; a nylon-tipped pen is often better than a ball point. If a pencil is used, it should have a soft lead.
- The pupil should be persuaded to sit up and give himself room to move; improved posture should help to reduce arm and hand tension. This also creates space for the hand to move freely across the paper. The non-writing hand should be placed on the paper to hold it steady. A pupil who hunches over his work to hide it might improve spontaneously as he becomes more confident – but may need to be reminded about sitting up.
- It helps if the paper is turned at a angle (15–20° is usually comfortable). For right handers, the paper should be placed slightly to the right of the body, with the lower left-hand corner pointing to the writer's middle. For left handers it will be the opposite way. Let the child experiment to find what is comfortable. An exaggerated angle to the body – at 90° or more – should be discouraged.
- There should be a good source of light, preferably from the left for right-handed children and vice versa.
- Squeezing exercises can help to reduce a tense grip, by making the pupil aware of his finger tension and, by contrast, to feel what it is like to relax the pressure. A small rubber ball (such as a squash ball) or a spring clothes peg can be used for this. These can also help to strengthen weak finger muscles if that is the problem.
- Some pupils feel more comfortable when they write on a sloping surface. They can more easily see what they are writing particularly when getting to the bottom of the page.
- The pupil's feet should be firmly on the floor in front of his seat so that his body is balanced.
- Correct height of desk top is important. If the pupil is too small, or too large, for the furniture, a good sitting position will be impossible. (This may seem too obvious to need a mention, but it happens!)

Left handedness

About 10 per cent of people are left handed, but there is not thought to be a causal connection between this and dyslexia. It creates particular kinds of difficulty for any writer because the natural inclination may be to work from right to left. It is much easier to pull the pencil across the page than to push it. Working from the left also means that the writing hand also gets in the way.

Right-handed people can be oblivious to the difficulties that left handers have to cope with and they often seem unsympathetic. Teachers should be aware of the general difficulties that left-handed children can encounter. When a left-handed person is also dyslexic the difficulties can be compounded. These will certainly be greater if an individual is uncertain about laterality, or has an additional motor difficulty, or poor memory for sequences of movement.

Left-handed writers can see only the letter they are writing: they cannot check what they have just written – which can make them feel very uncomfortable. Writing may also be smudged as the hand moves across the page. A non-smudge pen is essential; a fountain pen or a cheap biro is not ideal. It is important also to find a pen that flows smoothly. Some left-handed writers find that a non-joined writing style is more comfortable and faster because this removes the need to pull the pen through the joining lines.

Awkward hand positions and odd kinds of grip are often adopted. A hooked wrist position enables the writer to keep his hand above the words, but it places a great strain on the muscles and tendons of the fingers, wrist and forearm.

There are other factors too. Any implement designed for right-handed use, such as scissors and certain tools, and utensils with pouring 'lips', is going to be difficult. A right-handed person may forget that sewing needs to be set up to be done from the left and she may find it difficult to teach a left-handed child to tie shoelaces. The left hander might be slower carrying out any of these tasks (in technology classes, for instance) and do it less efficiently.

Organisation might also come out 'backwards' in other situations, e.g. putting books along a shelf – they will start from the right – and in laying out utensils and cutlery things will go wrong.

The left-handed dyslexic child might also try to read from the right.

Suggestions for helping

- Writing: the angle of the paper is important – 15–20° with the bottom right-hand corner pointing to the middle of the body. A sloping surface might also be more comfortable. The writer should be shown how to adjust the paper as he moves along the line so that he has maximum view.
- If he can be persuaded to keep his hand in a natural, relaxed position, he will find that the writing will appear beyond his pen hand after four or five words and he can then look back and check it. This requires a good deal of self-confidence because mistakes are more difficult to adjust when the writing has continued beyond the immediate word. Negotiation about how this can be done (neat crossing out and writing the correction above) might be possible. It may be necessary to give the pupil more support for spelling and, in cases of extreme awkwardness, he should be able to use a computer.
- Maths work may be more difficult too, because of the different directionality of sums.
- Wherever possible, marks or other indicators about where to start should be given. A cue

card with examples of sums with dots, showing the starting place for each, might be helpful. For writing, a Post-it note could be stuck on the page at the margin, or a red arrow shape could be clipped to the page pointing to the left and moved along as the page is turned.

Teaching the letter forms

The letter forms will be taught in the first place as part of the multisensory linkages work, in order of introduction for spelling and word building. However, when the focus of the work is the handwriting itself, the sequence of work is different. It is now advisable to group the letters according to similarity of shape and writing movement, so that they can be practised together and reinforce each other: *o c a d g q*; *e*; *s*; *f*; *b p h k*; *n m r*; *i t l j*; *u y*; *v w*; *x*; *z*. The grouping of *p* and *b* will depend on whether the open model ( ) or the closed 'ball-and-stick' model is used.

- Give extra attention to the shape of the letter, the starting and finishing points, and the direction of movement. Talk through these while demonstrating the form; use words that describe the movement through the shape: swing, round, back, up, over, down, flick (to describe the small exit line).
- Emphasise that all printed letters except *d*, *e* and *z* begin at the top and start with a downward, or down-curved, stroke.
- See that pupils make the letter forms at first using large arm movements, on a board or on large paper with thick felt pen or crayon, getting a good rhythmic swing through the shape. A baseline can be drawn if it helps. Note that

the movement is not always continuous: most letters will have a pause at one or two points, usually where the direction changes.

- Show the position of the letter on the line, with tall and long letters having ascending and descending strokes of the right length and at the right angle. Large forms can be made at first, to emphasise the points.
- Ask the pupil to trace a letter before he attempts his own version. After that, models for copying should have red and green spots to show where to start and stop, and arrows to indicate the direction of movement. The size can be reduced by stages until usual writing size is reached.

Comparison of the letters helps to spot the special features, and notice the differences.

- Names for shapes:
  - *h* for house has a chimney, *n* for nut does not
  - *n* is a one-tunnel letter, *m* has two tunnels
  - u has a rounded bottom, *v* sits on a spike
  - *w* can hold water, *m* cannot.
- The group of **a** letters must all have their tops closed. Compare **a** and *u*. An **a** form must end on the line, to distinguish it from *o* which is just a circle and joins from the top.
- Although direct comparisons can emphasise the differences and similarities, teachers need to be careful about presenting a choice between easily confused letters – *b/d* is the obvious one, but *f* and *t* can also be confused.
- Although the 'bed drawing' ( ) can be helpful for distinguishing the letters and sounds of *b* and *d*, some teachers may prefer to teach one

form and leave the other to look after itself: either emphasise the 'bat and ball' motif of *b* or teach *d* emphasising the starting place: it is the only letter with an ascender that does not start at the top. *d* starts like a *c*, which it follows in the alphabet.

Patterns and pictures

Handwriting patterns make a good preliminary or accompanying exercise for each kind of form. These can improve:

* directionality
* hand–eye coordination
* pen control and smoothness of flow
* regularity of form and even tops to the letters
* attention to detail
* automatic production of the particular shapes.

Patterns are particularly useful when joined writing is being taught. Fun activities such as completing patterns in pictures, maze tracking, joining dots, etc. are all useful general training.

Capital letters

Many pupils are not sure how to make these letters and it is often necessary to teach them as a separate topic. Each one should be associated with its lower-case letter on the reference page of the phonic dictionary. Some essential points to teach are as follows:

* Size and placing are simple:
  they all stand on the line
  they are twice the height of lower-case letter 'bodies'.

* It is incorrect to mix capital and lower-case letters within words and to use them within words except when writing in 'block' letters.
* 'BLOCK LETTERS' means capital letters: these are often required for filling in forms.
* M and N are sometimes found to be awkward: they have angular forms, not the rounded ones of the lower case *m* and *n*.
* In joined writing, a 'printed' capital letter can be used and this is not joined to the following letter.

Pupils often like to experiment with elaborate capital letter forms, adding curls and flourishes. In these cases, teachers could show the more decorative forms of older-style cursive writing, but it is best to encourage a plain style for general use.

Print or cursive?

The National Curriculum and the Literacy Hour emphasise the teaching of joined handwriting in the early stages of Key Stage 2 (KS2) but some pupils are not able to synthesise the necessary skills, and may still be printing long after their classmates are writing well. Before a decision is made about this, the teacher should consider the needs, and the age and stage, of the individual pupil. With writing, as elsewhere, it is important to look for the pupil's strengths and build on them. If a good print style is established, joined writing is the natural development. If not, the choice should be open. Factors to consider would include:

* the pupil's age and the extent of his difficulties
* his facility with a pencil, hand–eye coordination and physical 'togetherness'
* the school's handwriting policy

- possibly his general ability level.

If a child has great difficulty assembling the correct letters to make a given word, the extra attention to the handwriting task that is involved in learning joined writing might be too much to cope with.

The pupil who wants to 'draw' letters from the bottom may be helped by the fact that, in joined writing, the approach strokes of initial letters start at the baseline. However, the linking strokes within words differ; this is extra information to be remembered and good, even, joining strokes need a lot of practice. For beginning writers (and readers), the simplest printed forms might well be easier to master. In any case, the printed forms will have to be taught sometime, for the labelling of diagrams, printing on forms , etc. If a style of letter ending with a small hook is used (a h) it prepares the way for joined writing later on.

For a 9- or 10-year-old pupil whose handwriting is so poorly developed that a fresh start is essential, joining it up may be the best way to proceed. This will also avoid the ignominy of going back to what he might consider infant work. (See Appendix II for suggestions on handwriting workbooks.)

The advantages of joined writing

It may be necessary to persuade a pupil to move on from printing. Older students may be especially reluctant if they feel they have failed before, or they have developed a fast script style:

- It emphasises the whole word as distinct from individual letters and so helps with word spacing.
- It helps to establish directionality; this can be particularly important for letters such as *d* where starting in the right place is essential.
- The hand movement in joined writing can help to lead to more automatic writing of common words such as *the*, *was* and frequent letter sequences such as *ing*, *tion*, etc. (However, the teacher should not rely on writing coupled with visual memory alone for establishing memory for spelling patterns or irregular words. An oral component is an essential part of multisensory learning procedure.)
- Pupils' self-image and therefore their confidence may be improved if they can achieve a clear, even, joined writing style. It looks more adult.

Understanding the system

Although the letters should be grouped according to common shape, when showing the pupil how to join them one also has to look at how the strokes between them are formed. Pupils who have missed whatever instruction was given to their class often do not understand that the system of joining the letters is very practical. They should be shown that the joining lines are natural extensions of the letters, and that the exit line from one letter is the start of the entry to the next. These should therefore be as economical as possible to achieve a smooth and uncluttered flow of writing.

Joining strokes also act as separators, keeping the letters apart and producing clear forms. Writing otherwise becomes squashed up and difficult to read, e.g. *will betr rdn pit* . Some practice with separate letters, emphasising the exit strokes, might help in such cases, or an exercise in which printed letters are traced over and joining lines added.

Some key points for helping pupils to join up their letters are shown in Figure 11.1.

To loop or not to loop?

This depends on the chosen style and the school's handwriting policy – and what is easiest for the pupil. It may be easier for some children to make a loop on some tall letters than to trace down the letter line neatly and it is possibly quicker to make looped forms. *g*, *j* and *y* end in a curve and have to be looped if the writing flow is to be continuous.

Slope or upright?

Joined writing often slopes forward slightly; for neatness, the slopes must be at a consistent angle. Again the teacher should take into account what the pupil can do without difficulty. A slight slope is probably a quicker style for right-

---

- If the selected style uses an approach stroke for the first letter of a word, this should start on the line except when the first letter is a capital
- Most of the joining lines are formed by diagonal strokes; these are the easiest to make
- The joins between letters that finish at the top (*o, r, v, w*) are made by 'bridges' thus:

$$o \qquad r \qquad v \qquad w$$

The following letter therefore has an entry that starts 'in the air': *on*, *wh*, *ti*, *va*.

If these strokes are not made correctly it can lead to confusion and spelling mistakes (*o/a*; *u/v*; *r/n*) and writing that is difficult to read

- When *e* follows a bridge stroke the line must be dipped slightly because *e* starts in the middle. This keeps an even top to the word *we*.
- To make sure of closing the *o* group of letters, the approach stroke must go right round to the 'one o'clock' point before the letter itself is started:

$$o$$

- *s*, and the ball and stick form of *b* and *p*, can be troublesome because they end in a clockwise stroke. Should the writer lift the pen and re-start, or make a tracing stroke or small loop to the other side of the letter – which can look messy? *s* should be made in the way the pupil can most easily achieve a neat form, while still getting a good 'tuck back'. *p* and *b* can be solved by making the open *p* and *b* shapes. (Note that this turns the join after *b* into a bridge stroke.) The s forms, *s* and s can be a problem because their distinct shapes can be lost when they are written at speed

- *x* and *z* are difficult letters: *x* can be formed either by a forward moving line, *x* which is crossed after a pen lift, or by two back to back *c* forms that can be made (with practice) without lifting the pen. It is difficult to join *z* in a form similar to the printed letter because of the straight lines; it may be better to teach the more complex cursive form *z*.

- Crossing *t* and dotting *i* and *j*: these letters can be finished when the word is otherwise complete, so that the pen flow is not interrupted

- *f* is sometimes difficult – the direction of the return stroke can be tricky. Probably the neater form is the one that has both loops on the left, with the cross stroke lengthened to make a bridging join to the next letter *f*.

- Double letters can be tricky, particularly *ff*, *ss*, *zz*, and they sometimes need extra help and practice $\quad ff \qquad ss \qquad zz$

Figure 11.1 Points for helping with joined handwriting.

handed writers, and an upright style for left handers.

Children like to experiment with handwriting forms and in this way they arrive at a personal writing style. Although anything that catches their enthusiasm should, naturally, be encouraged, it is advisable to restrain unusual forms and elaborate flourishes in ordinary writing work. (These can be kept for personal work and special purposes.) A good firmly established style is a necessary base from which to develop.

Integration of tasks: handwriting + spelling

Handwriting should be practised as a separate exercise until it is well established and produced automatically. Although there are differences of opinion about separation of skills, and practice out of context, many pupils with learning difficulties cannot practise writing neatly if they are concentrating at the same time on spelling: getting new or difficult spellings right, e.g. in dictated sentences or in free writing. A reminder might be given about where to begin or join letters, but the main effort has to be directed elsewhere. On the other hand, if a pupil is using well-established spellings, correctly formed and joined letters should be expected.

The best way to combine handwriting and spelling is through practising common letter strings, such as consonant blends and word patterns. The kinaesthetic activity of writing a repeated pattern is then an additional way to rehearse spelling work. A writing workbook is useful for practice of printed and joined writing. (See Appendix II for suggestions.)

Help for the older pupil

By the time pupils are 13 or 14, poor handwriting is likely to be ingrained by years of habit and the speed of the scribble. Such pupils often think of writing as a speed test, not unreasonably, because they have to get down the maximum number of words in minimum time. (Young people whose handwriting is neat and well formed have been known to complain that they cannot write fast enough!) They will argue that, if improvement means slowing down, it is just not possible. If they are sufficiently motivated to try to change, they should be helped to make their own assessment and schedule.

1. Identify the general problem, e.g. is the writing illegible, or just untidy?
2. Select a few points that most urgently need work – and which will most easily lead to improvement – and work on them one by one, e.g. a poorly formed '*a*', or wrongly linked letters. A handwriting checklist can provide a useful benchmark for assessing priorities (Note 11.1, page 259).
3. Set small tasks so that there is some chance of success.
4. Put a time limit on the work, and reassess every few weeks.

If pupils write quickly, they should try to slow down the writing speed while they attempt to make improvements. Teachers can explain that, if we want to change something that is automatic, we have to slow down and think about it – which can be difficult. Even a small alteration such as making a habit of crossing *t* will need thought, while the previously learned actions are suppressed and the new series of movements is built up. This might be particularly difficult for dyslexic learners who have to put in greater efforts before a skill can be performed automatically, and it may therefore be more difficult to 'unlearn' it.

Separate practice to establish a hand routine will be useful first; this can then be speeded up before it is incorporated into a word – at first slowly, then faster. An analogy with sport can be helpful: think what is involved in changing a stroke in tennis, or improving a swimming style. Older pupils might like to time their writing speed, to see how fast they can write and still preserve improvements.

It is doubtful whether attempting to change a pupil's style is wise unless he really wants to try. The most that can be attempted, certainly in the short term, is the correction of gross errors that result in wrong spelling or illegibility, or possibly changing a very awkward, tense grip. Some pupils who are uncertain of spelling try to blame poor writing for their mistakes; helping the spelling can indirectly lead to clearer handwriting when the reason for illegibility is removed.

In cases of extreme difficulty, use of a word processor would be the long-term answer and pupils who are likely to go on to further and higher education will almost certainly need to acquire the necessary skills. However, there are occasions when most pupils (and many adults) cannot avoid writing by hand. With the right approach from the teacher, and some degree of motivation on the pupil's part, it is worth considering the possibility of improvement.

Chapter 12   Special topics

The topics in this chapter have been mentioned in earlier chapters and are now placed together for convenience so that some extra suggestions and comments may be made. Some topics will continue through the whole period of teaching; alphabet work, oral and listening work, and speech will be important to the regular programme although the emphasis may change at different times. The calendar and time are more likely to be the focus for a great effort at a particular point, and then need an occasional check thereafter.

Alphabet and dictionary skills

Dyslexic children should start on alphabet work in early lessons, as soon as they are ready to work on letter names. A set of plastic or wooden letters is recommended for this exercise; it is helpful if all the vowels are coloured red at first. Whether the letters are upper or lower case depends on the individual child. If he has been using only lower-case letters so far, then these should be used for the alphabet work. This might also help to ensure that he does not make rigid links between capitals and letter names.

As with other work, pupils' knowledge of the alphabet differs – some may already be able to say it fluently, some will be half-way there and others may know only a few letter names. Some know the names but may not have realised that letters also have sounds; this will be addressed in the phonic work already started.

For the pupil with little or no knowledge, the teacher should set out the whole sequence, helping him say the letter names. (A rainbow layout is convenient because it will fit on a small desk top.)

He should be taught that there are 26 letters – 21 consonants and 5 vowels – and which these are. He can learn the sequence a few letters at a time. The vowel function of y can be left until it comes up in the reading work.

Many children find The Alphabet Song helpful because it splits the letters into small groups, some of which rhyme, and ultimately it helps with the memorising of all 26 letters.

ABCD EFG HI,JK,LM NO,PQ RS,TU VW XYZ

(Some people use a version sung to the tune of 'Twinkle Twinkle Little Star' but this does not fit so naturally with the letters – it divides at P – and the tune has to be adapted at the end.)

This is a difficult memorisation task and needs plenty of repetition. If the pupil is given the alphabet written out on a strip of card, with the letters underlined as far as he has learnt, he can practise between lessons. (Some children learn it surprisingly quickly.)

Gradually, the pupil should take over the task of finding the letters and putting them out in the right order. Exercises and games can be played to help him remember the order (Figure 12.1).

The alphabet is sometimes used to help children's memorisation skills.

1. Draw a number of letters (random order) saying the names.
2. The pupil should attempt to repeat the sequence.

The number of letters can increase gradually until the pupil reaches a plateau. The letters for particular words (e.g. *because*) could be used, although this would give the task an additional long-term objective. This exercise is useful for training attentive listening and verbal rehearsal strategy.

It may also increase a pupil's confidence in his ability to remember and recall a sequence of items. (Children are often told they have 'a useless memory' and come to accept that.) It does not 'increase' the child's short-term memory capacity, but helps him to make better use of it (Note 12.1, page 259).

- Say the letters alternately with the child, singly and in groups of two or three. Keep the rhythm going
- Exercises in which the letters are tracked in order can help (see Appendix II for suggestions about materials)
- When the sequence is known, ask the pupil to draw the letters from their box in any order, putting each one in its approximate place in the arc
- Remove one or more letters, or change the order of a couple, for the pupil to spot the mistake
- Ask the pupil to do the same: the teacher has to guess the missing or altered letters with eyes closed, by running her hand over the sequence of letters. Pupils like to try this too
- Practise starting at different letters to help get over a habit of reciting always from A
- Try some 'Which letter comes before, after and between' questions. This would be done first by looking at the layout, later from memory with the layout to check the answer

Figure 12.1 Learning the alphabet.

For learning of the 'internal order' – essential for efficient use of the dictionary, directories, indexes, etc. – use a pack of cards showing groups of letters and dashes, such as A–C; UV–. A pupil can use this pack for practice on his own if linked groups, which are clues to each other, are put back to back on each card: FG–/F–H; –PQ/OP–.

Alphabet books can help the pupil to learn the letter sequence and the connection between the letter sound and name. They do not need to be at his reading level. Rhyming alphabets and picture books can all give valuable practice in their different ways and bring some fun into the work.

Dictionary skills

A simple dictionary can be introduced as soon as the pupil has some reading skill. The teacher should show how it divides into 'quartiles' and how this can reduce search time:

A to E, F to M, N to S, T to Z.

Mnemonics can help here: *Elephants Make Squirts*; *Earth*, *Moon*, *Sun*, etc.

Teachers should point out the significance of the guide words at the top of each page and encourage the pupil to use them. Alphabet sorting exercises can help to build familiarity with the method of sequencing words by successive letters, which again is essential for efficient searching. All this can be done in a fun way, perhaps against the clock, and with the pupil also setting tasks for the teacher.

Dictionary word searches serve many purposes:

- To practise finding the way around using knowledge of the alphabet
- For reading development
- To widen vocabulary and encourage pupils to think about the meaning of words
- To teach the concept of 'definition'
- To help develop more interesting writing
- For checking spellings(!).

Children often feel threatened by dictionaries – full of unintelligible words in small print, and boring, with no stories or interesting facts. If illustrated ones are used first, with lively pictures such as the *Beginner Books* or the Richard Scarry dictionaries and word books, the pupil may realise that they can be friendly tools, and learn to use them.

Language terms

Language Development is a major strand running through the programmes of study for the National Curriculum for English at all Key Stages, and it is given explicit attention at all levels of the Literacy Hour. It includes grammar, punctuation and vocabulary, language forms and registers, the differences between standard and colloquial English, and use of linguistic terminology. Some of these topics are integral to the work of the specialist teacher. It is impossible to teach writing skills without talking about words and sentences, and to refer to specific elements of language without such words as consonant, vowel, letter, syllable and suffix (Figure 12.2). Children will meet these language concepts, and the vocabulary for talking about them, in the classroom. The specialist teacher should ensure that they are understood and remembered. The Literacy Hour materials

---

- Terms to describe letters and sounds – consonant, vowel, phoneme, grapheme, digraph, blend, short vowel, long vowel, schwa, etc.
- The grammatical structures of written language: phrase, clause, sentence, paragraph
- Word classification: parts of speech – noun, verb, adjective, pronoun; suffix, prefix, morpheme, etc.
- Grammar words: singular, plural, tenses, different verb structures
- Punctuation: teaching about basic punctuation will occur in reading and writing work, but opportunities should be created to check that pupils are able to name other forms such as inverted commas

Figure 12.2 Essential terms for language work with the dyslexic pupil.

include a list of terms that children should be taught to use (see Appendix V, page 245).

One of the ways that children learn about the conventions of written language is by reading: sentence structures, punctuation, etc., are absorbed from books, comics and other printed sources. Not being readers, dyslexic children do not have easy access to such models. Nor, as their development as writers is delayed, do they have as much practice as other children at written sentence making. When these language skills are taught explicitly, they should be related to the reading and spelling work of the lesson wherever possible, but it will probably be necessary to use – or devise – exercises for structured practice and over-learning.

Oral and listening work

Oral work has a role in specialist teaching both as a foundation for written work, and to help dyslexic pupils with the Speaking and Listening Attainment Targets of the National Curriculum for English. (The version of the National Curriculum used in Wales calls this Oracy.)

It must be acknowledged that the time spent on this kind of work has to be limited if the pupil has only 1 hour a week individual or small group teaching. Nevertheless, purposeful oral work can be fitted into odd 5-minute spaces, and can be a break from concentrated phonic or reading work. For dyslexic children, it may have special relevance; for those who continue to have severe difficulties with writing, verbal expression will be an important supplement to writing for assessment and examination purposes.

Although many dyslexic children talk very freely, they do not always express themselves coherently. However, they are more likely to keep level with their peer group in oral work than in other areas of the English curriculum, and with a little help they might not fall behind at all.

In a one-to-one situation, teachers have good opportunities to get to know their pupils well, by listening to their accounts of what they have been doing, what is going on in school and at home, plans for the holidays, etc. They can encourage the children to express themselves clearly, without rushing and, if necessary, ask them to slow down and try again in a way that might be embarrassing in a class with others listening (Speaking and Listening ATs, Levels 2 – 4).

Older pupils should be encouraged to talk about their interests in a more formal manner: they might prepare a short verbal account of a hobby, a sport, a visit – some topic on which they have plenty to say (Speaking and Listening ATs Levels 4 and 5 and upward). This work can also relate to how they express themselves on paper.

Children can be helped to understand how the spoken and written forms of language differ by an exercise that makes the point explicitly:

- Make a tape-recording of a pupil's spoken language: ask him to give a short account of something that interests him.
- Next, he should write a brief account of the same thing – just a short paragraph.
- Finally, the taped version can be played back and the two compared.

It is interesting to look at the differences. In the spoken version there will probably be more words than in the writing, and the information may be expressed in an informal way, with hesitations and repetitions. The written version will show that, in writing, the information needs to be thought out more clearly than in speech; it will be expressed more concisely, the hesitations and pauses disappear, and it must have punctuation. By listening for the short pauses in the verbal version, and the up and down inflections, he may be able to see where punctuation is needed. This would be a suitable approach for dyslexic pupils of 13 and over.

The National Curriculum stresses that writing has different purposes: to inform, instruct, persuade and amuse – among others. All these purposes have their oral equivalent. It is useful to use each as a focus for oral work, both to help the pupil to express himself effectively and with regard to his audience and as a preliminary to written exercises (Speaking and Listening ATs at all levels). Again, a tape-recorder would be a valuable aid.

Listening

Right through the programme of work, attentive listening has been stressed for discrimination of speech sounds, memory for words and sentences, etc., often with the purpose of verbatim repetition. The National Curriculum Listening target is directed towards the appreciation and understanding of spoken language – the ability to concentrate on, and remember, verbal communication, and reflect or act upon it in various ways. (This is formalising the real-life purpose of spoken communication.) These too are skills that improve with practice. The habit of concentrated attention often has to be built explicitly and carefully for a dyslexic pupil;

short sessions of listening work can help to increase the attention span, and to point out that he is required to remember what is being said. (Sometimes, this just does not occur to a child – not only a dyslexic one!)

- Tell or read a story, or poem: the child must tell it back in his own words, or answer questions about it. (Make sure that the pupil knows what he has to do.)
- As a variation, this could be a message, or information, that has to be passed on.

Eye contact is important for helping to hold the child's attention. However, there are occasions when the speaker is unseen – on radio or the telephone – now frequently a 'mobile' (and the conversation is often on the move). A pre-recorded tape might simulate these situations.

Obviously the duration of such listening exercises will vary greatly from child to child; 15 or 20 seconds may be long enough for younger or more distractible children to begin with; this can be extended to 2 or 3 minutes for older ones. The objectives too will change. At the outset, the aim may be to train the pupil to sit still and remember a 'formal' communication; with a 14-year-old, it may be part of an exercise in note taking.

Speech

There are close links between the auditory discrimination of speech sounds and the articulation of words. Dyslexic children often do not correctly perceive individual sounds of speech in words that they hear; this might give rise to faulty pronunciation, which in turn creates spelling problems. A child who says *lickle* and *fink* has an inbuilt mis-cue every time he utters these words; it is almost impossible for him to know, in the first place, how they should be written and, when he has been shown, hard for him to remember. It is not always easy to see why such errors might be made. In a quick examination of spelling mistakes a *b/p* error looks like a visual inversion; in fact it could come from a difficulty with voiced and unvoiced conso-nants at the auditory or the spoken level. This may even be a residual problem from earlier uncertain-ty that is still reflected in the spelling of a particular word. The misspelling of *very* as *revy* might be taken for a visual sequencing error, when it is in fact linked to mispronunciations. (The boy in ques-tion – 12;6 years – did not pronounce either *v* or *r* clearly.)

It is usually the consonants that cause prob-lems, and consonant clusters and digraphs are bound to be more difficult than single sounds. Some children do have difficulty with short vowel sounds; /a/ and /e/ are can be troublesome because they are very close in pronunciation.

If a psychologist's report is available, it may be possible to check whether a child having this kind of difficulty has ever had help for it; if there are still major difficulties he should be referred back to the speech and language therapist. Whatever the case, the specialist teacher should include work in this area. The objective is not, naturally, to give 'therapy' but to give extra attention to the details of sounds in heard and spoken language. Some ways in which teachers can help are shown in Figure 12.3.

All these activities should be multisensory: in the end the pupil must also be able to discriminate sounds mainly by listening, but watching the teacher's mouth, or looking at letters while

---

- Encourage clear speech – slow down the 'gab-blers'. Ask the child to stand with his back to you and 'tell it slowly'
- Help pupils to listen to sounds: pronounce the individual phonemes in words clearly while the pupil listens and watches carefully
- Discuss the way particular sounds are made: use a mirror to see lip and tongue position. (Tongue out for /th/, in for /f/ and /v/.) Ask the pupil to place his hand on your throat to feel the vibration of a voiced consonant – then on his own throat to get a similar effect
- Distinguishing *b/p* sounds: ask the pupil to hold his hand just in front of his mouth. What difference does he notice when saying the two sounds (p has a puff of breath, b does not)

- Model pronunciation for pupils to listen and copy
- Help by analysing the sounds and their sequence in words such as *father*, *three*, *fifth*
- Draw attention to differences between sounds, e.g. by playing a 'mimimal pairs' game: ask the child to listen to pairs of words such as *free/three*, *fin/thin*, *first/thirst* (and non-words such as *famp* and *thamp*) and to say whether they are the same or different
- Use a tape-recorder so the pupil can listen to what he says. A 'Language Master' with target words for him to pronounce, record and check could be used for this

Figure 12.3 Helping children to speak clearly.

listening, can provide additional reinforcement while he is learning. The Edith Norrie Letter Case was devised to help children with speech and hearing impairment, as well as those with dyslexia (see Figure 14.1, page 211). Its consonant letters are colour coded for voiced and unvoiced consonants, and they are arranged in the box according to the place of articulation. This helps children to concentrate on the exact characteristics of phonemes. A small mirror is included. (Although we may not be fully aware of it, visual cues have an important role in our understanding of spoken communication – but this is more general than the reception of phonemes.)

Plastic letters will help by providing additional tactile experience when the pupil is learning how to say and write sounds and words that he habitually mispronounces. He may need help to remember, for instance:

- The link between /th/ and *th* (voiced and unvoiced). Two separate plastic letters may emphasise this.
- That the written word *thing* has five letters – even if he continues to say *fing*.

Obviously this kind of work needs to be carried out sensitively, because the pupil must not be made to feel inferior or self-conscious.

If a speech and language therapist is seeing the pupil, it is important to make contact so that the two professionals may exchange information and perhaps collaborate over aspects of the work.

The date and the time

Knowing the days and months, using a calendar, and telling the time can all be difficult because they draw on many aspects of understanding and learning. To be successful the learner must already know the vocabulary, and understand at least some of the concepts involved in this dimension (Figure 12.4).

Dyslexic children (and older individuals too) find it difficult to 'get the feel' of time, during the day, in the week or over a longer period. Children often do not know the date of their birthday or how long it is to a significant date – such as the end of term, or even Christmas. Facts about the organisation of days into weeks and months, and months into a year are difficult to grasp.

There is a great deal of variety in the way that time is presented. The learning of each form has its difficulties but eventually each one has to be familiar, particularly the conventional clockface and digital time. Even the way we refer to and write the time can be confusing for a learner; for instance we usually say 'twenty minutes past three' but write 3.20 – and we do not always say 'minutes'. Words don't always refer to the same number – 'quarter' can be 15 or 45 depending on past and to; this involves direction and getting the name right. Calendars, diaries and timetables can also be organised in different ways.

This kind of conceptual learning takes some time to assimilate and understand. By the middle years of primary school, children should be able to tell the time and read a calendar. By the age of 11, they will also need to be able to follow a simple timetable –

If they are to learn how to tell the time and read the calendar children must be familiar with the basic vocabulary and be secure with certain skills:

- be familiar with time and date vocabulary, including time prepositions
- know the day and month names in sequence
- read days and months, including abbreviations of the words
- be confident about laterality and direction
- have good counting skills
- know 5x table facts
- be familiar with half and quarters
- be flexible about the way calendars vary in their presentation
- be able to recognise and read numbers up to 31, and the four-digit number of the year
- for a digital clock – read numbers up to 59
- have some understanding about time, and how it is measured

Figure 12.4 Vocabulary and subskills needed for reading the calendar and telling the time.

namely a school timetable, which they will need from their first day in secondary school.

Calendar: learning the days and months

Learning the days, months and seasons can be difficult because there is no obvious logic or meaning to these names and sequences. Most children soon learn the days of the week. As well as being the shorter sequence, the child has repeated experience of all seven over a short period of time, and they relate to day-to-day experience. It takes much longer to meet all the months, and a year is a long time for a child. Knowing where to start can also be a problem; a mnemonic for January is useful – but it has to be specific to the pupil.

The teacher should use a calendar to show how the days, weeks and months succeed each other, and then write the names in a circle so that Saturday is seen to be followed by Sunday again, and December by January. (The Flanders and Swann version of 'January brings the Snow' makes this memorably clear.)

Remembering the sequence can be helped by a simple visual aid (Figure 12.5). A similar aid can be made for the days of the week. Using the months to study syllable division for reading and for spelling by syllables fits well with this learning exercise.

1. Fold a piece of stiff paper or card down the middle – top to bottom – and open it up
2. Write the months, evenly spaced from top to bottom, on the right-hand side of the fold
3. Cut the card into strips (up to the fold) with one month on each strip and fold them back, out of sight as each month is said
4. To check memory, fold all the words out of sight. As the pupil recites the months he brings each strip round to check his progress through the year
5. When the year is known the strips can be detached and used to practise placing the months in the right order as they are picked at random out of a pile
6. The seasons can be added on the left of the card when the months are known

Figure 12.5 Visual aid for learning the months.

Reading the date

A strip calendar is simplest to use because it is arranged from top to bottom in a line. This is probably the most useful as it often doubles as a wall diary.

'Block' layouts are more difficult to read and may need explicit explanation.

- Explain how the days of the week are arranged across or down.
- Look at the pattern of the month. The numbers are the days in the month.
- Look at the name of the month. Find today's day name. Read today's date, e.g. Monday, June 5th, or Monday, the 5th of June.
- Show how the dates for Mondays are arranged under (or along from) each other.
- From one line or column to the next, the numbers are a week apart. Work out a few easy examples.
- Look at the end of the month. The line is not complete. Show that this is because the calendar is arranged in whole months. There is nothing missing.

Cut up a large calendar and place two months to show how successive months run on from one to the next, or ink in the blank spaces.

Writing the date

The simple numbers-only method means that the number of the month must be known. Pupils will learn the convention in the early school years, but it is worth checking that they really know what they are doing. They should also know how to write the date in words, including the abbreviations 1st, 2nd, 3rd, 4th. These sometimes catch them out in the numbers after 10.

It is now conventional to insert 0 for days and months under 10 – for forms, etc. With older pupils, this too should be checked and explained if necessary.

Telling the time

The clockface is better than a digital display to start with because it shows the whole hour and will help the learner to understand the relationship between minutes and the hour. It is more difficult to understand from a digital display how much time has elapsed within the hour – unless the time reader is good at mental subtraction.

The amount of detailed demonstration and explanation needed will vary from one pupil to another. However, it is useful to observe the sequence: hours; half-past, quarter, all for the right, 'past' side of the clock before doing the same for the left, 'to', side. The details of the other times (5, 10, etc., first 'past', then 'to') can come after the four main quarters.

A real clock, showing all the numbers, is needed as well as a teaching clock and some drawn clockfaces for practice. Refer to the moving hands of the clockface to establish the relative speed of the hands and the direction of movement. (A watch is not really big enough.) Put in as much explanation and practice as needed at each stage.

- Use a clock with clear minute marks. Let the child watch the clock to observe the passage of a minute (don't bother about seconds to start with), then 5 minutes, to understand what the clock is measuring.
- Look at the sizes of the two hands and observe how the long hand moves faster: this is the minute hand and it moves faster than the hour

hand, which is smaller. (I tell a story about a runner with long legs who moves faster than one with short legs.) It has to go round once while the hour hand moves from one number to the next.

Hours

- Change to a teaching clock. Look at how it is organised into 12 sections with smaller marks between. Ignore the minutes to begin with.
- Show the hour hand. Take it right round the clock saying the hours in turn. Let the pupil practise this.
- Explain that the hour hand must go right round between midnight and midday (dinner-time) then again between midday and midnight, i.e. 12 hours each – 24 hours in one whole day. Give plenty of examples.

The pupil should practise at each stage both reading the time and drawing in the hands to show a time.

Half-hours

Think about what 'half' means. (Do not think about half as a fraction if the child is worried about fractions.) Think about other expressions of half to relate it to real life: half-time in a match; half a bag of chips; half an apple; half-full; half-finished; half-way.

Make a drawing (or find one) of a cake – and cut it in half.

- Establish where half way round comes. The whole is one hour, therefore: half an hour.

Quarters

- Use the cake picture to work out what a quarter is. Relate this to the clock – half-way between the hour (12) and half way round: a quarter.

Minutes

- Look at the marks between the numbers and count them between 12 and 1.
- Establish that there are five marks between the numbers all the way round, and 12 numbers: $12 \times 5 = 60$; 60 minutes between 1 hour and the next.
- Work out the minutes for half and quarter past: half past = $6 \times 5 = 30$ minutes past quarter past = $3 \times 5 = 15$ minutes past. Write out the 5× table if the child can't say it.

(This section could follow the half and quarter practice if preferred.)

The right-hand side: 'past' time

- Explain the term 'past'. The hand (or the time) has gone past the hour. (Look at the way the hands move.)
- Practise saying the half-pasts for each hour.
- Using a drawing of a clockface, write in some hours and half-hours for the child to read.
- Say some times and ask him to write them on small clockface drawings and read them.

The two halves of the teaching clock will be in different colours to show the past and to sides.

The other numbers 'past'

- Count 5, 10, 15 minutes – past whatever hour it is.
- Count 20 past and 25 past, then half past.
- Work them with the 5× table. Count the minutes if necessary.

Work some examples with the clock, and writing and telling the time on the small clockfaces.

The left-hand side: 'to' time

- Work out the third quarter as with quarter past.

State that this is called 'a quarter to' – discuss the logical reasoning: the hand (or the time) is going to – that is towards – the hour. Work some examples.

The rest of the 'to' time

- Climb from the 6/30 minute/half-hour, back to the hour, counting backwards in 5s from 30.
  Work out the minutes (in 5s) left between the half-hour (30 minutes) and the hour. These are all called 'to'.
  Do some practice examples – first with 45 minutes – a quarter to – then with the other 5s, on the teaching clock and the small clockfaces. (One number on the clock tells the time exactly ('10 to'). Can the pupil spot which it is?)
- Look at the pattern: quarters are opposite each other; times with the same name are at the same angle from the hour and half-hour.
  '20 past' – '20 to'; '25 past' – '25 to' tend to be the most difficult to remember.

Work plenty of examples using the whole clock.

'Time' words

Revise and discuss some 'time' words.

- Quarter, half, three-quarters of an hour: what do they mean?.
- How do you talk about them in minutes?
- When is midday? Noon? Midnight? Tell, and show on the clock.
- What do am and pm mean?
- When is it: morning, afternoon, night, evening, daytime, night-time?
- What is clockwise? and anti-clockwise?
- When does the day – date – begin and end?

Simple time sums

How long is it from 1 o'clock to 2 o'clock and from half past 2 to half past 3?

Work out other times, going on to more difficult sums only when the whole task of telling the time is secure. (For digital time and the 24-hour clock see Chapter 9, page 139.)

Chapter 13

Computer technology in lessons with dyslexic children

Computers and information technology (IT) offer a new route into written language for people who have difficulty with reading and writing. It is a continuously changing field and teachers using computers with pupils will need to keep in touch with specialist sources of information about new developments. Communications technology is also important for dyslexic learners. Like everyone else, they will want to 'surf the web', and use the internet and email to get information and send messages.

This chapter gives an overview for non-specialists in the field of ways in which computers and IT can help dyslexic pupils, particularly those having specialist tuition, with the skills and subskills of reading, writing and mathematics, and with study skills.

As to terminology, 'computer' will be used with reference to the pupil working with a machine – running software and word processing. IT, or ICT (Information and Communication Technology), will be used when the reference is to use for specific information and communication purposes.

The dyslexic individual and IT

A computer, like any other piece of equipment, can be used as a teaching resource in whatever way the teacher and pupil need it:

- as a tutor for basic literacy and numeracy skills via ready-made software
- as a word processor, for creating, editing and printing written work
- to run other software such as dictionaries and multi-media encyclopaedias
- for communication and information: access to communication networks – electronic mail (email) and the world-wide web (the web or the net)
- simply as a computer – to write programs, and carry out computing procedures.

While the last point will not be of direct concern to the individual basic skills teacher, it is worth remembering that many dyslexic individuals have the aptitudes that are needed for computer work, i.e. good logical reasoning faculties and, often, graphic and design skills. It is possible that they are successful here because programming languages, as a medium of communication, are consistent and reliable. They do not have tiresome shifting vowel combinations, or odd silent consonants. Perhaps, too, they work rather like many people with dyslexia, who learn best if the information is given in small steps, one instruction at a time, and yet require a global view, a general plan, before the work on detail is begun. Preparation of computer work has to be undertaken in a highly sequential, structured manner within a prepared framework. Those who are familiar with the disorganisation shown by many dyslexic youngsters and students may be surprised by their success at working in this very precise field. Perhaps the very structured method that computer work demands provides the discipline that they need.

Dyslexic pupils should be encouraged to look closely at computer science courses and to use ICT as widely as possible in the curriculum. It is not only valuable for boosting their self-confidence, it is also important for further education and career prospects (Note 13.1, page 260).

Computers for teaching

The teacher giving one-to-one or small group tuition will want to know:

- how to use the computer in the most purposeful way to help basic literacy and numeracy skills and
- how dyslexic learners can get maximum benefit from ICT in general.

The answers will depend – as so often – on the amount of time available, on where the main focus of the work is at any particular time, and on the knowledge and skills of the teacher. If the pupil is working mainly on basic spelling and reading skills, software for back-up and revision might be of most immediate use. In the long term, the greatest benefit (for school and college purposes) is likely to be from its function as a text processor.

Basic skills

Dyslexic learners need a great deal of repetition and practice to master the subskills of literacy to the point of automatic response and recall. As this can become very boring, IT can be a valuable medium for extra practice. It is a mistake to view an exercise presented on computer as no more than an animated worksheet – and therefore not worth time or money. An on-screen moving, talking program that can monitor the user's responses is a different medium and has a different role from a pen and paper worksheet – even though it may use few of the resources of 'real IT' (Figure 13.1).

The multisensory approaches essential for this kind of learning are almost all available through IT. Although synthetic speech is greatly improved, digitally recorded speech is preferable in programs for basic skills and is now nearly always used. Pupils can hear real speech sounds and they may be able to record in their own voice lists of words, or sentences, for later work. It may not be long before the computer is also able to 'hear' a pupil's oral response (e.g. in a word-recognition task).

Handwriting can be demonstrated on the screen and touch screens can help to teach letter shapes and joining strokes. Hand movement over

Reading and spelling:
- letter knowledge – alphabet and alphabet order
- basic sound–symbol correspondences
- phonemic awareness and phonological skills, e.g. sound segmentation, rhyming, letter order
- spelling principles, patterns and conventions
- word attack for both reading and spelling
- word recognition
- immediate links can be made between reading and writing simply because words on the screen look like 'print'

Handwriting:
- demonstration and practice of letters and letter formation

Mathematics
- memorisation of number facts
- enhanced illustration to help understanding of shape and volume
- understanding of difficult concepts, e.g. place value, fractions and decimals
- providing a bridge between concrete and symbolic learning
- practising and learning the details and sequence of methods of computation

Figure 13.1 IT help for essential basic skills.

the keyboard can reinforce spelling knowledge through motor memory – although this depends on the learner's familiarity with the letter layout.

It has been found that children working with a computer often concentrate better and spend more time on a task than they do in conventional situations. This increases the chances of effective learning.

It has particular advantages for those who have difficulties:

- The 'high-tech' image can be motivating and boost self-esteem.
- Learners can work at their own pace: the computer will wait all day if necessary.
- There is no need to worry about poor handwriting skills or messy work.

- Many programs can be customised for the individual.
- Many programs, e.g. 'adventure games', can stimulate the child in a way that 'print' does not.
- The computer is impersonal; the learner is less afraid of mistakes and does not resent losing.
- Different formats for repetition can be offered, so it does not become tedious.
- It can offer the possibility of a new start.

Why use the computer in a one-to-one lesson?

People often assume that the computer releases the teacher to do something else, but there are all kinds of ways that IT can be used profitably in one-to-one work:

- A program can be used to focus on a point at the initial teaching stage to introduce spelling points and principles.
- The teacher's help may be indispensable if the pupil is to work on his own later. It will nearly always be necessary to explain how a program works. The teacher must make sure that the pupil can read and respond to the screen messages and remember what to do.
- A program may have many options; some of the planning and enabling software has different levels and many functions. Help is needed to get into the different levels or use all the facilities.
- A pupil may not be able to work unaided; he may need help to read instructions or use the keyboard.
- A child can be helped to use a program that is in some ways too difficult – but that his peer group enjoys. (Is this any different from reading Roald Dahl to him?) Helping him to have fun is important.
- For specific phonic work the presence of the teacher is essential. Oral response to the letters and words on the screen is important and will need to be encouraged. Sharing a spelling program gives opportunities to talk about spelling patterns.
- If the whole of a particular task is just a little too difficult, the dyslexic pupil might get other benefits from using a program, such as carrying out a sequence of operations in the correct order and using the mouse or cursor keys to move around the screen. Directionality itself can be practised.

- It is always illuminating to watch how the pupil works.
- Oral work: IT can create all kinds of opportunities here – describing what is happening, sequencing the tasks verbally or talking through particular operations. Some dyslexic children have difficulty with naming, finding the right words and organising ideas. Many programs can be a focus to oral work, e.g. programs that stimulate descriptive expression, adventure programs where discussion is part of the exercise, and memory and thinking skills tasks.
- Compiling the pupil's own word lists: a pupil may want to use a program's editing section to store vocabulary for his own learning – or perhaps for other pupils to practise. Some programs will allow own-voice input and the teacher's help will be necessary here.

Using software

Computers can be excellent aids to learning in areas where much repetition and practice are needed. Programs that aim to reinforce spelling by games and exercises have obvious potential for bringing interest and fun to the task. Variety of approach in itself may be a motivator and so increase the chances of learning. Pupils can usefully spend time following up points that have formed part of a lesson, or getting some routine practice in areas of difficulty, e.g. in a lesson on a group of consonant blends, or on vowel digraphs, the work might be divided between instruction from the teacher and use of a program on the same topic.

Spelling

Choosing suitable programs

The criteria for choosing programs are the same as those for selecting any resource: first the quality of the program itself should be considered, and then whether it can help the pupil who is to use it. The teacher should be very clear about what she wants from it, about what it actually does (not always what it sets out to do) and how it presents the tasks, e.g. if a program has penalty features that are more exciting than the rewards, the results might not be what the teacher expects.

It should be possible to select exactly what needs to be practised and to set up the program to either a number of examples in each set of words, or a time limit. Programs with content that can be 'customised' for the individual pupil, changing or adding material, are perhaps the most valuable of all.

Integrated Learning Systems

Some schools now use Integrated Learning Systems (ILS) for spelling work. In these the computer directs the progression of work, the amount of repetition and revision that is needed, and when the pupil should move to the next section. A program will branch between sections or vary the difficulty level according to the success in each unit. (It might require a 95 per cent correct rate before the user can move on.) These may not be structured in the same way as an individual teacher plans the work, so caution is needed before a pupil is directed to practise independently in the ILS program.

Phonic work

If software is to be used alongside a phonic programme, it is especially important to look for those with content and structure that fits in with the teaching programme. Figure 13.2 shows guidelines about choosing suitable programs.

More general considerations

Age level

Programs should match the pupil's age and interest level. Many programs for basic phonic skills are designed for beginning learners in Key Stage 1 (KS1). Although the material might be just what the teacher needs, a pupil whose self-esteem has been damaged by failure may feel even worse if he thinks it is babyish.

Games

Programs designed as games naturally set tasks that are intended to be fun: the user might have to catch the right string of letters to fill gaps, or zoom a character round a maze.

There is often a time factor to encourage a quick response, and beating the clock is part of the fun, but this should be adjustable. Speed can be an important part of the learning process, because the aim of practice is to reach the point of automatic correct response; there is a 'trade off' between speed and accuracy, and finding the right balance is an important part of learning. But the early teaching and learning have to be done more slowly before a pupil is exposed to a game that penalises mistakes or poor time.

- The content should be based on phonic principles
- The tasks set should not place undue emphasis on visual memorising of whole words
- Words should be grouped to emphasise spelling patterns or principles from which the pupil can generalise, rather than on the learning of individual words
- They should make the right demands on the user. Dyslexic pupils may be confused by some kinds of task, e.g. anagrams, or a choice between right and wrong spellings; programs that make extensive use of such tasks are best avoided
- There should be enough repetition at each level
- Reading content should be at the right level for the individual pupil
- The screen design should be clear and not too 'busy'
- Pupil response: pupils should be expected to type in complete words, not merely finish incomplete ones or respond by choosing between alternatives by pressing a key
- Transfer to paper: correct answers in the program do not guarantee correct spelling on paper. Follow-up in handwriting can help to ensure transfer – perhaps with an exercise based on the same words. Some programs have printout worksheets
- It should be possible for the pupil to work on his own. Ease of setting up a program – choosing the right lists and setting options, and on-screen instructions – preferably using icons – are essential

Figure 13.2 Guidelines for choosing programs for phonic work.

Timing

The interval between screen changes can be important; programs that shift too quickly between tasks may not give the pupil a chance to look at a correct answer and take it in. Something that looks slow to the teacher may be right for the pupil.

Variety

Programs vary in their screen display and in the ways that the learner interacts with the machine. Individual preferences are bound to differ among pupils as well as among teachers.

It is useful to have two or three different packages for pupils to have a change and choose the one they like.

'Visual dictation': look, cover and type routines

The best programs use well-structured vocabularies, based either on phonic principles or on spelling patterns. Words are usually presented on the screen one by one and can be read aloud by the computer, using sampled (real) speech. The pupil can therefore both read and hear each word as part of a 'look, listen, cover and type' learning routine. The word must be remembered, and typed in. This in itself helps to link spelling and reading; it is also a meaningful memory exercise.

A number of options are usually available: hearing the whole word, letter-by-letter rehearsal or read only. There may also be a 'test' option on which the computer says each word unseen for the pupil to spell.

The teacher working individually with the child should help by discussing memory strategies as she would in other situations. If a list is being set up a for an individual pupil it is useful to be able to highlight the awkward bits, or put them in a different font if the program allows. Editing routines that allow own-voice input and feedback are especially useful.

Sentence dictation

It is standard practice in spelling work with dyslexic children to extend work on individual words by the same vocabulary in sentences for dictation.

- *Acceleread Accelerwrite* (IanSyst) is based on the principle of 'own-voice' dictation and aims to link reading and spelling through the reading and writing of sentences. This is a complete reading and spelling program. The pupil reads and remembers a sentence, dictates it to himself and types it, reads it and hears it read back from the screen reader (synthetic speech at this point).
- *Sentence Pumper* (Xavier – Acorn only) is designed to run alongside a spelling program. Sentences appear that must be read and remembered before being typed in. Selected letters may be masked and teachers can provide whatever support pupils need. There is also an unseen dictation option. This program has an editing disk for teachers to write their own sentences. (The sentence editor can also be used to present other material. This disk has been used for learning long words, for cloze exercises by masking words, and for helping pupils to learn curriculum-related material.)

Pupils on their own or in groups

Although the teacher may decide to supervise this kind of work, it is much more usual for children to work at computer tasks on their own whenever they can operate the program. In any case, they often prefer to get on with such tasks by themselves – some spend their breaks in the IT room and are happy to work on spelling programs.

Many older pupils can set up the programs themselves, choosing the time of presentations or asking for help from the program if they need it. Taking charge of his own learning in this way can help a pupil to monitor his own work; it can also boost his self-esteem – which can be reduced or even non-existent when he is dependent on the teacher for assessment.

Working in pairs, or in a small group, can also be profitable. The computer's vertical screen transforms the working situation here; several children can participate in a computer activity, just because they can see it. In a group, children can give each other peer support and each one can contribute in whatever way is possible. It allows for discussion, and takes away the isolation that the computer can create.

Feedback

Pupils need to get the right kind of feedback from the computer. This can sometimes be difficult for a teacher to gauge: what might seem a slow response to an adult may be right for the child. Errors on the screen should also be considered. Although there are times when teachers want to draw attention to the details of spelling mistakes, it is probably better that computer spelling programs do not display errors on the screen. Presenting a poor example may be counterproductive. Apart from this, the computer cannot distinguish between a genuine error and a wrong key press – so the correction may be misdirected and even confusing.

The style of response from the machine is important: indication of right or wrong with a clear message. The kind of message also needs to be considered, whether spoken words or display features. A spoken message that is delivered in the same way, time after time, might eventually irritate even a small child, especially if the program allows too many wrong tries. Messages, jingles or moving characters can be motivating to begin with, but they become an irritant if they slow down or interrupt the work. Most pupils want to get on with the job and finish. Just getting it right can be an important motivator.

The system for getting to the right answer is equally important. Programs should allow one or two more tries, but then provide help without making a fuss. Feedback for the teacher is essential, e.g. an error analysis showing every key press.

Precision teaching

In group or class situations where spelling and reading programmes include practice with structured lists, the daily 'probe' can usefully be done with IT. The machine presents the target words, marks the pupil's response and sets the appropriate lists for the next step in the learning program. The work at word level can be planned around the computer.

Children with severe spelling problems, who need frequent opportunities for revision of a limited number of words, would probably benefit from this daily testing routine. Vocabulary from any structured programme could be used in this way.

At present it is more difficult for the computer to monitor reading responses, but when the machine becomes able – without prior training – to recognise anyone's voice it will be a huge help for monitoring of reading skills.

Transferring skills from computer to pen and paper

Even pupils who use IT for most of their course work still have to write by hand at times. With a few exceptions, they will not be using IT in tests and exams. Reversion to writing brings back the factors that hamper work – handwriting, poor spelling and habit.

If they are using software for spelling it is important to use methods that facilitate the transfer to pen and paper. Saying letter sounds aloud (or in their minds) as they type them will help memory as it does in other multisensory work. They should also practise the words in handwriting. Spelling tests after a computer session might be the best way to ensure learning – but this would probably be impractical (and unpopular!). The teacher will have to be well organised and canny, e.g. creating opportunities for the pupil to use the same words in worksheets or other follow-up exercises.

Some adventure and curriculum support programs have worksheets and other follow-up material that forms an integral part of the work; this is probably the best way to make the link between the two modes of learning.

Some software for basic skills and spelling

Alphabet: *Talking Animated Alphabet* (Sherston)
Handwriting: *Kid's Designer* (Semerc) can be used
    on a touch screen or a separate graphics tablet
Short vowel sounds and rhyming:
    Sounds and Rhymes (Xavier)
    Chatback (Xavier) own voice recording of
    sounds

Spelling:
  Wordshark (White Space)
  Soapbox (Xavier) includes editor for new lists with own-voice input
  Gamz (Inclusive Technology): an IT version of card games – *Swap* and *Fix*
Memory:
  Thinkin Things 2 & 3 (Iona; TAG)
  Mastering Memory (CALSC)

Reading

All kinds of software for reading are available, with real or synthetic speech support. Most of it has built-in routines which give instant help when pupils need it. The links between the printed and spoken words can be made very directly when the 'voice' is activated by the pupil moving a mouse or by touching the screen and looking attentively at the words while listening. IT can also provide the medium for practising essential reading subskills – word recognition and word attack – and for increasing reading speed.

Word learning

Every spelling practice program that displays whole words gives good word-recognition practice at the same time, particularly if it speaks the completed word. (This can also help a pupil who has trouble saying long words correctly.) This is particularly helpful for irregular words but is also useful for core subject vocabulary, e.g. maths.

The learning stages would be:

- The pupil looks at/reads the word to be spelled and hears it spoken. He can be encouraged to beat the computer by saying the word before he hears it.

- He types in the word after it has disappeared.
- He checks if it is correct and hears it read back.

(The most effective programs for word recognition will be those that do not allow an incorrect entry so that the on-screen word is always correct.) Flashcard presentation can be an effective aid to learning because the exposure can be timed to individual need. This can also be self-checking but the pupil would have to keep his own record of correct responses.

Practice can be even more effective if the initial sound input has been in the user's own voice, because this will give a stronger connection with the word in his memory. A program that recorded the user's response could be helpful for teacher feedback.

Word attack

Teachers can make effective use of IT for teaching blending and syllable division skills. A spelling program that uses letter–sound pronunciation and shows words building up on screen is a useful medium for blending practice. Syllable division for a whole range of vocabulary can be taught effectively on screen using any editing or word-processing package, especially one that has good synthesised speech.

Although this may seem no more than an exercise transferred from paper, the action of the cursor and space bar to move syllables apart and join them again can raise it to a different level. It is certainly more acceptable for older learners. It is helpful to change the colour of selected syllables (such as suffixes or root words), make them bold or put them in different fonts. Syllables may be said separately and as the whole word, so the pupil will be able to check on his own version. It may be possible to raise the pupil's interest in the way words are constructed by encouraging him to play around with this kind of exercise.

Talking books

'Books on the screen' offer a good way into the enjoyment of reading. The medium may help a reluctant dyslexic reader simply because he does not think of the computer as a book: turning the pages by pressing the space bar may not be associated with failure. The added attractions of computer presentation – animated illustration, puzzles to be solved – might also help to motivate someone to the effort of the reading task. Often, hidden activities can be brought up by clicking on parts of the picture. The best packages have activities that are related to the story and require some response from the reader. The story should also be available as a book.

For independent use there should be support at different levels. Readers should be able to hear the whole story first, guided by the cursor if they wish, then read it themselves with whatever level of help they need – single sounds, whole word or sentences. Syllable division – if it is available – is especially useful for coping with more difficult text.

IT versions of reading schemes give children with difficulties access to the same stories as their classmates (for example: *Oxford Reading Tree, Fuzz Buzz, Wellington Square, Cambridge Reading*). This can keep them up with the group – but they do not learn to read independently by listening to and looking at text. It will be an advantage if there are printed follow-up materials for activities at different levels to build phonological skills and word recognition, and sentence and text exercises to extend comprehension.

For successful learning the IT version must enable the child to:

- read the story in its printed form; the teacher will need to check levels of accuracy and fluency
- recognise the words from the story in other texts at the same level
- build up a lexicon of essential vocabulary which can be recognised in any other text.

Do IT books help the pupil with severe difficulties? Getting into a book and experiencing language in its written form is so important that learning time can be spent very purposefully in this way – even though it is not likely to rub off into actual reading skill. Hearing books read and seeing the text may help word recognition if the child repeats a favourite program often enough, especially if the learning is transferred quickly to a printed book. A teacher sharing a session can make connections explicit and encourage reading of some parts without the sound. For maximum teaching value, there will have to be additional subskills work to fit the child's level of need.

Adventure programs

Reading often isolates children from each other but, when they use adventure programs in pairs or in groups, it can become a social experience. This makes it much more fun, besides helping to get round the reading difficulty. The dyslexic pupil may learn by hearing the others read the text and they may encourage him to try joining in. Even if he opts out of the reading, he will gain valuable reasoning experience, and social experience too. These programs demand the active use of comprehension skills: information has to be collected and decisions made; the child must remember what has gone before, and carry out logical reasoning tasks. As well as all this, oral discussion between members of the group and cooperation in the problem-solving activities mean that the pupil gets valuable, all-round language experience. When dyslexic children are able to work with their classmates in this way, they will be extended and stimulated by the activity and should be able to make their own contributions to the group. Their logical reasoning skills and innovative ideas (dyslexic people are often 'lateral thinkers') will enable them to take an active part in the group discussion.

If the teacher is aiming to extend a child's reading skills through this medium by independent practice, the text will need to be at the right level to be read without too much support from the computer. (Writing can become a social activity in the same way – see page 200.)

Comprehension work

For more proficient readers, the computer offers further possibilities in programs that aim to develop comprehension skills. Cloze programs are useful for teachers wanting to create their own exercises, using material right across the curriculum. As the teacher will select the text, the reading level can be matched to individual pupils' needs. When used on the computer the pupil can get instant feedback – again a powerful motivator.

A program with text which must be reconstructed from a mix of letters and dashes – or is even displayed entirely as dashes (such as *Tray*) – will be quite difficult for dyslexic learners. More confident pupils might enjoy them but they will probably need the support of a teacher or another pupil. *Tray* cannot be completed without all-round skills: knowledge of spelling patterns, understanding of syntactic structure and good guesses based on the use of cues as the context develops. These are the skills of the proficient reader. Such exercises can have a place in the resources of the dyslexia teacher if they are used cautiously, with preparation of text at the right level and teacher support, and they are approached with a sense of fun and challenge.

More conventional comprehension exercises can usefully be presented on the computer because there can be immediate feedback to multiple choice. Exercises that present questions as the passage develops (not just at the end) help the pupil to interact with the text and process meaning. Programs that practise skimming and scanning a passage for information can also be useful. Text is displayed for a limited length of time (set by the teacher or pupil) before multiple choice questions are presented, which encourages quick but accurate reading.

Reading and comprehension skills can be transferred into wider curriculum fields by using subject software, particularly topics that relate to the environment and day-to-day life where pupils can draw on their general experience. Maps and charts are especially useful for one-to-one work because they allow for discussion of directionality and spatial awareness.

Collaboration between individual tutor and class teacher or subject specialist would be especially useful if this kind of comprehension work is planned.

Software for reading skills

Flashcards (Eurotalk): used with the teacher's own word lists.
SCANiT (Maia Learning Systems) (Flashcards)
Adventure program with chart: *Badger Trails* (Sherston).

Other language skills

Software following the Literacy Hour structure provides resources at all three levels (word, sentence and text) for group and individual work. Teachers working with dyslexic children may be able to arrange for follow-up activities in the classroom. Careful selection of program and content will be needed; it is best to look at the software with the pupil's needs in mind.

IT can also be used to teach and practise aspects of grammar and punctuation. Software can be used as a focus for oral work and many dyslexic pupils need help when they need to comment on, or analyse, language and the way it is used. Punctuation also needs to be discussed. Programs can present examples to raise awareness of punctuation; those that have a speed factor may help automatic response by promoting quick decisions. If the tasks are in sentence context, improvement in reading fluency could result from a timed punctuation exercise.

Using a talking word processor, teachers can create their own materials at all three levels – word, sentence and text – to support their tuition.

Software

English Keywords (Sherston): glossary of support for English language terms (read-aloud option)
Making Sense with Words (Inclusive Technology): practice for reading and language skills
Children's Dictionary (Dorling Kindersley): interactive dictionary with pictures and sounds
Punctuate (Xavier): this has a sentence context with an optional timed game and a quiz
The Punctuation Show (Sherston): quiz format.

For teachers' use

Reading Schemes (NASEN): IT version of The NASEN Guide to Reading Schemes
SMOG (Inclusive Technology) works out the reading level of any text (including worksheets made by the teacher)
Crosswords and *Wordsquare* (both SPA) for creating puzzles.

Word processors

This section looks at ways in which ICT can be used to support writing skills for dyslexic children and students, including study skills techniques.

When parents consider buying a computer for a child, they nearly always think first about what programs are available to help spelling. In fact, in the long term it will probably have far greater value as a tool for producing written work. For a dyslexic student, it will be essential.

Using a word processor cannot be guaranteed to turn a writing-shy pupil into an enthusiastic writer. Some detest using the keyboard; they cannot find their way around it and lack the motivation to learn. For those who think they have nothing to say, or who find it very difficult to express themselves in language, even the glamour of technology may not break down the barriers. For many dyslexic pupils, it is just the opposite, and they should be given the opportunity to learn and develop word-processing skills as early as possible, certainly by the time they get to the middle years of secondary school.

There are many reasons for recommending this. Of course they are also the reasons why many people become enthusiastic about word processors but, for dyslexic individuals, whose difficulties make writing such a struggle, the advantages stand out very sharply (Figure 13.3).

It is important that dyslexic pupils have instruction in word-processing technique, especially if they are producing course-work and projects with the computer. They may not be able to read a simple handbook and (like anyone else) might be put off by the frustrations that can limit the scope of self-taught users. As soon as they start they should

be taught how to delete and move text, and how to OPEN, SAVE and PRINT files and pieces of work. Having control over the machine can be very liberating; it is more likely to be the pen-and-paper environment that is not user friendly.

Hearing the work

For dyslexic pupils, a major advantage of using IT for writing is that a screen text reader or a 'talking word processor' means that they can hear what they have written – as often as they like. A choice of voice is often offered (male or female; high or low voice; even a child's voice). Grammatical mistakes (e.g. -*ed* omitted) will stand out; spelling mistakes – apart from homophone errors – will show up as mispronunciations. (Even good readers find it difficult to proofread their own work.) It is not only mistakes that will show up: awkward expressions stand out when they are heard and poorly organised work might be more obvious when read aloud.

- Handwriting is eliminated
- Typing gives the writer a greater chance to think about what he is writing – unlike handwriting, where learned hand movements and fast scribble can produce mistakes
- It is easier to spot mistakes on screen where the text is clear
- Work can be drafted, corrected, moved around and edited without the need for repeated re-writing
- A printed copy can be corrected away from the machine, by a teacher perhaps
- Everything can be saved and re-used easily, allowing work to be done in short sessions

- Presentation: the final printed version is legible and looks good
- Spell checkers can overcome the inhibition about writing that may come from poor spelling, as well as the stigma of being a 'lousy speller'
- Different styles and sizes of fonts and of text display can encourage pupils to think about presentation and how it can be adapted to suit different purposes for writing
- Optical comfort is important: a choice of different colours of screen background and different sizes of text on the screen can be helpful

---

Figure 13.3 The advantages of word processing for dyslexic pupils.

Keyboard skills

Teachers have different opinions on whether touch typing is necessary for word processing.

At the very least, keyboard familiarity is essential for competent use. A 'hunt-and-peck' style is inefficient and slow; it can throttle a reluctant writer as surely as clumsy handwriting. I do not think it matters if the user looks at his hands and the upper-case letters on the keys worry the teachers more than the pupils. It is of course, useful to be able to watch the screen, seeing the writing develop, but not at the expense of numerous mistakes. For a poor speller, the letters on the keys may even act as mnemonics at times. The QWERTY keyboard can enhance kinaesthetic memory, helping pupils to spell certain high-frequency words (*the*, *there*, *we*, *were*, *was*) and some spelling patterns (*-ed*, *-ght*, *-tion*) more reliably than by writing, simply by the position of the letters. This would build into touch-typing skills.

On the other hand, touch typing gives the advantages of fluent keyboard operation and takes out the bottom level of the task. It is difficult to make generalisations about whether dyslexic pupils find much greater difficulty than others in learning the skill. With a good teaching system and plenty of practice, they probably master the keyboard as well as anyone else, although they may take longer. It is possible that those who do not, never find their way around efficiently by sight either.

Programs are available for keyboard practice as well as for teaching touch typing; some of these structure the practice so that they are also spelling tutors. A reasonable minimum might be to ensure that the pupil uses both hands, certainly more than two fingers, and uses his thumbs for the space bar. It is useful also to show that, if the fingers settle over the 'home keys', they are then in a position to reach all the keys easily. Appropriate use of fingers and finger placement can develop from that point. It would be a mistake, however, to insist on touch-typing proficiency before a pupil is allowed to use a machine for writing. Practice comes with doing, and this should in itself provide the motivation to improve.

Stickers to change the letters to lower case might be used to start with younger children who have not learnt capitals. For children who find the QWERTY layout difficult, it is also possible to have an overlay that will convert the keyboard to alphabetic order. An alternative is to use a program that shows the keyboard on-screen or, for limited writing purposes, the letters in an arc on screen.

Software for keyboard skills

First Keys to Literacy (especially good for younger pupils)
Type to Learn (Sunburst)
Magictype (IEP Books).

Spelling checkers

Dyslexic pupils commonly avoid difficulties by restricting themselves to easy words. A spelling checker can give them confidence to use whatever words they need. Making good use of such tools requires the writer to be able to read the options that it offers. However, it is often much easier to choose between alternatives than produce the spelling from memory in the first place. It helps if these can be read aloud by the machine.

For someone with intractable spelling problems, the spelling checker can be a demanding friend. Some cannot respond to the more extreme spelling errors or to words that are written phonically; most cannot correct wrongly used homonyms, although some software will identify them and offer definitions. Strategies for using it have to be developed. If the first two – preferably three – letters are right, there is more chance that suitable alternatives will be offered. If an error cannot be recognised, but the attempt can be heard, there is more chance that it can be altered to a nearer match. Some spelling packages, and some of the small hand-size spell checkers (especially the *Franklin* range), are designed especially for dyslexic users and these are more helpful.

Predictive spell checkers attempt to predict each word from the first two or three letters, using letter pattern and syntactic information, and offer a number of possibilities, rather like a continuously changing word bank. The writer can select the one he wants by a single key press. The system automatically builds up its dictionary as the writer proceeds. It thus reflects the vocabulary of the user. The resident dictionaries are quite small (1000–3000 words), but these can be extended according to pupils' developing language skills and to cater for particular subject areas. However, the user must remember to check and correct words (by asking tutors perhaps) before they are saved.

Selecting the right word from the choices is a major difficulty for users whose reading is poor. Here, a screen reader is needed that can work in tandem with the checker. Some enabling software provides both of these plus a thesaurus, grammar checker and an on-screen keyboard.

Pupils should be encouraged to use the checker and the thesaurus to sharpen their appreciation of the right word for a particular context and to broaden their vocabulary. As early as possible they should be taught how to make use of these facilities, starting with simple versions.

Starting to write

Dyslexic pupils can be encouraged to try out their ideas at a very early stage by using a writing program designed for younger children. The simplest ones allow deletions to be made, and can print out in large letters; the work can be saved for further editing. Most allow text to be moved and offer a choice of print styles. Desk-top publishing packages enable the production of much more sophisticated work, but even the simplest program, by enhancing the appearance of the end-product, should encourage a pupil to try some writing.

From the very start the pupil can be shown how to delete and insert. In this way, he can change and add to what he is writing as his thoughts develop, and he sees how ideas can grow. All this is absorbed into the text without a trace of the process! Mistakes disappear and the evidence of labour over the mechanics is suppressed. The pupil can be praised for his ideas and for his final production, so there is no feeling of inadequacy. If a teaching point is needed, print-outs taken at each stage as a record of the process can be used to look back, with the pupil, at the way he has developed the work, which could be a very positive experience.

Getting a piece of handwritten work to a good enough standard for display can require several drafts and still not reflect the quality of the ideas.

Word-processed work, decorated, mounted and displayed on the classroom wall, can do a great deal to enhance the self-esteem of a struggling learner. A poem is possibly a good way to start; lines can be short and a poem needs fewer words than other kinds of writing but can still be effective.

In classrooms where there is only one computer, pupils may not be able to produce their work using the computer alone; they may be able only to type in a completed (and corrected) effort. It is especially sad for the dyslexic pupil if he is not able to use the facility that can take so much of the labour from his work. If priority time is allowed to any group of children, the dyslexic ones have a strong claim to it.

Writing as a group activity

Small groups of children can more easily work together using a computer than by pen and paper simply because the vertical screen is easier to see and they can adapt the content as each one adds ideas. Two or three children can work together on a piece of writing so that it becomes, as with adventure programs, a social and collaborative activity. Here again, there is much that a dyslexic child can gain. He can participate in the oral discussion, contribute to the ideas and help to develop a theme in a way that might otherwise be difficult for him; another child can cope with the mechanics of the spelling. The final result 'belongs' to the group, but the individuals will still recognise it as their own work.

Writing and reading activities integrate very naturally in this kind of work. The words, as they appear, are those that the group has decided to write and they have been spoken aloud – hence the reading-back task is a very immediate language experience. So often, the dyslexic child does not correct his mistakes when he writes on paper; at the time he does not recognise them as errors, although he may do so later – if he reads what he has written. On the computer it is so much easier to monitor the work as it goes along. In the group situation it is possible for the dyslexic pupil also to read someone else's work; he might even recognise someone else's mistakes and correct them! The dyslexic pupil is learning a way into work, as well as helping with the immediate task.

Support for writing

Dyslexic pupils often cannot get into a writing task without help. As noted earlier they do not know how to start, and how to organise what they want to say, even if they have plenty of ideas and information. Many teachers use word processors to make word banks and support sheets – story outlines, structures and writing frames for 'desk work'. This kind of material can model the way to set about the organisation of written work, as well as helping the generation of ideas and argument.

It could also be used on screen and saved in individual files for continuing work before being printed out. IT has the advantage that the pupil, in the early stages, is able to merge his ideas with the teacher's support features to create a unified piece of writing. The supporting frameworks can be reduced over a number of sessions until, in time, all the work is generated by the pupil himself. The disadvantage might be that – unless they are made in a software 'shell' – they are not 'fixed', so the supporting structures move around or can be accidentally deleted.

Talking Textease (Softease) can be used to make 'talking labels' for worksheets and diagrams. (If teachers are preparing work to be used on a different computer – perhaps prepared at home and used in school – it will be necessary to check that files can be transferred from the original source to the classroom computer. It must be admitted that it takes time to devise and produce this kind of framework material.)

Software

There is plenty of commercial software to support writing but it takes time to become familiar with programs so that they can be used effectively. Teachers wanting to explore this area should consult the specialist literature (see Appendix II) and, if possible, try programs before buying. An overview is given here of how software may be used, with a few example titles.

Writing support packages often incorporate a simple word-processing program or are used with a standard word-processing package. They often have a spell checker and speech feedback to provide an extra level of support. Graphics and pictures can be added to stories. Users can often record their own speech and sound effects can be downloaded from files to add interest. These features do not depend on the written word and they allow the dyslexic child to make use of their often considerable skills in verbal language and design.

The combination of a support structure for content, a spell-checking facility, and being able to hear (and check) what he has written can do wonders for a child's general confidence and enable him to produce excellent work.

Problems with typing can be helped by a keyboard overlay that converts QWERTY to an alphabetic layout. A keyboard – or letter – display on screen in standard or adapted format might be easier for some pupils; clicking on keys with the mouse removes the need to look up and down from screen to keyboard. Some word-processing packages include this facility.

Word-processing software that includes spell checkers

- *Clicker 4* (Crick): word grid + talking word processor. Integrates reading and writing by enabling the pupil to hear and read what he has written. Supportive features: *Clicker* word-grid; pictures; facility to record sounds to insert with writing; spell checker. Can be used with the web and email.
- *Penfriend* (Penfriend Ltd): word processor with predictive spell checker and punctuation aid; on-screen keyboard. Can be used as a screen reader for other software text.
- *Talk Write* (Resource) and *Talking Pendown* (Logotron) are both for younger writers.
- *Texthelp Read and Write* (IanSyst) is for older students.
- *Write Outloud* and *Co-Writer* (both Don Johnson)

All these are 'dyslexia-friendly' packages.

Story writing
Programs give ideas for writing and prompts to provide details of character, place, etc.; questions and structures help organise ideas and move the story along.

The pupil is able to change details, add and amplify points as he wants. Pictures are often available.

- *I Can Write* (Resource) for younger children. Begins with a sequence that allows the child to provide details about him- or herself. Offers a number of topics for stories with supporting vocabulary on pull-down lists. The supplied words can be heard.

Writing with Pictures (rebuses)

Pupils whose reading and spelling are very poor could be helped by the use of rebuses. Pictures, icons, letters and numbers are used to represent words, for example, the walking man on an exit sign is a rebus. Many children's puzzles use them, e.g. an eye to mean 'I', and they turn up in word play as in URYYY for 'you are wise'. (The developing language of text messaging uses this kind of shorthand.) Software provides the words for the selected pictures, which helps word recognition and reading.

- *Inclusive Writer* (Inclusive Technology).

Word banks

These can stimulate ideas as well as providing the keywords for topics. They help to extend writing by encouraging use of more interesting words, adjectives, etc.

- *Clicker Plus*: grids of words and pictures provide vocabulary that can be imported into the writing just by clicking on the words needed. The program has speech sound. *Clicker* is under continuous development and has a users' support network on the web. Grids are available for teachers to make their own word banks. Pictures can be downloaded into the program from other sources. On-screen keyboard.

Writing frames

These help to structure the work in an appropriate way for a genre by providing sentences and phrases. The completed frame can then be used as an outline and edited – showing the child that drafting and editing are much more than correcting spelling. Using the frame as a first draft, ideas and discussion can be added. Print-outs can be taken at various stages of the work and further edited by hand using colour – e.g. showing where improvements can be made, for instance by moving text.

- *Word Bar* (Crick) provides sentences and phrases to help with the structure of different genres of writing.

Data collection software

Structures can guide a child through the stages of recording his observations, for example, of a science project (perhaps the sowing and growing-rate of seeds) or a practical exercise in a technology lesson (the construction of a layout of roads and bridges).

It is the kind of activity that could be used to good purpose in the one-to-one situation when the teacher wishes to make links into curriculum work. (Subject teachers should be able to advise about suitable programs.)

Software for planning

Computer versions of brainstorming and planning techniques provide structures for generating ideas, collecting and organising information. Material can be developed, collated, edited and arranged, ready for the final version to be produced. They allow the student to work at different levels by building up card 'stacks' that are stored one behind the other. These can be opened and changed, merged and displayed as continuous text when needed. Older students can also use the structures for making notes for revision. This kind of software is used alongside a standard word processor and other software – spell checkers and screen text reader.

A student using this kind of software would probably need support from a teacher to get full use from the package at the start.

- *Think Sheet* (Fischer Marriot) is for younger writers
- *Inspiration* (IanSyst) is a more complex package, based on Mind Map techniques.
- *Kidspiration* (IanSyst) for KS3 pupils has symbol and picture files.

The desk-top publisher *Pendown* also gives facilities for planning essays.

ICT to support school and course work

It makes sense for dyslexic pupils to use lap-top and portable computers in the classroom. Note taking, copying from the board and taking dictation can all be done more efficiently than by handwriting – but good keyboard skills are essential. (It requires the pupil to be organised too, e.g. he must make sure that batteries are regularly recharged.)

Not many pupils take exams or tests using IT – even if they use it regularly to produce homework and most of the course work. The criterion is the candidate's 'normal' way of working in class work. It seems unreasonable to expect a pupil who has used a computer regularly as his means of writing to revert to handwriting for a $1\frac{1}{2}$- or 2-hour examination. If a case is made to the Examination Board, it must be supported by timed samples of word-processed work and handwritten work. If permission is given, the computer must be used exactly as a typewriter, without editing and spell-checking facilities (Note 13.2, page 260).

Early introduction to IT and practice for skills does not need the latest technology. As new machines come on to the market, there is much pressure on schools to upgrade their hardware. Many special needs teachers have to make do with older models and these should not be despised. Some of the original software is still running and still useful – especially programs for practising spelling and learning the keyboard and simple word-processing programs.

Voice recognition software

Systems that enable the writer to talk to the machine, and by-pass the need for spelling, have been greeted as the solution to the dyslexic person's difficulties. Individuals differ in how they get on with voice recognition software (VRS). For some, particularly older users, it can give excellent results. The systems themselves vary, depending on the complexity of the software. At present the more powerful systems have to be trained to the user's voice and the percentage of accuracy of their word recognition is, in general, in proportion to the amount of training (or 'enrolment') that is given.

After the introductory enrolment the process is then incremental, although a tutor should keep an eye on the spelling of added vocabulary.

Some systems may not give good results for younger users, with light, higher voices, or for boys whose voices are breaking. They can also be upset by background noise, making use in a classroom difficult.

Dictation skills must also be considered: speaking work, an assignment or essay – even in draft version – to the computer, or making notes, is a different skill from writing. Inexperienced writers will need to organise their thoughts and ideas before they are spoken. For this reason the discrete speech models (which require a pause between words) may be more suitable for dyslexic users than those taking continuous (natural) speech. Help with organising and planning work will be of benefit to pupils learning to use VRS. Linking the software to a screen text reader is essential, so that the work can be read back for checking. It will almost certainly need to be run through the spell checker for mishearings and it will not be able to distinguish between homonyms.

There may be some 'spin-off' in a student's reading and spelling skills. One user has reported that, when she speaks a word and sees it on screen in the correct spelling, it improves her chances of being able to recognise it in print, whereas previously she looked for her own – extreme phonic – versions of words. (The VRS – correctly instructed at the enrolment stage – will print *fink* as *think*, and similar individual speech characteristics.) She compared her reading of English to the experience of someone trying to read an unknown language.

Optical character recognition (scanners)

Reading remains very difficult for some dyslexic individuals, especially when they are faced with texts for study at Further and Higher Education levels. Scanning software, which enables the student to access the text, is an essential study aid.

Text 'read' by the scanner into the computer can be used in whatever way it is needed, but the student must be careful when using material from published sources that are under copyright.

- It can be read aloud by the synthetic speech processor and extracts or references can be down-loaded for use in whatever way they are needed.
- Graphic material and pictures can be scanned for use in coursework.

Students at A-Level (possibly at GCSE) could also find a scanner useful and younger age groups might wish to use personal pictures – photographs and so on – in their written work.

Audio-tape on cassette recorders

- Taped books: this may be the single best use for audio-tape, giving access to dimensions otherwise closed off to disabled readers. Books on tape are an essential tool for individuals who need to work very hard at the word or sentence level, resulting in limited concentration span and poor comprehension. Where there is choice, a tape may be better than a scanner, because the voice is human and the way a text is read can help understanding. The advantage of a scanner is in having the text available in electronic form for use in written work.

- Taping lessons and lectures: getting a good recording will depend on the equipment used – and possibly also on the way that the teacher or lecturer delivers the session. A standard cassette may not pick it up efficiently. A separate microphone should always be used, so the tape does not also record machine noise. Supposing that the taping is successful, it has to be listened to, and notes made if the content needs to be recalled later. Students who use audio-tape may find that a speed control helps when they work on the playback.
- Dictation of essays, course work, notes for assignments and revision: for continuous writing, good organisation of thought is needed, as well as the ability to speak in the way that language is written. Using tape to record notes either from reading or to prepare work for writing or for revision might be easier. There is some evidence that listening to own-voice-recorded notes is an effective way to revise. Help with techniques for using audio-tape could be needed.
- As a personal memo pad: this could be very useful, e.g. to take details of homework – as it can be done quickly and does not depend on speaking 'continuous text'.
- The chief disadvantage with audio-tape is the problem of finding the right place on the tape. Recorders that allow searching from pause to pause are useful, but the user has to remember

to put these in. It is also useful to make spoken cue headings after a pause – making it easier to recognise each section.

Personal organisation

Some students depend on their pocket-size computers, entering all their personal facts, keeping a diary and timetables, making notes, keeping accounts and so on. Entries can be printed off via the computer. Spell checking is usually available, but as these systems are mostly for personal use, correct spelling is not essential. Students need to be encouraged to become well organised about their day-to-day life as well as their school and college work. These little machines are often great motivators when other systems – such as hand-kept diaries, and calendars – have failed.

Communication and information

Internet and web

In its multidimensional aspect, 'cyberspace' seems to be a wholly new medium, quite unlike our previous two-dimensional experience of literacy. Dyslexic students in GSCE and A-Level classes will want to 'surf the net' – like all their friends – and subject teachers may expect them to use the web (or the school intranet – or internal web) as a source of information. Skills with these technologies are essential for any dyslexic student going on to further study, as well as for more general purposes. When tuition about using the web is given to mixed groups, the dyslexic student may be left floundering, so that a little individual help from a teacher who understands their difficulties could be valuable. These are also 'transferable skills': reading, locating and categorising text (compare skimming through exam papers); writing addresses and search words accurately. Reading – or listening to – the accessed information requires the same higher-order comprehension and writing skills as print, pen and paper. If pages are downloaded and printed, they turn into conventional literacy tasks – and can be highlighted, marked and have notes written on them.

- Finding the way around the access page: screen text can be very small and some screens are busy and confusing. Knowing what is important, understanding the layout and where to enter the address is the first step.
- Accuracy: long website addresses can be difficult to copy – punctuation and case must be accurate and can be difficult to check. Searching for on-line information may also depend on spelling the keywords accurately; they will need to be reminded about attention to detail. Students should know how to copy and insert on-screen addresses and how to store as 'bookmarks' the addresses of those sites of most interest.
- Reading the screen: a screen text reader – or talking web browser – will be useful in the access stages and will be essential for helping the user to get through the mass of information that is available. This may depend on the site having a parallel version of the webpages.

The student will need to know how to operate these support devices.

- Following links: collecting information by going from one site to another can lead to confusion. The student with poor short-term memory will need to develop a way of keeping track of his path and what he has found. A hand-written flow chart, or Mind Map, with a few drawings or notes could be the answer – but the student may value a teacher's help in arriving at a personal strategy. (This will be useful for other study purposes too.)
- Referencing information: new conventions are building up about this. References will always require the date of access because web pages are constantly updated and changed. It is advisable to download and print pages that will be used for course work.
- Downloading: copying and saving parts of the text for inclusion in course work. It is vital that a student understands the boundaries of copyright and the dangers of plagiarism. He may not have registered warnings given by teachers to a class or group.

Email

This can be a boon for dyslexic individuals, particularly the way the system works and the conventions of usage that are developing. The most useful are likely to be:

- Facility: sending, replying to and storing messages is much easier than writing letters.
- Reading: with the right software, messages can be read aloud on screen.
- Informality: messages can be short and without conventional layout or 'top and tail'.
- Communication: the message has priority – spelling and typing errors are not only tolerated,

a whole new lexicon is growing up around email. Many words are spelled without vowels and single letters and other symbols are used to express whole words.

The dyslexic writer seems to take confidence from all this. The conventions and usage – including short-cuts – have to be learned. Although some kinds of quick help from a teacher may be valuable, anyone offering to help her student with ICT could find that the student, in fact, becomes the instructor. There could not be a better confidence-builder (for the student!).

Mathematics

IT can support maths in many ways, particularly in making the bridge between the concrete and symbolic stages of maths that many children need. Software is able to make 'objects' and pictures, move, rotate, change, switch colour, appear and disappear. It can present forms in simulated three dimensions or flatten them into a 'net'. The resulting templates can be downloaded through a printer and assembled into real three-dimensional models, making possible transformations from simulated to real objects.

This interactive character of 'on-screen' maths is possibly the most important factor because the pupil is able to watch and do. This can provide for the maths experience something like a practical, real-life situation, and make direct links between the real world and its more abstract representation.

When the child is working with numbers, it takes away the need for handwritten work, as it does for writing. It can also can provide support for the computation processes of arithmetic. If 'talking help' is available, it can bring success to the child who cannot work out how to tackle a problem, or remember how to do, for instance, long division. It can also read the instructions or explain difficult words. IT can provide a multisensory teaching approach for maths and this should be one of the criteria for selecting software for use with dyslexic learners.

Teachers working with pupils singly or in small groups have an opportunity to demonstrate, explore and talk through many maths topics. Oral discussion is especially important to find out how much the child understands, and to explain and teach the extensive vocabulary of maths.

It is especially important to find out whether an individual has a preferred learning style (see below and Chapter 9) because this may indicate the kind of software that would be most suitable. The chief advantage of using IT might be that it can take away some of the fear that surrounds maths in its conventional form by the fun factor, and by its seemingly magical quality.

Some ways that software can be used

One of the most useful purposes for software can be to help children learn to use the skills that underlie competence in maths. Among the most important are the ability to:

- follow and remember instructions in sequence
- put things in the right order – of event, occurrence, size, number, etc.
- sort and classify items into categories
- understand direction and orientation
- recognise and remember patterns

- estimate size or totals
- visualise how objects might look from another angle.

The development of more general reasoning and memory skills can also be helped through using software for mathematics.

In all these areas computers can be valuable both as a focus for teaching and to provide resources for individual work. IT may be able to provide feedback and help systems that are more comprehensive in maths than in much language software, because maths is in many respects a 'closed' system, with right and wrong answers.

Work in all these areas can be presented first with 'real' objects, or situations, before being replaced with words, concepts or numbers. Number knowledge itself can be presented as games or activities supported by spoken instructions and help options. Animated demonstration of fractions, decimals and percentages, and the relationships between them, is especially useful. Equations can be explained in a similar way, with demonstration and opportunity to experiment, e.g. with on-screen balances and see-saws. Verbal explanations make more sense if there is a visual or a physical understanding.

All the 'desk' aids that pupils have met in the classroom, such as number lines, number squares and grids, cue cards and calculators, can be found in software versions, often with speech, but in an interactive, oral presentation. Even when they use software, children may need help from the teacher to make the step from, for example, representation by 'concrete' examples and pictures to the more abstract language of concepts and symbols and numbers. They may need an explanation in language when they meet each new topic. After that, children may be more able to work with numbers on their own.

Individual learning styles

Too many verbal explanations may not be helpful for dyslexic children who prefer to learn in a visual, global way. They will probably benefit more from presentations where patterns can be seen and in which they can experiment. They may be more likely to carry out arithmetic computations in an unconventional way than others who feel more secure when learning in a sequential manner. Inevitably, they will meet the specialist language of maths and will have to learn what it means. If this can be firmly associated with images instead of being described and conceptualised, it will be easier for them to learn. It is not only 'visualisers' who will benefit: the 'verbalisers' (who may underestimate and undervalue their own visualisation skills) will probably find the terminology easier to understand and remember if it is illustrated as well as described.

Software

- *Maths Keywords* (Sherston) is an IT talking dictionary. Links between definitions allow a browser to follow a pathway of explanations. It is illustrated with a good range of pictures that further explain the terms.

Learners of both kinds will benefit from activities in which problem-solving is the objective such as themed, or adventure, programs, before numbers alone are involved.

- *Maths Circus* (three different packages) (4Mation) offers a variety of tasks that work on concepts and set problem-solving puzzles before moving into numerical tasks. It is fun and non-threatening, with very little text – and this can be read aloud by the computer.
- *Numbershark* has about 30 different games that provide practice in number, including the 'four rules', as well as games that involve tasks of sequencing and memorising number facts. Numbers are presented in different ways so that pupils with different learning styles can see them as number lines, on a numberpad, an abacus, etc.

Presentation

Programs that set number tasks in more conventional ways need to have a very uncluttered screen and present only a small number of items at any one time. The quantity of language – story, instructions and explanations – also needs to be limited. Even if text can be read aloud, it will not help the child whose memory is poor. Adventure programs that set number tasks as their standard 'move-on' factor need to be very clear.

Software that focuses on problems and puzzles is especially suitable for working with children in pairs or threes because it is an excellent medium for encouraging discussion; language and communication skills benefit as well as the maths.

Learning tables

Visual and oral presentation can provide an extra layer of help here. Software may help but the memory factor is still a difficulty.

- *What to Do When You Can't Learn Your Times Tables* (Semerc)
- *Numbershark* games (White Space)
- *The Interactive Calculator* (Inclusive Technology) may be the next best answer. This has a number of features, including speech and a guess option to encourage the child to estimate the answer.

Chapter 14

Using visual and multi-sensory aids, games and other materials

For pupils trying to master the writing system, teaching aids and games can help to make more real the abstract principles and concepts of language and literacy. Teachers use all kinds of such aids to support multisensory teaching, but three items are essential for this kind of work. They can be bought or made, but they should be on hand at all times, especially for younger pupils and beginners.

Essential multisensory aids

Letter–sound flashcards

These are used for teaching the Linkages and for many other purposes: for introducing letters and sounds; as cue cards while the pupil is learning new spellings; to help focus attention on particular sounds, etc. They are also needed for the Linkages drill routine.

The Alpha to Omega Flashcard box (Heinemann) is a useful resource. As well as single sounds it has consonant and vowel digraphs, consonant blends and assimilated consonants, and cards for teaching essential rules such as soft *c* and *g*.

Plastic or wooden letters

These are necessary for learning the alphabet, for additional multisensory tactile work and for all kinds of word-building activities. Colouring the vowels red is recommended.

A box of letters for word building and general work with sounds

Printed letters are better than plastic 'outline' shapes for this purpose; they are clearer and look more like written letters. It is important to have them in a good storage box, with the letters separated, or valuable time is wasted hunting for them. Besides, the letter layout in the box can be useful in itself as a visual aid.

A number of the educational suppliers have sets of letters, but most are not in compartmented boxes. Scrabble tiles are fine too. For all these the storage/display problem needs to be considered. Figure 14.1 shows the Edith Norrie Letter Case.

The Letter Case has some special features that derive from the original maker's work as a speech therapist:

- The letters are arranged according to articulation of the sounds, and not alphabetically (although of course this can be altered if the teacher prefers the alphabet layout)
- The vowels are coloured red
- Voiced/unvoiced consonants are printed in green and black respectively
- Consonant digraphs are given as single phoneme units
- A small mirror is provided for the pupil to look at his mouth shape where this is distinctive
- Basic punctuation marks are included, so that sentences can be constructed

---

Figure 14.1 The Edith Norrie Letter Case. It is designed for use with dyslexic pupils.

Other multisensory aids

A good variety of visual aids means that pupils can do the 'same thing' in many different ways, which helps to enhance the multisensory approach. Plenty of commercial aids are available but most of the materials suggested below are easy to make:

- Tactile letters, with sandpaper or felt surface for helping memory of letter shapes.
- A short-vowel cue card, with the vowels and key pictures. This is useful when building the early dictionary page and in sentence dictation.
- Finger puppets for work on vowel sounds, blending and other oral activities.
- Word wheels and slider cards which help children to practise generalisation of sounds from one word to another and to practise adding long-vowel -e.
- An alphabet strip for the pupil's desk.
- 'Phonic' pictures for all kinds of spelling groups but especially for short vowels and long-vowel -e.
- Suffix cards for practising suffixing rules: put them next to root words (also on card) covering -e or leaving a space to double a consonant.
- 'Flip' cards for helping word blending and phonic generalisation skills. These can include initial and final consonants, consonant blends, suffixes and prefixes, and compound words.
- Other 'word-cue' cards can be made as needed, to remind pupils of word patterns, spelling 'rules' or individual difficulties. (Examples have been mentioned in earlier chapters.)

It is useful to remember why handling cards and moving them around has, at some stages of learning, an advantage over merely writing letters on paper. The physical act of picking up the cards, moving them around, placing them correctly, can make a stronger impact on the learner. It takes out the writing task and allows more attention to be given to the reason for deciding what to do, e.g. why a consonant should be doubled or -e dropped. The sounds/words should also be said aloud and it is good practice –

certainly in the first stages of learning a 'rule' – for the pupil to say what he is doing and why.

'Word-sums' on paper are at the next stage of practice.

Games

Many aspects of games make them useful as teaching aids, but some general, underlying principles about the way that children (and others) learn give games an even more important role in the resource bank. Most of the children referred for specialist help have had only negative experiences of literacy. They have failed too often and 'switched off' – afraid to try again. Children develop different tactics to cope with the low self-image that failure can give, including clowning and bad behaviour, but many prefer to hide their feelings and keep out of the way. They often adopt the 'lazy – lacks effort' label that is applied. Some of these children can be difficult to reach but, whichever way they react, they cannot begin to turn around until they experience some success, and of course this is difficult if they are too afraid to try. Although it would be an overstatement to describe all dyslexic children as 'emotionally damaged', the way that an emotional reaction to early difficulties can shut down the process of learning should not be underestimated. A low-key approach, which they do not find threatening, can help children to summon up courage for another go (Note 14.1, page 260).

Most children enjoy games, although they may be surprised when a teacher first brings a game into a lesson. They like a challenge – when it is different from the usual classroom work – and, above all, they like to win. Games therefore have to be carefully chosen and targeted at the right level. It also helps if there is a chance factor – so the teacher doesn't always lose.

There is a huge difference between getting something right in the course of a lesson (a mere tick) and getting it right in a game where you win. One is routine and boring, the other is special and exciting. (Which would you tell your mum about?) It can be a revelation when a quiet child turns into a fierce competitor, desperate to carry on.

When should a game be used? Many teachers keep the fun bit till the end and see it as a reward or a relaxation. This takes a limited view of what a game is for. A game that is the vehicle for new work, or used as an immediate follow-up, must come much earlier.

If the pupil arrives in a strung-up mood, still carrying difficulties from earlier in the day, a game might help him to relax (Figure 14.2). There is a

---

1. End of the lesson:
   - reinforce and consolidate the teaching points made in the lesson
   - send pupil back to class in a positive frame of mind
2. Middle of the lesson:
   - allow a teaching point to be consolidated before moving on to a new topic
   - provide a break when the child may be tired after a concentrated spell of work
3. Beginning of the lesson:
   - put the pupil in the right frame of mind to learn; he might have had a difficult time in an earlier lesson
   - quick revision of previous work – linking it to new material to be done in lesson

Figure 14.2 When to use a game.
(I am grateful to my colleague Julia Keeves for these points)

case for being flexible about it – and being prepared to change one's plans.

Although the pupils do not think about it, it is obvious that games must be aimed at learning – most of the time. They must therefore be selected with care. Commercial games are numerous (and vary in price), but teachers often produce their own. Whether buying or making games, teachers should keep some guiding principles in mind (Figure 14.3).

Making games

You do not have to be creative or artistic to make simple games to help with routine topics, or with special points as they come up. For points that need a lot of repetition (long-vowel -e and many others), a variety of formats – different race tracks etc. – keeps up the interest while the objective stays the same. It can also help learning for the same point to be presented in different ways.

Although games can be made very quickly, it is worth taking a little trouble over them. Write the words neatly with strong lines, or word process them (large font, bold) and make the bases colourful. Pupils will then respond more readily. Many pupils get enthusiastic about the simplest games and most children like to think that a game has been made specially for them. (They can be very encouraging!) If they like drawing they may like to help and it gives them some ownership of their lesson.

For versatility and maximum value, games are best made open-ended so they can be used with different word banks.

- What is the objective? Teaching, practice, revision, testing can all be done with a game
  Be clear about which it is
  Teaching: make especially sure it is multisensory
  Practice or revision: restrict the variety. If too much is included, the points will not come up often enough, especially if practice is intended
  Testing: this can cover whatever the teacher wants to survey – but be careful to avoid failure
- What is the task? Word recognition, sentence reading, spelling, a phonic topic?
- Will the task achieve the objective?
  Reading single words: is it enough to read words once or should they be repeated?
  Spellings: how will they be remembered? Are they to be 'spelled out' or written down?
  Specific point practice – such as b/d/p, ch/sh: keep it short and use it often
- It should not take up much lesson time – ten minutes at most
  Two quick games may be better than one longer game
- There should be plenty to do – a task at nearly every move, for maximum learning time
- It should be fun – and there must be a game factor, which means someone must WIN!!
- A few simple layouts on A4 sheets can be as effective as something more complicated
  Keep them in a file and offer a choice
- There should be a challenge – it should stretch the pupil, so he feels he has achieved
- A solitaire activity can be a challenge if it is timed. Older pupils will accept this kind of 'game' more readily than one that involves 'play'

Figure 14.3 Points to consider when using games.

Practical points

- Don't write specific points on the layout: use penalty squares instead and draw words or tasks from a pile of cards.
- If writing on the layout is essential, laminate the game board and use a non-permanent overhead projector marker that can be wiped off, or photocopy the blank sheet so it can be used for another topic.
- Find – or make – different kinds of race boards – car-race track, obstacle course – but keep them simple and short; 30–50 spaces are enough. Use two dice for the longer ones.
- Make race tracks etc. interesting with themed bonus and penalty points.
- Use novelty game pieces – markers, counters, cars, men, etc. to match the theme and different kinds of spinners, dice and shakers.
- Velcro is useful for holding pieces on games boards, when playing and for storage.
- Get different kinds of blank dice and customise them – vowels, consonant blends, colours.
- For very short games, use dice numbered 1, 2, 3. For longer games, use two dice.
- For timed activities, use different kinds of timer – a novelty kitchen timer, a minute sand-timer or a stop watch.
- When making games, think out the rules clearly. Keep them simple and write them out. (Try them on someone else first.) Be prepared to be flexible. Pupils enjoy changing the rules.
- A game-board of A4 size (at most a folded A3) is big enough for most purposes. Think about carriage and storage. Keep it in a plastic wallet or box with all the bits safe.

- Good packaging and ingenious details can enhance appeal.
- Blank playing cards are ideal if a bank of card sets is being built up. Old Christmas cards are useful for trying out games but they do not give a good, uniform finish and it can be difficult to cut them to equal size.
- If making a lot of cards, think about storage so they can be got out quickly and are ready to use.
- Pictures: there are lots on various clip-art files. If you don't have access to ICT, a small picture dictionary (e.g. Ladybird) can be cut up and stuck on card.

Word games

Open-ended word games, such as Scrabble, Lexicon and Boggle, are quite difficult for dyslexic pupils, particularly the younger ones. They cannot see the possibilities that random sets of letters offer. Anagrams and Hangman can be a problem for the same reason, although some children do like Hangman – probably because it allows them to hang the teacher.

Crosswords, on the other hand, offer more possibilities and they offer a great deal of scope for reading and spelling practice. The kind of crossword play that allows the building up of a word pattern – rather like Scrabble, but with no limit on letters – can be a good introduction for less confident spellers, especially if they have a list of possible words.

- Crosswords: as a variant give the list of words to the pupil to fit into a grid or pattern. Let him make up the clues, which is good word play.

- Word searches are popular and can give useful word-reading practice.
- Word squares and fitting words into shapes (selecting answers to clues) are useful for calling attention to the details of letters and letter order, and for reading practice.
- Keep some photocopied blanks.

Some simple games

'Snail Race'

Objective: practice of short vowel sounds, either from oral/auditory stimulus or recognising and matching vowel letters.

This is best played with a set of short-vowel picture cards, but a vowel dice will do.

- Mark the sixth face of the dice with an asterisk. Draw a 'snail shell' spiral and mark it off into about 50 squares. Write the vowels on the squares.
- Each player in turn draws a card, says the word illustrated and identifies the vowel, or shakes the dice and sounds the vowel, gives a suitable word, then moves to the appropriate square.
- If * is thrown, move to the next same vowel – or perhaps the next in the alphabet.
- The first to the centre wins.

'Serpents'

Objective: word-reading or spelling practice.

- Draw a suitably contorted serpent and divide it into segments.
- Write R or S (read or spell) or other coded instructions on most of the segments. (As an alternative, read or spell according to odd or even dice throws.)
- Have a bank of cards with the words to be practised – sight words, spelling topics, etc.
- Throw a dice to move.
- When the player lands on a task segment, he must complete it successfully or forfeit his next go.

Teachers can handicap themselves by making deliberate mistakes for the pupil to catch them out.

Suffixing game

Objective: to practise the 'simple join' and the 'doubling' rule.

- Make sets of cards for *cvc* and *cvcc* root words, vowel and consonant suffixes, and some spare single consonants.
- Place them in three separate piles face down between the players.
- The players in turn draw a card from each of the piles and turn them over.
- Two points are scored immediately if:
  - the three cards form a word (*cvc* + correct extra consonant + appropriate suffix) or
  - the root and suffix form a word without the extra consonant, e.g. a *cvc* root + *ly*; a *cvcc* root + vowel suffix. In this case, the player returns the extra consonant to the pile and says why he is discarding it.
- If no word can be made the player keeps the cards in his bank and may use them to supplement the next three cards turned over.
  The possibilities for making words will gradually increase.

- If a word is made using one of the cards in the player's bank, a point is scored.
- When all cards have been used (or an agreed number reached), the players each read out the words they have made.
- The player with the most points wins.

(The rules are not unchangeable!)

Long vowel -*e* words can be added to this game. In this case, the pupil would place the suffix over the -*e*, or not, according to whether it begins with a vowel or a consonant, and again discard the extra consonant.

Extension of the game: teachers could also use these materials flexibly to introduce a suffixing rule. A number of words could first be built with the cards, and the use of the extra consonant explored. The pupil can then experiment for himself, trying out different ways of including, or not including, extra letters and reading the result.

Other phonic games and multisensory activities are mentioned in earlier chapters.

Other materials: worksheets and exercises

All teachers use worksheets to follow up a point and give their pupils structured practice.

There is no shortage of published worksheets, for purposes of all kinds. Many are photocopiable and all teachers will have their own favourites. It can be difficult to choose between them. Some points to consider are given in Figure 14.4. A list of titles and sources is given in Appendix II.

After a worksheet has been done – as a follow-up in class or for homework – the points should be tested in the next lesson, ideally in a sentence-

A few questions to ask include:

- Do they fit in with the sequence of the phonic programme you have been following?
- Are the tasks meaningful – not mere gap filling?
- Are they self-checking? If so, can the pupil just copy the answers – does he need to remember anything?
- Is there plenty of space, the material not tightly packed?
- Are the printing and the layout clear?
- Are the instructions clear and can the pupil read them?
- Will the activity help the pupil to remember the points being covered.
  (If not, why is he doing it?)

Figure 14.4 Choosing worksheets for spelling work.

writing context. This may seem too obvious to state, but it is easy to assume that because the work has been done correctly it can be remembered.

Teachers often make their own worksheets despite all the available material because nothing quite fits their particular purpose. It is handy to keep a format on word processor that helps with the layout. When designing these, it may be possible to avoid giving the pupil so much information that he can complete the exercise by copying or merely following a pattern.

Worksheets for language development, vocabulary, grammar and sentence writing

Teachers will want to work on a number of literacy skills, such as punctuation, writing complex sentences, parts of speech and wider language usage – meanings of 'sayings', proverbs, etc., where dyslexic learners do not fully understand the idioms – and, again, worksheets offer practice material. The same guidelines apply as for spelling and the presentation is even more important here.

Too much on the page will be an immediate 'turn off'. Many exercises – however excellent – often ask for too much. Dyslexic learners need to take time to read accurately and understand, so that a whole page of tasks may take too long to complete. There is also the question of generalising the points that are practised to their own writing. It may be more effective to use the worksheet as a teaching aid and help the pupil to create examples, using the worksheet as a model. If it is possible to find out what kind of work is going on in class – or what has been done recently – it may be useful to support that. If an exercise is set for homework, it is better to set less and have it done with full concentration. Photocopy half the page and enlarge it.

Typeface and fonts should make clear distinction between instructions and exercises, and there should be plenty of guidance, with examples, about what the pupil has to do. Again, look at the reading level of the instructions. Sometimes there is a mismatch between that and the level of the task itself. Are the instructions intended for the pupil or the teacher?

Appendix I

Talking to parents

Dyslexic children who succeed at school have nearly always had firm support and a great deal of help from parents. It helps if teachers are able to make contact with parents. It is easier with younger pupils – schools are smaller and parents visit more often, if not on a daily take-and-fetch basis. It may be possible to talk to the parents of older pupils on the phone.

It is useful to explain to parents how the work is being organised. If there is a Statement, or other funded provision, the parents will have agreed to this but they may still be hazy about what is going on. There are often assumptions and preconceptions about what 'specialist help' will be – or what it can do. At the least it will enable the teacher to introduce herself and ask about the child's history.

Parents often need reassurance about how the teaching is going. If one or both are themselves dyslexic, they may be unable to help with reading and writing, and they may feel awkward about acknowledging this. There may be particular ways in which they can help and it can be useful to keep in touch. Teachers also will have preferences about how parents can become involved in the work. There are several different areas to consider.

Personal support

This could be the most important factor for dyslexic youngsters. Children often try to hide their worries and fears, and parents sometimes need to be encouraged to listen out for these and to acknowledge them. Dyslexic children often feel quite useless. If they make a lot of effort for not very good results, it shakes their self-confidence and self-esteem. They can need a lot of reassurance that they are OK and worthwhile individuals.

Parents can help to convince them that high flying success in schoolwork and exams is not the only way people count. Often children do not recognise their own strong areas – or they refuse to accept that these are important. Do their teachers show that these are valued? Discuss ways in which parents can convince them that everyone has strengths and encourage them to work at what they are good at. Other family members (especially grandparents) and friends can make a big difference here. The crucial factor can be the way that dyslexia is explained to the child. If he or she, and everyone else, understands that there is a reason for the problem, and the effects it can have, the worry and the fault-finding are often reduced.

Helping with homework

This is often the first thing to be mentioned. It is helpful to discuss it with parents. Teachers also have agendas and it is important to find out what parents can do. What the child wants has also to be thought about and negotiations may be needed.

- Reading a book *to* children is often the parent's most important contribution.
- Paired or shared reading is helpful for the child's own practice.
- Parents reading homework books or worksheets aloud may be appreciated.
- Discuss ways of organising the child to do homework – preferably at a sensible time. If homework proves very difficult, it may be better to try to arrange follow-up work in school time.
- A teacher should explain what she will be asking the child to do.
- It is useful for parents to know where details of homework are written. Teacher's instructions should be very clear, and written down. (We think we have explained clearly but, after a gap of several days, explanations are not remembered.) Can parents give written feedback?
- Discuss how much correction the parent should

do. Most teachers like to see writing without corrections.
- Encourage parents not to criticise – but to give genuine praise and always to reward effort.
- Helping with learning: discuss with the parents the way that the child seems to learn best – repeating things, drawing, remembering visually, etc. They might also like to know about learning aids: tables tapes, games, etc.
- Marking: teachers should explain how they will mark or comment on work. Parents worry if spelling mistakes are not corrected, and some find it hard to accept that the content can be more important than correct spelling.

Learning spellings, number bonds and tables

These are the areas in which parents often report the most (horrendous) efforts. The class spelling lists are usually too difficult for the dyslexic child. If this is causing problems, perhaps the teacher could negotiate with the class teacher about adjustments. Otherwise, perhaps the parent could be shown how to sort the words into order for easier learning.

Parents are often glad to have tips for helping with learning. The most important could be to resist overload: learn words or number facts, a few at a time; 5–10 minutes at one sitting is better than all at once. Revise/go over the ones done the day before. (A look at one of the aids to memory books might be useful.) Suggest a box of magnetic letters and numbers.

Parents might help the child to make some useful cue cards:

- number words
- days of week and months
- alphabet

- table square
- home and school address and telephone nos
- parents' work telephone nos.

Store them in a pocket-size plastic wallet. Keep it in a handy place (pencil case?).

Helping to organise the work

Bringing the books

Probably the most important role for parents is to get the child to school on the day of his lesson, with the right books: reading book, phonic dictionary and homework.

Working space

It can be useful to find out where the child does homework and under what kinds of conditions. Is there a quiet place? Are the books safe from younger siblings?

Tools

Parents often like to know what will be helpful.

- Pens and pencils: encourage them to get a kind the child likes. (Very cheap biros often smudge; a soft pencil rubs out better; some children like a thicker implement – it can be easier to hold, but try a variety.)
- Watch (especially for older children).
- Electronic spellmaster: a Franklin is a good buy because it is designed to be dyslexia-friendly.
- Calculator.
- Computer: parents often ask advice about this. Encourage the parent to think about what it is really for. They often ask about programs for

helping to learn spellings and maths. Explain the advantages of word processing. The British Dyslexia Association has good advice leaflets.

Further referrals

Vision

Teachers should check with parents about what routine tests have been done. If glasses have been prescribed, does the child bring them to school and wear them? Even if the eyesight is 'normal' there could still be a problem with colour sensitivity or other visual difficulties.

Children may have commented to parents about lines of print moving around, and the parent will know if there have been frequent headaches or sore eyes. It can be useful to check out with a parent the kind of mistakes that are made in reading, e.g. reading words in the wrong order or missing a line, missing words out or putting extra words in. These could indicate a vision problem.

Parents may grumble at a child for doing untidy, messy work and for failure to develop neat handwriting. They may not realise the possibility of visuo-spatial difficulties. They might be able to seek a referral through their doctor to a specialist optometry clinic.

Hearing

Is there a frequent complaint that a child does not listen, or forgets most of what he hears? Is this intermittent – does it suddenly get worse for no apparent reason? Has there been a hearing test?

It may even be related to the child's mucus level – does he eat a lot of dairy produce, which can affect some children's hearing in the same way as a heavy cold might do. A check with the doctor or a nutrition specialist might help.

Speech
Does the child speak clearly and articulate sounds correctly? If there is a difficulty segmenting sounds for spelling, does this reflect something about the way words are said? Mothers will have information about early speech development, whether there has been speech therapy and so on. If an earlier difficulty is now leading to errors there may be a need to seek a referral for advice.

Movement
Clumsiness is also a point to talk about. Parents often get cross with a child who frequently knocks things over. Unsuccessful efforts to ride a bike, play football or swim, might indicate a problem. Again, they might be advised to chat to their doctor, or to ask the SENCO about a chat with the PE teacher.

A persistent difficulty, especially if the child is worried about it, could be a reason for seeking a referral to a children's occupational therapist or physiotherapist.

Parents are sometimes very keen to get specialist advice from clinics and advisory centres. While it is sensible to take action in time for the child to benefit from help, the parents' anxiety to find an 'answer' can put a child under a lot of pressure if he or she is 'overinvestigated'. Parents often welcome a chance to talk over their worries and an individual teacher taking an interest may help them to take a more relaxed approach.

Let's Discover Dyslexia Sandon, P and Myers, S. Watts Books 1995 and *Keeping Ahead in School* Mel Levine Educator's Publishers, Cambridge, Mass. (for older children) provide explanations that children can understand. (From SEN Publishing)

Appendix II

Programmes, resources and books for teaching and assessment

The titles and materials quoted here have all been found useful for teaching dyslexic learners. However, the lists are a tiny sample of what is available and can only be a guide on where to start and where to look. These are listed in sections as follows:

- Phonic teaching programmes
- Materials for multisensory phonic teaching
- Books and materials for older students
- Books: readers and other books for development of reading skills
- Dictionaries
- Handwriting
- Mathematics
- Computer software and ICT.
- Assessment and test materials
- Approaches to teaching and practical guides
- Where to see resources

Phonic teaching programmes

Brand, Violet. *Spelling Made Easy*. Baldock, Herts: Egon Publishers, 1976. Four books. A programme of spelling and reading work from introductory level to top juniors. This also provides useful phonic reading/dictation material related to the spelling work.

Brand, Violet. *Remedial Spelling*. Baldock, Herts: Egon Publishers. Wordlists and sentences. Especially suitable for older pupils.

Combley, Margaret. *The Hickey Language Course*, 3rd edn. London: Whurr Publishers, 2001.

Ellis, Sula, Ellis, Tony, Davison, Jackie and Davison, Mick. *Lifeboat*. Stourbridge: Robinswood Press, 2000. Reading and spelling programme (worksheet based).

Hornsby, Beve. *Alpha to Omega*, 5th edn. London: Heinemann, 1999

Miles, Elaine. *The Bangor Dyslexia Teaching System*, 3rd edn. London: Whurr Publishers Ltd, 1998.

Materials for multisensory phonic teaching

Alpha to Omega Flashcard Pack. London: Heinemann. From Learning Development Aids (LDA) (Living and Learning), Duke Street, Wisbech, Cambs PE13 2AE.

Edith Norrie Letter Case. From the Helen Arkell Centre, Frensham, Farnham, Surrey GU19 3BW.

Hickey Reading and Spelling Cards. For use as part of a structured teaching programme. From the Helen Arkell Centre.

Linking Letters. Learning Materials Limited, Dixon Street, Wolverhampton, WV2 2BX. These include vowel digraphs, which are not included in the *Edith Norrie Letter Case*.

Magnetic plastic letters sets (upper and lower case) from branches of the Early Learning Centre.

Magnetic letters, foam letters, alphabet jigsaws, phonic dominoes and other materials: Formative Fun, Education House, Horn Park Business Centre, Broadwindsor Road, Beaminster DT8 3TT and Smart Kids (UK) Ltd, 169B Main Street, New Greenham Park, Thatcham, Berkshire RG19 6HN.

Wooden letters. From SEN Marketing, 618 Leeds Road, Outwood, Wakefield WF1 2LT.

Flip Cards that Teach. From Better Books, 3 Paganel Drive, Dudley, West Midlands DY1 4AZ.

Phonics Flicker word builder books: *cvc* words and onset and rime. From LDA.

Rhyme and Alliteration Picture Cards. From LDA.

Sound Beginnings: a phonological awareness pack. Early phonological skills. From LDA.

Games

Blend-It, *Odd Bods*, *Pounce* and other phonic games. From HELP Educational Games, 29 Churchill Close, Didcot, Oxon OX11 7BX.

I Spy, short-vowel rhymes matching game; consonant blends dominoes and other early games to develop phonological skills. From LDA.

Managing Homophones, *Win-Wine-Winner* and other games (many suitable for older pupils), *Phonic Rime Time* (Hugh Bellamy) and other reading materials. Many in photocopiable form. From Bob Hext, Crossbow Games, 41 Sawpit Lane, Brocton, Stafford ST17 0TE.

p/b/d/ games; race-track word-building games and other games. From Learning Materials Ltd, Dixon Street, Wolverhampton WV2 2BX.

SWAP and FIX cards. Packs for vowel spellings, suffixes and prefixes: *GAMZ* (Also available as software.) (Older pupils like these games.)

Stile. Self-checking tray and work books. Different phonics topics, reading, spelling and maths. From LDA.

Phonic spelling workbooks and phonological materials

Brand, Violet. *Spelling Made Easy Worksheets*. Baldock, Herts: Egon Publishers. Introductory level and three books 1 and 2.

Briggs, Sue. *Learning can be Fun*: Book 1 *Alphabet Sequencing*. Book 2 *Syllable Division for Word Attack Skills*. From SEN Marketing.

Hornsby, Beve. *Alpha to Omega Activity Packs*. London: Heinemann. Three books, spelling and language usage.

Leach, Judith and Nettle, Gillian. *Read, Write and Spell*. London: Heinemann Educational Books. Four workbooks covering whole basic phonic programme. Also as worksheets.

Lewis, Patricia. *Spell It*. Oxford: Blackwell Educational. Four books for practice to accompany a spelling programme.

Lipscombe, Louise. *Sound Activities Worksheets* (two levels, four books). Baldock, Herts: Egon Publishers, 1998. Worksheets with word searches, crosswords and other word games to support *Spelling Made Easy* teaching programme and stories.

Steggles, Eira. *Rhymes and Strings*. Scunthorpe: Desktop Publications, 1995. Worksheets. Phonic reading and spelling through poems.

Thought Tracking, *Word Tracking* and other activities for development of phonic skills. Progressive grades of difficulty (re-usable versions available). From Ann Arbor Publishers, PO Box 1, Belford, Northumberland NE70 7JX.

Vivian, Virginia. *Literacy Strategies for the Classroom – Specific Learning Difficulties, Dyslexia*. Croydon Special Education Needs Support Service, Croydon 1998. Games and phonic activities. From Davidson Information Centre, Davidson Road, Croydon CR0 6DD.

Wendon, Lyn. *Letterland*. London: Collins, 1997. Available from Letterland Ltd, Barton, Cambs.

Wilson, Jo. *Phonological Awareness Training* (PAT). Four books (beginners to two-syllable words), onset and rime worksheets. From Educational Psychology Publishing, University College London, 26 Bedford Way, London WC1H 0AP.

Books and materials for older pupils

Spelling

Hackman, Sue. *Spelling*. Sevenoaks: Hodder & Stoughton. This has information about spelling as well as providing exercises and routines for learning.

Klein, Cynthia and Millar, Robin. *Unscrambling Spelling*. Sevenoaks: Hodder & Stoughton, 1989.

News Worksheets, *Word Play*, *A Speller's Companion* and other titles. From Brown and Brown, Keeper's Cottage, Westward, Wigton, Cumbria CA7 8NQ.

Pratley, Rhiannon. *Spelling it Out*. London: BBC Books, 1988.

Rak, Elsie. *Spellbound* and *The Spell of Words*. Cambridge, MA: USA Educators Publishing Service, Inc., 1972. From Better Books.

Steere, Amey, Peck, Caroline Z. and Kahn, Linda. *Solving Language Difficulties, Remedial Routines*. Cambridge, MA: USA Educators Publishing Service, Inc., 1966 From Better Books.

Walker, Marion. *Resource Pack*. From 14 Weston Close, Dorridge, Solihull, W. Midlands B93 8BL.

Wood, Elizabeth. *Exercise Your Spelling* and *Strengthen Your Spelling*. Sevenoaks: Hodder & Stoughton, 1990. Photocopiable.

Writing, comprehension work, thinking skills

(Many of these publications are photocopiable.)

Bentley, Diana. *False Teeth and Vampires* and other titles (cloze passages). From LDA.

Dubberley, Sue. *English Workout*. Hutchinson Publishers. A wide range of work on different aspects of language.

Hutchinson, Lynn. *Reading, Writing*. Sevenoaks: Hodder & Stoughton, 1993. Developing comprehension and language skills.

Hutchinson, Lynn. *Cloze Plus* and other titles. London: Edward Arnold/Hodder.

Looking and Thinking, and *Reading and Thinking*. From Learning Materials Ltd, Wolverhampton. For helping comprehension skills.

Picture Writing and the *Really Useful Picture* series. From Learning Materials Ltd.

Culshaw, Chris and Waters, Deborah. *Headwork*, Books 1–4 and *English Headwork*, Books 1 and 2. Both for pupils in lower secondary school. *Headwork* books contain exercises in problem-solving, matching, comparing, and sequence, classifying and interpreting information. Reading practice presented as thinking skills.

Waters, Deborah. *Primary Headwork*, Books 1 and 2. Oxford: Oxford University Press.

Blueprints series: *Spelling Book*, *Writing Book*, *Phonics Book* and other basic skills for literacy. London: Nelson Thornes.

Specials series: *Grammar*, *Writing for a Purpose*, *Study Skills*, and other titles. Dunstable: Folens Publishers.

Study skills

Buzan, Tony. *Use Your Head*. London: BBC Books, 1989. Distributed by BBC.

Leach, Robert. *How to Improve Your Memory*. London: Collins, 1994. For older students.

North, Vanda and Buzan, Tony. *Get Ahead*. An easy introduction to mind mapping. From Buzan Centres Ltd, 37 Waterloo Road, Bournemouth BH9 1BD.

Ostler, Christine. *Study Skills: A Pupil's Survival Guide*. Godalming: Ammonite Books.

Ostler, Christine and Ward, Frances. *Advanced Study Skills*: A Student's Survival Guide for AS, A-Level and Advanced GNVQ. Wakefield: SEN Marketing Publications, 2001.

Rowntree, D. *Learn How to Study – A Realistic Approach*. London: Warner Books, 1998.

Books: readers and other books for development of reading skills

Phonic material for beginning readers, especially suitable for complementing spelling work.

Earliest reading

Groves, Paul. *Bangers and Mash*. Longman. Twenty-four books.

Harris, Colin. *Fuzz Buzz*. Oxford: Oxford University Press.

Huxford Laura, Reason Rea and Wilson, Jo. *Rhyme World*. Oxford: Heinemann, 1998. Reading scheme for Key Stage 1. For oral/auditory work as well as reading.

Jackman, John and Frost, Hilary. *Sound Start* stories. London: Nelson Thornes. Earliest phonic reading: short vowels, consonant blends, vowel digraphs. Core book and six booster books at each stage.

Westwood, Jo. *The ZED Project*. Earliest phonic reading. Five books, short vowels and some sight words. From IEC Books Ltd, 77 Orton Lane, Wombourne, Wolverhampton WV5 9AP

(See illustration on page 43.)

Next stages in reading

For younger children:

Butterworth, Ben. *Trog Books*. London: Nelson.
Oxford Reading Tree. Oxford: Oxford University Press. Particularly Levels 4–8.
Sparklers. Cheltenham: Nelson Thornes, 2000.
Starpol. Oxford: Ginn & Co. Ltd, 1998
Zoom. Ginn & Co. Ltd. Graded readers for KS2. Reading age 5–7 years; six levels, eight books at each level.

For older pupils (about 9–14 years)

Fastbacks and *Five Minute Thrillers* from LDA
Headwork Reading. Oxford: Oxford University Press. Age group 11–14. Four levels of reading age 6–9.
High Noon Books, *Perspectives* and other series from Ann Arbor Books. American books with tales of adventure, mystery and thrillers. Interest levels for 10–14 years, reading ages graded 7–10.
Hotshot Puzzles. Oxford: Oxford University Press. Stories with clues to be solved. Four levels.
Impact. Ginn & Co. Ltd. Graded readers for Y5 and Y6. Non-fiction, re-telling stories, humour.
Orme, David. *Orbit 7*. Cheltenham: Nelson Thornes. Mystery and creepy stories.
Treetops. Oxford Reading Tree. Interest range 10+; reading age 6–9 years.
Zone 13 readers. Cheltenham: Nelson Thornes.

Teenagers

Chillers (mystery and horror). Basic Skills Agency and Hodder & Stoughton. Interest level 13+ years/reading age 7–9 years.

Jackson, Anita. *Spirals*. Cheltenham: Nelson Thornes.

Standard reading books

Ahlberg, Alan and Ahlberg, Janet. *Happy Families*. Viking Kestrel, 1988.
Books with cartoons, e.g. Deary, Terry. *The Grott Street Gang and Magic of the Mummy*. Hemel Hempstead: Simon & Schuster.
Dr Seuss Beginner Books – numerous titles. Collins.
Jets books: *Desperate for a Dog*, *Houdini Dog* and other titles. Young Knights Books.
Streamers series – Hippo Books. Scholastic Publications Ltd.
Young Knights series – Hodder & Stoughton.
Young Lions and *Picture Lions* series – Collins.
Young Puffins – two levels: *Read Alone* story books for first solo reading and building confidence; *Story Books* for children who have developed reading fluency.

Barrington Stoke Publishers

Barrington Stoke was established to produce a range of specially written fiction for dyslexic and reluctant readers in the age range 8–14 years. Books are edited so that style of writing, including length of words and sentences, is within readers' attainment level, without reducing the quality of writing. Specially designed font, careful lay-out and buff, matt pages make for comfortable reading. Bright covers and good illustrations enhance the appeal. Wide range of themes. Titles for older teenagers and young adults are being added. Titles include:

Bertanger, Julie. *Bungee Hero*

Douglas, Hill. *Alien Deeps.*
Dowland, Colin. *Weevil K Neevil.*
Johnson, Pete. *Runaway Teacher*
Masters, Anthony. *Bicycle Blues*
Oldfield, Jenny. *Extra Time*
  Teenage titles:
  From Barrington Stoke Publishers, Belford Terrace, Edinburgh EH3 4DQ, SEN Marketing and bookshops.

For a guide to the age levels of reading books

Hinson, Mike and Gains, Charles. *NASEN A–Z: A Graded List of Reading Books.* A guide to reading ages of the graded readers in most frequent use. From NASEN House, 4/5 Amber Business Village, Amber Close, Amington, Tamworth B77 4RP. Also on CD-ROM and at http://www.nasen.org.uk with sample pages of some books.
The Fog Index of Readability. How to make a readability analysis is explained in Appendix III.

Poems

Foster, John. *A First Poetry Book.* Oxford: Oxford University Press, 1979.
Foster, John. *A Very First Poetry Book.* Oxford: Oxford University Press, 1984.
  Also other titles in the same series.
Harris, Rolf. *A Catalogue of Comic Verse.* Sevenoaks: Hodder & Stoughton, 1988.
McNaughton, Colin. *Making Friends with Frankenstein.* London: Walker Books, 2000.
Milligan, Spike. *A Children's Treasury of Milligan.* London: Virgin Books.
Rosen, Michael. *Uncle Billy Being Silly.* London: Puffin Books, 2001.

Information books

Usborne Publishing Ltd (London) for all kinds of information books.
Deary, Terry. *Horrible Histories.* London: Scholastic, 1996.
Ganeri, Anita. *Horrible Geography.* London: Scholastic, 2000.
Oxford First Encyclopaedia. Oxford: Oxford University Press, 1998.
Science: Pople, Stephen. *Foundation Science to 14.* Oxford: Oxford University Press. This is listed as an example of the kind of classroom course book that would be ideal for a dyslexic learner. Information is supported by pictures, diagrams and charts; although the print is small, the pages are well spaced and the different sections are colour coded. Technical and science vocabulary is in short sentences and short paragraphs, mostly as labels or captions to the graphic content.

Dictionaries

Eastman, P.D. *The Cat in the Hat Dictionary. Beginner Books.* London: Collins.
Fergusson, Rosalind. *The Dean First Picture Dictionary.* London: Hamlyn Publishing Group Ltd, 1989.
Junior Dictionary. London: HarperCollins, 2000.
Primary Dictionary. London: HarperCollins, 2001.

Specialist dictionary: words listed by phonic reference

Moseley, David and Nicol, Catharine. *Aurally Coded English. The ACE Dictionary.* LDA.

Spelling dictionaries

Hawker, G.T. *Spell it Yourself.* Oxford: Oxford University Press, 1981. Quick reference for spellings, wordlists only, including suffixing.

Stirling, Eileen. *A Spelling Checklist for Dyslexics*, and *Which is Witch? – A Dictionary of Homonyms*. Also subject wordlists. From the author: 114 Westbourne Road, Sheffield S10 2QT.

Handwriting

Teaching Handwriting. A Guide for Teachers and Parents by Jean Alston and Jane Taylor. Lichfield: QED. 2000.

Writing Left-handed Jean Alston. Dextral Books. From SEN Marketing Ltd.

The Handwriting File Kath Balcombe. From SEN Marketing.

Handwriting: A Teacher's Guide. Jane Taylor. London: David Fulton. (Includes checklists).

Write from the Start (pictures and patterns for beginners) and other materials and handwriting schemes. From LDA.

Exercise books with special ruling for handwriting, LDA Tacey.

Pencil grips from LDA or Taskmaster Ltd, Morris Road, Leicester.

Mathematics

Maths Made Easy. Structured series from Introduction (numbers 1–10) and six further books. Also the *Money Book* and *Time*. Worksheets and materials for teaching and practice. Also on CD. From Egon Publishers.

Essential Facts and Tables: a quick reference book of maths and language terms for non-specialists. From Prim Ed, PO Box 51, Nuneaton, Warwickshire CV11 6ZU.

What to do when you can't say your tables and *What do you do when you can't add and subtract.* Steve Chinn. Baldock: Egon Books.

Computer software and ICT

Information

The best guide to ICT developments for dyslexic learners is the Computer-Users' Bulletin published by the Computer Working Party of the British Dyslexia Association. All the software included is vetted by members of the group; it is updated regularly.

See also the Educational Software Database, BECTa. http://vtc.ngfl.gov.uk/resource/esr/

Titles

Software titles are given in Chapter 13. Except where noted, all are available for PCs. The software is suggested as suitable for dyslexic learners but there are many other titles. For further recommended software and addresses of software developers, see the publications of the British Dyslexia Association and other literature.

Suppliers

Software can be bought from:

AVP. The Big Black Catalogue. School Hill Centre, Chepstow, Gwent NP6 5PH.

Rickitt Educational Media (REM), Software Directory, Great Western House, Langport, Somerset TA10 9YU.

Neither firm supplies goods on approval but the developers often do.

Support and advice

Teachers using computers with children may obtain support and advice on ICT from the following (among others):

British Dyslexia Association, 98 London Road, Reading RG1 5AU
(http://www.bda-dyslexia.demon.co.uk).

British Educational and Communications Technology Agency (BECTa), Millburn Hill Road, Science Park, Coventry CV4 7EZ
(www.becta.org.uk).

Granada Learning/SEMERC Granada Television, Quay Street, Manchester M60 9EA
(www.semerc.com).

Exhibitions

Computer software and hardware can be seen at the annual BETT (British Educational Training and Technology) exhibition, in London in mid-January and at other special educational needs exhibitions.

Assessment and test materials

Publishers' catalogues contain many titles. The following tests include some of the most recent and revised editions of earlier tests. All are suitable for individual administration. Some publishers will provide inspection copies.

Reading tests (norm referenced)

Single-word reading

Graded Word Reading Test. Windsor: NFER-Nelson. Age level 6 to 14. It has been noted that dyslexic children in the early stages of learning find this test exceptionally difficult.

Wide Range Achievement Tests (WRAT 3): single-word reading. Age range 5 to 75. Obtainable from The Psychological Corporation or the Dyslexia Institute, Gresham Road, Staines, Middlesex.

Sentence and passage reading

Salford Sentence Reading Test, Bookbinder, G.E. revised and re-standardised. Sevenoaks: Hodder & Stoughton, 2000.

NFER Group Reading Test II. Windsor: NFER-Nelson. Sentences for completion by selecting words from lists. Age range 6 to 14. For group administration but can be used with an individual pupil.

Neale Analysis of Reading Ability, 2nd revised edn (NARA II). Neale, Marie D. Windsor: NFER-Nelson, 1997. Age range 7 to 12.5.

New Reading Analysis by Denis Vincent and Michael de la Mare. Windsor: NFER-Nelson. Age level 7 to 13.

The two last tests assess a number of reading skills and strategies because they use passages for the reading task. Scores are given for reading accuracy and comprehension. These are expressed in broad bands rather than as a single reading age score in years and months.

Phonic and Word-recognition tests

Carver, Clifford and Moseley, David. *Word Recognition and Phonic Skills (WRAPS)*. Sevenoaks: Hodder & Stoughton, 1994. Ages 5 to 8. Group or individual.

Wordchains. Windsor: NFER-Nelson, 1996. Age range 7 to adult. The task is to recognise letter clusters within a string of letters, and whole words within a chain of three or four words presented without spacing. As many letters or words as possible must be divided in 3 minutes (group or individual).

Spelling tests (norm referenced)

Vernon, P.E. *Graded Word Spelling Test*. Sevenoaks: Hodder & Stoughton. Age range 6 to 17.6.

Wide Range Achievement Tests (WRAT 3). Spelling – single words.

Young, D. *Parallel Spelling Tests*. Sevenoaks: Hodder & Stoughton. Age range 5 to 11. These tests are in the form of a bank of words, presented in the context of sentences, from which items for tests may be chosen.

Diagnostic tests (not norm referenced)

Early language development

Boyle, J. and MacLellan, E. *Early Language Skills Checklist*. London: Hodder Headline, 1998.

Reading

Arnold, Helen. *Diagnostic Reading Record*, revised. Sevenoaks: Hodder & Stoughton, 1998. Passages for making a reading analysis.

Spelling

Cotterell, Gill. *The Phonics File: Diagnostic spelling tests*. Wisbech: LDA. Age range 9 years and up. These are designed for use with children who have spelling difficulties, and look especially for knowledge of phonic patterns and principles of spelling. It includes The Checklist of Basic Sounds which can be used in conjunction with the tests. (LDA)

Vincent, Denis and Claydon, Jenny. *Diagnostic Spelling Test*. Windsor: NFER. Age level 7 to 12, and older children who have difficulties with spelling. This is for group administration but can be used for individuals.

Mathematics (norm-referenced tests)

Gillham, Bill and Hesse, K.A. *Basic Number Screening Test*. Windsor: Hodder & Stoughton, 2001. Age range 7 to 12.

Wide Range Achievement Tests (WRAT 3). Mathematics test; 7 to 75.

Diagnostic test

Morfett, Chris. *Mathematics*. Croydon: Croydon Special Education Needs Support Service, 1998. From Davidson Information Centre, Davidson Road, Croydon CR0 6DD.

Tests of cognitive ability (norm referenced)

Non-verbal reasoning

Cognitive Abilities Test (CAT). Windsor: NFER-Nelson. Age range 7 to 15.

Cognitive Profiling System (CoPS) and *Lucid Assessment System for Schools* (LASS). Beverley: Lucid Creative Ltd. Age range 11 to 15.

NFER-Nelson Non-Verbal Reasoning Test. Windsor: NFER-Nelson. Age range 7;6 to 15;6.

RAVENS Coloured Progressive Matrices (Easy). Oxford: Oxford Psychological Press. Age range 5 to 11 and *RAVENS Standard Progressive Matrices* (Average). Oxford: Oxford Psychological Press. Age range 11 to adult.
Non-verbal reasoning tests. Group or individual administration.

Vocabulary knowledge tests

British Picture Vocabulary Scale. Windsor: NFER-Nelson. This test can help to identify children who have difficulties in the understanding of spoken language, or of verbal expression.
Crichton Vocabulary Scale. Oxford: Oxford Psychological Press. Age range 6 to 11. May be read to the pupil.
Mill Hill Vocabulary Scale. Oxford: Oxford Psychological Press. Definitions and multiple choice questions. 11 to adult. May be read to the pupil.

Phonological skills tests (norm referenced)

Frederikson, Norah, Reason, Rea and Wilson, Jo. *Phonological Assessment Battery (PhAB).* Windsor: NFER-Nelson, 1997. Six tests: alliteration, naming speed, rhyme, spoonerisms, fluency, non-word reading. Age range 6 to 14;11.
Gathercole, Sue and Baddeley, Alan. *Children's Test of Non-Word Repetition.* London: Psychological Corp., 1996. Age range 4 to 8.
Phonological Abilities Test (PAT). London: The Psychological Corp. Ltd, 1996. Six tests: rhyme identification, rhyme production, word completion, phoneme identification, speech rate, letter knowledge. Age range 5 to 7.
Snowling, Margaret and Muter, Valerie. *Children's Test of Non-word Reading.* Bury St Edmunds: Thames Valley Test Co., 1996.

Tests for specific learning difficulty/dyslexia (norm referenced)

Newton, Margaret and Thomson, Michael. *The Aston Index.* Wisbech: LDA, 1982. The Index provides a range of test material to assess reading and spelling attainment (the Schonell Word Recognition Test and Spelling Test), auditory and visual memory and graphomotor skills. Age range 5 to 14.
Miles, T.R. *The Bangor Dyslexia Test.* Wisbech: LDA, 1998. Partially standardised. The test looks for difficulties that are typical of those shown by dyslexic children, such as left–right uncertainty and with repeating sequences, e.g. arithmetic tables and months of the year. Age range 7 to adult. It is intended as a preliminary screening test.
Dyslexia Early Screening Test (DEST): age range 4;6 to 6;6. Rapid naming, bead threading, phonological discrimination, postural stability, rhyme detection, digit span, digit and letter naming, sound order, shape copying.
Dyslexia Screening Test (DST): age range 6;6 to 14;6.
Dyslexia Adult Screening Test (DAST): 14;6 to adult.

These last three tests are authored by R. Nicolson and A. Fawcett and published by The Psychological Corporation Ltd. The *DST* and *DAST* tests have 11 subtests including naming speed, timed reading and spelling, non-word reading, fine-motor skills (bead threading), postural stability and verbal fluency. *DAST* also has tests of cognitive ability.

Approaches to teaching and practical guides

Alston, Jean. *Assessing and Promoting Writing Skills*. Tamworth: NASEN, 1995

Arnold, Helen. *Listening to Children Reading*. Sevenoaks: Hodder & Stoughton, 1982.

Augur, Jean. *This Book Doesn't Make Sense*. London: Whurr Publishers, 1996.

Barton, Geoff. *Writing to 14* and *Comprehension to 14*. Oxford: Oxford University Press. These are class course books but they provide useful material and reference on strategies for different aspects of language work for teachers working with individual pupils.

Bristow, Jacqui, Cowling, Philip and Davies, Bon. *Memory and Learning. A practical guide for teachers*. London: David Fulton, 1999.

Cotterell, Gill. *The Phonic Reference File*. Wisbech: LDA, 1993. Word lists, checklist of basic sounds, diagnostic spelling tests.

Crombie, Margaret. *Specific Learning Difficulties (Dyslexia). A Teachers' Guide*, 2nd edn. Glasgow: Jordanhill College of Education, 1997.

Fisher, Robert. *Teaching Children to Think*. Cheltenham: Nelson Thornes, 1995.

Gilroy, D. and Miles, T.R. *Dyslexia at College*, 2nd edn. London: Routledge, 1996.

Hall, Nigel and Robinson, Anne. *Learning About Punctuation*. Clevedon: Multilingual Matters, 1996.

Hornsby, Beve. *Before Alpha*. Abingdon: Souvenir Press, 1996. Teaching the under 7s.

Hornsby, Beve. *Overcoming Dyslexia*. London: Macdonald Optima, Macdonald Co., 1984.

Layton, Lyn, Deeny, Karen and Upton, Graham. *Sound Practice. Phonological Awareness in the Classroom*. London: David Fulton, 1997.

Ott, Philomena. *How to Detect and Manage Dyslexia*. London: Heinemann, 1997.

Payne, Trevor and Turner, Elizabeth. *Dyslexia: A parents' and teachers' guide*. Clevedon: Multilingual Matters, 1998.

Pollock, Joy and Waller, Elizabeth. *Day to Day: Dyslexia in the classroom*, revised edn. London: Routledge, 2000.

Pollock, Joy and Waller, Elizabeth. *English Grammar and Teaching Strategies*. London: Routledge, 1999.

Poustie, Jan. *Literacy Solutions: A practical guide to effective strategies and resources for dyslexia and other specific learning difficulty conditions*. Taunton: Next Generation.

Portwood, Madeleine. *Understanding Developmental Dyspraxia. A textbook for students and professionals*. London: David Fulton, 2000.

Reason, Rea and Boote, Rene. *Learning Difficulties in Reading and Writing: A teachers' manual*, 2nd edn. Windsor: NFER-Nelson, 1994.

Reid, Gavid. *Dyslexia: A practitioner's handbook*. Chichester: John Wiley, 1998.

Stirling, Eileen. *Help for the Dyslexic Adolescent*. 1986. From 114 Westbourne Road, Sheffield S10 2QT.

Thomson, Michael. *Dyslexia: A Teacher's Handbook*, 2nd edn. London: Whurr Publishers Ltd, 1998.

Thomson, Patience and Gilchrist, Peter. *Dyslexia, a Multidisciplinary Approach*. Cheltenham: Nelson Thornes, 1999.

Todd, Janet. *Individual Education Plans – Dyslexia*. London: David Fulton, 2000.

Walton, Margaret. *Teaching Reading and Spelling to Dyslexic Children*. London: David Fulton, 1998. Particularly useful for parents.

Handwriting and Motor Skills

The Handwriting Review. Published by the Handwriting Interest Group. For details write to Janet Tootall, West Hill High School, Thompson Cross, Stalybridge, Cheshire SK15 1LX.

Sassoon, Rosemary. *Handwriting – A New Perspective and Handwriting – How to Teach It*. London: Nelson Thornes, 1989.

Nash-Worthiam, Mary and Hunt, J. *Take Time! Exercises for dyslexic/dyspraxic pupils*, revised edn. Stourbridge: Robinswood Press.

Mathematics

Chinn, S.J. and Ashcroft, R. *Mathematics for Dyslexics*, *A Teaching Handbook*, 2nd edn. London: Whurr Publishers, 1998.

Henderson, Anne. *Maths for the Dyslexic*. London: David Fulton, 1998.

Henderson, Anne and Miles, Elaine. *Basic Topics in Mathematics for Dyslexics*. London: Whurr Publishers, 2000.

ICT

Crivelli, Victoria. *Write to Read with ITC* (British Dyslexia Association Computer Committee series). Wakefield: SEN Marketing Publications, 2000.

Hillage, Di. *Count on your Computer* (British Dyslexia Association Computer Committee series). Wakefield: SEN Marketing Publications, 2001.

Keates, Anita. *Dyslexia and Information and Communications Technology. A guide for teachers and parents*. London: David Fulton, 2000.

McKeown, Sally. *Dyslexia and ICT. Building on success*. Coventry: BECTa, 2000.

Providing for candidates with special assessment needs during GCE (ALevel), VCE, GCSE and GNVQ

Backhouse, Gill. *A Practical Guide*. Evesham: The Professional Association of Teachers of Students with Specific Learning Difficulties (PATOSS). Available from the PATOSS office: PO Box 10, Evesham, Worcestershire WR11 6ZW. A guide for teachers carrying out assessments and writing reports.

Where to see resources

A large range of books, materials and software can be seen at the exhibitions arranged by the Educational Publishers' Council and NASEN: London Special Needs Exhibition (November), Birmingham (March), Bolton (May) and the BETT computer exhibition (January).

Information on new developments in computers – hardware and software (programs) – can be found in the journals and publications of groups such as BECTa and the British Dyslexia Association Computer Users' Bulletin (subscription).

Teachers looking for books and materials will find it useful to obtain the catalogues of publishers and suppliers such as those mentioned.

Specialist booksellers for books and materials on dyslexia and other specific learning difficulties are:

Better Books, 3 Paganel Drive, Dudley, West Midlands DY1 4AZ.

SEN Marketing, 618 Leeds Road, Outwood, Wakefield WF1 2LT.

For resources for left-handed individuals
Anything Left-handed, 57 Brewer Street, London W1F 9UL

Many of the materials and resources listed are stocked by more than one supplier. The prices can also vary.

Appendix III

Estimating the readability of books

This is usually done by making a detailed analysis of the vocabulary in the text but it is just as important to get an impression of the whole book as well.

An overview would include a number of factors:

- Length of book; length of chapters
- Overall design
- Print features, e.g. font, font size, line spacing, number of illustrations, captions
- Style, e.g. length of sentence, number of words of more than two syllables per sentence; complexity of grammar and language, e.g. passive voice; complex tenses; abbreviated forms
- Dialogue: how is it arranged? Are the speakers indicated clearly?
- Relationship of text to pictures: how are they spaced?
- Do the pictures help with decoding?
- Relation of picture captions to text: how much help do they give?

- Speech bubbles: what kind of text do they carry – a short version of the text or other features, e.g. exclamations?

If a reading age figure is needed, a reading age analysis can be carried out – but this is a mechanistic process and the 'score' should not be rigidly interpreted. Long sentences with short words may give a low score, but a struggling reader might be better able to read shorter sentences with more two-syllable and the occasional three-syllable words.

Fog index

1. Take a sample of text – approximately 150 words.
2. Calculate the average number of words per sentence.
3. Count the number of words that contain three syllables or more. Calculate the percentage of these to the total number of words.

4. Add together the average of words per sentence, and the percentage of long words: Divide this total by 2.5. This will give the RA.

For example:

average number of words per sentence: 12
percentage of words with 3 syllables: 18

12 + 18 divided by 2.5 = 12. Fog index
RA = 12.

(This is only one of a number of methods for calculating reading ages.) An easier option would be use a computer program e.g. SMOG Readability published by Inclusive Technology. This uses the SMOG formula for text analysis.

Appendix IV Further reading and reference addresses

Adams, Marilyn Jager. *Beginning to Read*. Cambridge, MA: Educators Publishers Inc., 1990.

Beech, John R. and Singleton, Chris (eds). *The Psychological Assessment of Reading*. London: Routledge, 1997.

Bryant, Peter and Bradley, Lynette. *Children's Reading Problems*. Oxford: Blackwell, 1985.

Clay, Marie. *Becoming Literate. The construction of inner control*. London: Heinemann Education, 1991.

Fawcett, Angela (ed.). *Dyslexia: Theory and good practice*. London: Whurr Publishers, 2001.

Given, Barbara K and Reid, Gavin. *Learning Styles. A guide for teachers and parents*. St Annes-on-Sea: Red Rose Publications, 1999.

Miles, T.R. *Dyslexia: The pattern of difficulties*, 2nd edn. London: Whurr Publishers, 1993.

Miles, T.R. and Miles, Elaine (eds). *Dyslexia and Mathematics*. London: Routledge, 1993.

Miles, T.R. and Miles, E. *Dyslexia – A Hundred Years On*, revised edn. Milton Keynes: Open University Press, 1999.

Miles, T.R. and Varma, V. *Dyslexia and Stress*. London: Whurr Publishers, 1999.

Miles, T.R. and Westcombe, John (eds). *Dyslexia and Music: Opening new doors*. London: Whurr Publishers, 2000.

Montgomery, Diane. *Spelling*. London: Cassell, 1998.

Oakhill, Jane and Beard, Roger (eds). *Reading Development and the Teaching of Reading*. Oxford: Blackwell, 1999.

Peer, Lindsay and Reid, Gavin (eds). *Multiculturalism, Literacy and Dyslexia. A challenge for educators*. London: David Fulton, 2000.

Pumfrey, Peter and Elliot, Colin D. (eds). *Children's Difficulties in Reading, Spelling and Writing*. London: Falmer Press, 1990.

Riddick, B. *Living with Dyslexia*. London: Routledge, 1996.

Snowling, Margaret. *Dyslexia: A cognitive perspective*. Oxford: Blackwell 2001.

Thomson, Michael. *The Psychology of Dyslexia*. London: Whurr Publishers, 2001.

Wray, David and Lewis, Maureen. *Extending Literacy*. London: Routledge, 1997. An account of the EXEL Project and the development of writing frames.

Journals

Basic Skills: Magazine of the Learning Skills and Development Agency. London.

British Dyslexia Association Handbook: for teachers and parents. Carries articles and up-dates information. Published annually.

Child Language and Therapy (three issues per year): London: Arnold.

Contact (three issues per year): the BDA members' journal.

Dyslexia: An International Journal of Research and Practice: British Dyslexia Association. Chichester: John Wiley.

Dyslexia Review: The Dyslexia Institute Journal, 133 Gresham Road, Staines, Middlesex

Reading Literacy and Language: Journal of UKRA the United Kingdom Reading Association. Oxford: Blackwell

Support for Learning and *The British Journal of Educational Research*: NASEN.

Sources for information

Organisations for dyslexia, special educational needs and other specific learning difficulties

ADO: The Adult Dyslexia Organisation, 336 Brixton Road, London SW9 7AA (www.futurenet.co.uk/charity/ado/index.htm)

BDA: The British Dyslexia Association, 98 London Road, Reading, Berkshire RG1 5AU, has many leaflets and other publications on dyslexia and dyslexic learners in mainstream education. Leaflets can be downloaded from the website: www.bda-dyslexia.org.uk

Handwriting Interest Group: Secretary: Felicitie Barnes, 6 Fyfield Road, Ongar, Essex CM5 0AH www.handwritinginterestgroup.org.uk

NASEN (National Association for Special Educational Needs): has booklets with ideas for games and other activities. Lists available from York House, Exhall Grange, Wheelwright Lane, Coventry CV7 9HP and www.nasen.org.uk

PATOSS: The Professional Association of Teachers of Students with Specific Learning Difficulties, PO Box 10, Evesham, Worcs WR11 6ZW: www.patoss-dyslexia.org

(A varuable list of resources is published annually.)

Centres for teaching, assessment and specialist training courses

Dyslexia Institute (Staines): www.dyslexia-inst.org.uk

Dyslexia Unit: University of Wales, Bangor. www.dyslexia.bangor.ac.uk

Helen Arkell Dyslexia Centre (Farnham, Surrey): www.arkellcentre.org.uk

Hornsby International Centre (London): www.hornsby.co.uk

For information on dyslexia and other specific learning difficulties

ADD: Attention Deficit Disorder Information Services (www.addiss.co.uk).

AFASIC: Association for All Speech Impaired Children (www.afasic.org.uk).

Colour and Visual Sensitivity Information Group (Visual/Optical difficulties) c/o Visual Perception Unit, University of Essex. www.essex.ac.uk/psychology/overlays

Dyscovery Centre (Cardiff): www.dyscovery.co.uk. Also carries out assessments and arranges teaching and therapy.

Dyslexia Research Trust, Magdalen College, Oxford: for information on research, mainly on vision problems, genetics and nutrition. (www.dyslexic.org.uk).

Dyspraxia Foundation: Information about developmental motor-coordination difficulties (www.dyspraxiafoundation.org.uk)

Royal College of Speech and Language Therapists: For information on aspects of speech and language difficulty and kinds of help that can be given. (www.rcslt.org).

Other useful websites and addresses

- BBC Education: Phonic resources and activities can be accessed online and worksheets downloaded. www.bbc.co.uk/education/schools
- Department for Education and Skills (www.dfes.gov.uk).
- National Literacy Strategy Publications. NLS materials and other resources are available from the DfES Publications, PO Box 5050, Sherwood Park, Annesley, Nottinghamshire NG15 0DJ. Tel. 0845 6022260 (Lists can be seen on the DfES website).
- www.dyslexichelp.co.uk: links to other sites, information and commercial (especially useful for parents).
- The Left-handed Shop: Information and products. www.anythinglefthanded.co.uk

- Listening Books (The National Listening Library): enquiries about membership: 12 Lant Street, London SE1 1QH or www.listening-books.org.uk
- NFER publishers for information on tests and testing: www.nfer.ac.uk
- www.psych-ed.org: General information about dyslexia, links to other sites, spelling information (common words lists) and readability check for texts.
- Resources Discovery Network: for information on special education and government publications. Resources lists with linked sites and links to organisations, for special educational needs. www.sosig.ac.uk
- Writing frames and other teaching strategies. Information and materials for downloading. www.warwick.ac.uk/staff/D.J.Wray/resources.html

Specialist teacher training courses

Part-time professional development courses on dyslexia can be followed at institutions in many parts of the UK. Entry criteria are usually Qualified Teacher Status and a minimum of 2 years of full-time teaching (or the equivalent in part-time work). Courses carrying BDA accreditation status include modules of practical teaching and assessment work. Teachers successfully completing courses at the higher level of accreditation (AMBDA) are recognised by the Joint Examinations Board as qualified to make recommendations for special arrangements in examinations.

Information about courses may be obtained from the BDA. Leaflets with details of accreditation criteria can be accessed via the BDA website.

Appendix V

Checklists

1. Tackling Dyslexia wordlists

2. The 'Literacy Hour' wordlists

3. Terms for language teaching

1. Tackling Dyslexia wordlists

The Checklist of Basic Spelling Patterns and the List of Irregular Words (Figures V.1 and V.2, pages 242, 243) have been devised to provide a guideline for teachers on what to teach and to offer an 'at-a-glance' record of pupils' progress for parents and teachers alike.

The items on the Checklist have been arranged roughly according to order of teaching, but this must not be taken as rigid. Items have been grouped, for convenience according to similarity of sound or spelling; however, it is preferable to teach words with similar sounds but different spelling patterns on separate occasions. Depending on the level of the pupil, teachers may find it helpful to make additional checklists to record in more detail progress on certain items, e.g. knowledge of alphabet and consonant blends.

The Irregular Words lists are in three sections. Lists A and B contain common words, most of which are not covered by the patterns on the Checklist. Some have been included because they are known to present particular difficulty. Where a number of irregular words share a similar spelling pattern or meaning they have been linked. Words in Group A are more common than those in Group B. The third set, in numbered groups, are not all irregular words. Group 1 shows high-frequency 'open-syllable' words. Group 2 words are important sight words with the less frequent /z/ sound of s; the rest are high-frequency 'sight' words with similar features which can be usefully taught together.

If teachers decide to use the national Literacy Hour word lists (see below), these might be rearranged on principles similar to those in the checklists.

Progress

Six boxes have been provided against each item on both lists; the first three concern reading, the second three spelling.

- Box 1 is to be dated when work on that item is introduced.

- Box 2 is to be ticked when the pupil can read the item in a 'focused' way.
- Box 3 may be ticked when it is evident that the pupil can read an item in context 'automatically' without recourse to analytical skills.
- Box 4 is to be dated when spelling work on that item has commenced.
- Box 5 is to be ticked if the pupil can spell the item in a focused spelling test.
- Box 6 may be ticked when the pupil produces the correct spelling in a free-writing situation.

Ticks in both boxes 3 and 6 would indicate that items had been sufficiently mastered to expect transfer of skills into other contexts.

2. The Literacy Hour wordlists

Lists of high-frequency words included in Literacy Hour work are printed here so that teachers may be informed about the work of the classroom. They may also want to cover the same word lists as the class teacher.

The Reception Year (YR) and Key Stage 1 (KS1) lists contain essential high-frequency words that are important in holding text together. The Literacy Hour Framework for Teaching states that 'familiarity with these words will enable children to get pace and accuracy into their reading at an early stage.' and recommends that pupils should be taught to recognise them in and out of context. They should be taught in shared text work with the whole class, but they will need to be reinforced by other activities.

List 1: High-frequency words

Reception year

I	up	look	we	like	and	on	at	for	he	is	said	go	you	are
this	going	they	away	play	a	am	cat	to	come	day	the	dog	big	my
mum	no	dad	all	get	in	went	was	of	me	she	see	it	yes	can

Years 1–2

about	after	again	an	another	as	back
ball	be	because	bed	been	boy	brother
but	call(ed)	came	can't	could	did	do
don't	dig	door	down	first	from	girl
good	got	had	half	has	have	help
her	here	him	his	home	house	how
if	jump	just	last	laugh	little	live(d)
made	man	may	more	much	must	name
new	next	night	not	now	off	old
once	one	of	our	out	over	people
push	pull	ran	saw	school	seen	should

(continued on page 244)

Figure V.1 Checklist of basic word patterns and spelling sounds.

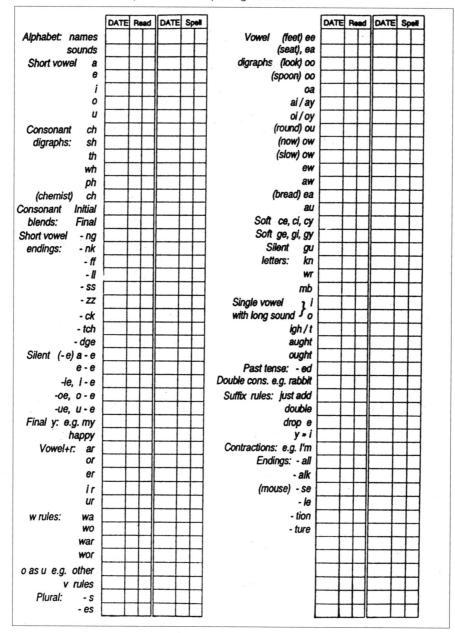

Please note that permission is given to photocopy this sheet; the sheet can then be enlarged.

Figure V.2 Common irregular words.

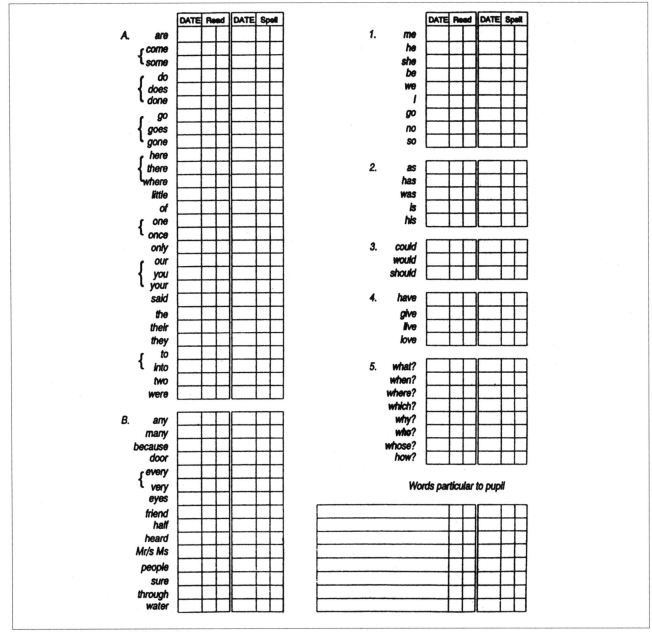

Please note that permission is given to photocopy this sheet; the sheet can then be enlarged.

High-frequency words years 1–2 continued

sister	so	some	take	their	them	then
there	these	this	three	time	too	took
tree	two	very	want	water	way	were
what	when	where	who	will	with	would
your						

Plus:

- Days of the week
- Months of the year
- Numbers to 20
- Common colour words
- Pupil's name and address
- Name and address of school.

List 2 provides medium-frequency words to be taught through years 4 and 5. It is expected that children will be able to read most of the words with little or no difficulty but that there may be some difficulty in spelling some of them.

It is recommended that teachers check that they can all be read and written easily, and that words should be grouped in various ways to facilitate learning.

above	across	almost	along	also	always	animals
any	around	asked	baby	balloon	before	began
being	below	better	between	birthday	both	brother
brought	can't	change	children	clothes	coming	didn't
different	does	don't	during	earth	every	eyes
father	first	follow(ing)	found	friends	garden	goes
gone	great	half	happy	head	heard	high
I'm	important	inside	jumped	knew	know	lady
leave	light	might	money	morning	mother	much
near	never	number	often	only	opened	other
outside	own	paper	place	right	round	second
show	sister	small	something	sometimes	sound	started
still	stopped	such	suddenly	sure	swimming	think
those	thought	through	today	together	told	tries
turn(ed)	under	until	upon	used	walk(ed) (ing)	watch
where	while	white	whole	why	window	without
woke(n)	word	work	world	write	year	young

3. Terms for language teaching

Essential phonetic and phonological terms and conventions

Children should be familiar with most of the following so that talk about language is possible. (Notes are for the convenience of teachers who may be new to language teaching.)

- Consonant: a letter that is not a vowel; *y* can be a consonant or a vowel.
- Consonant blend: consonants sounded rapidly one after the other but still keeping their identity as separate phonemes (*br*, *st*, *pl*, *spl*).
- Consonant blends in final position: *nt*, *mp*, *ld*, etc. are more correctly referred to as 'assimilated consonants'.
- Digraph (vowel or consonant): two written letters making one sound (*sh*, *ch*, *th*, *ck*; *ai*, *ay*, *ea*, etc.). Diphthong also means a sound written with two letters; it is probably more helpful in our work to use the term digraph and make the distinction between consonant and vowel sounds, especially as the term makes explicit the relationship between sound and spelling.
  Note: *ar*, *ear*, *or*, etc. are not vowel digraphs or consonant blends: the vowel sound is modified by the consonant and a correct description would be '*r*-modified vowel'. For brevity they may be referred to as 'vowel + *r*'.
- Double letters: *ff*, *ss*, *ll*, etc. are not blends or digraphs – just double letters, a convention of spelling. They count as a single phoneme.
- Grapheme: written letter or letters to represent a phoneme. A grapheme may be more than one letter, e.g. *k*, *ck*, *tch*; *ough*.

- Morpheme: a unit of meaning (*er*, *ing*, *trans*, *wait*, *struct*, *carpet*). Note: 'morpheme' is not synonymous with 'syllable'.
  trumpet – two syllables – one morpheme
  trumpeting – three syllables – two morphemes
  waited – two syllables; wait is a whole word; *ed* is a unit of meaning
  construct – two syllables, each is a morpheme
    con (prefix) can be added to another word (*conduct*)
    struct (root but not itself a word) is a unit of meaning and can form part of another word.
- Onset: the letters of a syllable before the vowel.
- Phoneme: a single speech sound (/s/, /a/, /sh/, /ee/, /igh/, /ng/). (Note: a single sound may be written with two or more letters.)
- Rime: that part of a syllable that contains the vowel and the letters that follow it. (The part that would rhyme if there was another word to compare.)
- Sound: a vowel or consonant phoneme: and its position: initial/beginning/first, middle/medial, final/last/end.
- Schwa: an unstressed vowel. The vowel loses its distinctive sound – often sounds like a grunt (*about*, *collar*, *colour*, *garden*) or may not be sounded (*general*, *interest*).
- Voiced/unvoiced consonants: when some consonant sounds are pronounced a vibration can be felt if the hand is placed on the larynx:
  b, *d*, *g*, *v*, *z* are voiced sounds (they cannot be whispered easily).
  Contrast *p*, *t*, *c*, *f* and *s* (the unvoiced pairs to the phonemes in the first list).
  Some children need help to distinguish all these sounds.

m and *n* are nasal consonants; they have a vibration but this is in the nose. Again children may find it helpful to distinguish *m* and *n* in words by putting their hand on their nose and feeling the buzz (contrast *sad*/*sand*; *lip*/*limp*).

- Vowel: *a*, *e*, *i*, *o*, *u*, and sometimes *y* acts as a vowel. Every syllable must have a vowel, otherwise it cannot be pronounced. Vowels are made by shaping the inside of the mouth by tongue and palate with no distinctive effects of articulation – friction, voicing or movement of the lips. A child with poor phonemic awareness may have difficulty perceiving and segmenting vowel sounds, or appreciating the difference between those that are made near to each other in the mouth (a/e; e/i). For this reason vowels are best taught in an order with maximum contrasts.

Essential grammatical and language usage terms that dyslexic children should know and use

- Parts of speech: noun, verb, adjective, adverb, pronoun, conjunction.
- Grammar: nouns: singular, plural. Verbs: tense – present, past, future; person – 1st, 2nd, 3rd. Root word, suffix, prefix. Word, phrase, sentence, paragraph; clause, subject.
- Letters: alphabet; capital letter; lower-case letter.

- Punctuation marks: full stop, comma, question mark, bracket, speech marks (inverted commas), exclamation mark, apostrophe.
- Style: the way an author writes.
- Dialogue: what characters say in a story, sometimes shown in speech bubbles.
- Labels: title, heading, caption.

National Literacy Strategy language terms

These are technical words that class teachers will use in the Literacy Hour. It is not suggested that they will teach the words formally, but it is expected that they will form part of children's developing vocabulary for talking about language. The lists span Reception to Year 6; the first four are printed here.

Reception year

Word	Sentence	Text
alphabet	Capital letter	beginning
alphabetical order		book
grapheme		cover
letter		end
onset		line
phoneme		page
rime		recount
sounds (first, middle, end/final)		rhyme
word		story
		title

Year 1

Word	Sentence	Text
consonant	full stop	author
letter sound	question	blurb
final, initial	question mark	caption
lower case	sentence	character
plural	speech marks	contents
spelling pattern		diagram
upper case		dictionary
vowel		fiction
		illustrator
		index
		instruction
		label
		layout
		lists
		non-chronological writing
		non-fiction
		play
		poem
		predict
		report
		setting
		signs

Year 2

Word	Sentence	Text
antonym	bold print	anthology
compound word	comma	explanation
digraph	exclamation mark	fact
prefix	italics	flow chart
syllable	punctuation	glossary
synonym		heading
		key phrase
		keyword
		nonsense poem
		notes
		poet
		publisher
		riddle
		scan
		setting
		skim
		story plot
		sub-heading
		theme
		tongue-twister
		verse

Year 3

Word	Sentence	Text
apostrophe	adjective	alliteration
definition	bullet points	audience
homonym	conjunction	bibliography
root word	formal language	calligram
singular	grammar	dialogue
suffix	informal language	encyclopaedia
	noun: collective,	fable
	common, proper	legend
	pronoun: personal,	myth
	possessive	onomatopoeia
	verb	parables
	verb tense	performance
	1st, 2nd, 3rd	poetry
	person	purpose of
		writing
		sequel
		sequence
		structure
		thesaurus
		traditional story

Year 4

Word	Sentence	Text
diminutive	adjectives:	abbreviate
font	comparative,	argument
homophone	superlative	chorus
pun	adverb	cinquain
simile	clause	debate
	colon	discursive
	connective	writing
	hyphen	discussion
	paragraph	editorial
	phrase	epitaph
	possessive	fantasy
	apostrophe	adventure
	monologue	free verse
	opinion	Haiku
	playscript	jingle
	science fiction	narrative
	summary	persuasive
		writing
		rhyming
		couplet
		stanza
		voice

Appendix VI The National Curriculum and the Literacy Hour

The Literacy Hour was introduced into schools in England in 1998, as the recommended (but not statutory) way to implement the National Curriculum for English. The rationale underlying this approach is that of whole-class teaching and of direct teaching of skills.

To achieve this, the teacher's time is divided systematically between instruction to the whole class and individualised work with groups. The hour is therefore divided into four segments.

1. Whole-class teaching (15 minutes): 'shared text work' on reading and writing. This gives the teacher opportunities to make links between the two.
2. Whole-class teaching (15 minutes): 'focused word work' at Key Stage 1 (KS1). Word and sentence work – spelling and written expression, grammar and punctuation (comprehension and composition) at KS2. The detailed work in this section includes much phonics and phonological awareness teaching.

In both whole-class segments a high level of interaction between teacher and children is expected.

3. Group work (20 minutes): the children work cooperatively or independently within their ability groups on word or sentence work, reading or writing. The teacher works with two groups in each session on 'guided text work' – reading or writing.
4. Whole class (10 minutes): this is the time for reviewing work, reflecting on it, following up teaching points, and allowing children to present their work to the class.

The categorisation of activities as word level, sentence level and text level makes explicit the different kinds of skill that children must be taught.

The content of the Hour is set out in the Framework for Teaching. This expands the programmes of study as they are set out in the National Curriculum, and specifies them in detail in a termly timetable of work. Supplementary documents and resources for teaching are provided.

The Literacy Hour content is aimed at children of average attainment. It is expected that they will learn (at least for reading purposes) much of the work in the basic phonic programme by the end of KS1, with spelling to be consolidated in the next 2 years.

Additional group work, with additional literacy materials, is provided in Year 2 (Y2) and Y3 for children with learning difficulties who cannot keep up with the rest. From 2002 this will be extended to children in Y1, in keeping with the policy that children with special needs should be identified early and help should be provided within the class. (Baseline assessment at school entry should help to ensure such identification.)

Most dyslexic children should be picked up early under this system; with the right kind of help those with moderate difficulties might be given a good start. It will still be important that teachers monitor their progress because underlying difficulties can re-surface when the demands of work get more difficult, e.g. they will still need more time to learn and assimilate new work, and increased amounts of practice before it is generally applied. Children with more severe difficulties will continue to need individual help.

In school year 2000–2001, the Literacy Hour arrangements began to be extended into secondary school, starting with Y7 and going on to Y8 and Y9. The same kinds of segments are proposed, but, with the emphasis now on using and developing skills and the literature syllabus, some adjustments will probably be needed.

For children with special needs, it is acknowledged that Y7 is a critical year for catching up, and additional time on literacy will be provided.

The documents emphasise that literacy teaching is not confined to the English syllabus. It extends right through the curriculum and every subject specialist must deal with the literacy work appropriate to their subject needs. In a similar way, teachers working with dyslexic pupils – especially in secondary school – can contribute by using subject material as a focus for reading, spelling and writing. This might help pupils to take their specialised work back into the classroom.

Appendix VII   Notes and references

Chapter 1

Note 1.1, page 1

Schools in Wales and Scotland place a similar emphasis on phonic instruction, although the Literacy Hour structure as developed for use in English schools has not been adopted as policy in Wales or Scotland. All children in Wales learn Welsh as well as English, which may affect the pattern and pace of learning.

Note 1.2, page 2

These three factors are interrelated. Although they all give rise to problems that are directly observable in children's performance at reading and writing tasks, it is probable that the difficulties with phonology underlie the other two. Such difficulties mean that direct attention has to be given to individual sounds in spoken and written words. This takes up resources of working memory.

The term 'working memory' refers to the memory function by which incoming sensory stimuli are processed for future use. 'Information' in this case means information from the sensory activity through which we respond to words, whether printed or heard. It can be stored in the working memory for a short time only (about 18 seconds). During this time it must be changed into a form for storage in an appropriate 'place' in the long-term memory. If the processing is slowed down by a neurological difficulty, such as a difficulty with phonemic information, the working memory will not be able to process and clear quickly enough – as a telephone switchboard might become jammed by too many callers. Instant, automatic processing of the incoming 'messages' is necessary.

All learning involves the working memory and so does any task that requires information to be held and analysed: its limited capacity can be seen in tasks such as remembering telephone numbers or verbal instructions, or visual copying from a notice. Efficient functioning of the working memory is a key factor in the learning of basic skills for reading and spelling, and in subsequent literacy activity. Processing and retention can be helped by verbal or subvocal repetition.

See Baddeley, Alan. *Working Memory*. Oxford: Basil Blackwell, 1986.

Note 1.3, page 2

The role of phonological skills in reading and writing activity has been examined in detail in many research studies. There is still a great deal of discussion about the development of children's ability to segment and categorise sounds, and the nature of the contribution that this makes to reading. Much of the debate turns on how far this skill develops independently or whether it is a consequence of early literacy development. An account of this research can be found in:

Goswami, Usha and Bryant, Peter. *Phonological Skills and Learning to Read*. Hove: Laurence Erlbaum Associates Ltd, 1990.

Note 1.4, page 3

For a readable account of the way that oral language may be stored and retrieved from the memory, see:

Aitchinson, Jean. *Words in the Mind*. Oxford: Basil Blackwell, 1987.

Note 1.5, page 5

An account of the difficulties which dyslexic children and older people experience can be found in many publications. See, among others:

Edwards J. *The Scars of Dyslexia. Eight case studies in Emotional Reactions.* London: Cassell, 1994.

Miles, T.R. *Dyslexia: The pattern of difficulties*, 2nd edn. London: Whurr Publishers, 1993

Miles, T.R. and Varma, V. (eds). *Dyslexia and Stress*. London: Whurr Publishers, 1995.

Chapter 2

Note 2.1, page 7

The detailed material that goes into lessons can be found in:

Miles, Elaine. *The Bangor Dyslexia Teaching System*, 3rd edn. London: Whurr Publishers, 1997.

This is a syllabus of phonic work and an approach to teaching spelling and reading skills which gives systematic attention to the phonological and linguistic characteristics of written language. It was developed over a number of years as the working material for the team of teachers at the Dyslexia Unit, University of Wales, Bangor. An earlier programme, published in Miles and Miles may be considered a precursor to the BDTS:

Miles, T.R. and Miles, E. *Help for Dyslexic Children*. London: Routledge, 1983.

Other programmes that use a phonic approach are:

Hornsby, Bevé and Shear, Frula. *Alpha to Omega*, 5th edn. London: Heinemann Educational, 1999.

Brand, Violet. *Spelling Made Easy*. Baldock, Herts: Egon Publishers Ltd, 1984.

This makes direct links between spelling and reading by means of stories.

Note 2.2, page 8

The work in this programme is now set out in a recommended sequence in the syllabus of phonic work in the Literacy Hour.

Many teachers working with individual pupils have their own preferred order. There will be differences of detail but all will follow the major principles that are described here.

If teachers base their work around a programme of published worksheets (such as *Lifeboat*, Robinswood Press, 2000), it will be more difficult to vary the order because the work will be cumulative and, at each new step, it will be assumed that the pupil has worked on all the preceding points in the programme. Teachers need to be aware of pitfalls if they dip into different programmes for their materials.

Note 2.3, page 13

A number of studies have shown that tracing the letters of a word, while saying the letter names simultaneously, is a successful method of learning to write words. The important factor lies in the linking of the sensory channels of movement, vision and speech, and hearing. Tracing methods were advocated by Samuel Orton and also by Grace Fernald working in America in the 1930s. While Orton's theory was that this would strengthen phonological skills, Fernald's long-term objective was to train children to memorise whole words by visual means alone.

Note 2.4, page 13

A technique of teaching through a holistic tactile and visual approach has been developed by Ron Davis and described in his book:

Davis, R. *The Gift of Dyslexia*. London: Souvenir Press, 1994.

It is taught by trained tutors in a one-to-one situation.

Note 2.5, page 14

The *Phonological Awareness Training* programme by Jo Wilson is published by University College London. Further details and the photocopiable materials are obtainable from the publisher. For address see page 224.

Chapter 3

Note 3.1, page 20

For an account of children's language development and a guide to helping children with speech and language difficulties, see:

Stackhouse, Joy and Snowling, Margaret. *Dyslexia, Speech and Language: A Practitioner's Handbook*. London: Whurr Publishers, 1996.

Note 3.2, page 26

The visual difficulties now known as Meares–Irlen syndrome were first described in the early 1980s by a teacher and a psychologist (independently of each other) – Olive Meares (1980) and Helen Irlen. They suggested that coloured acetate overlays could help. Irlen subsequently developed a system for testing individuals who experienced difficulties and prescribed overlays and, where appropriate, tinted lenses.

Equipment for use by opticians and orthoptists was developed by Wilkins in the mid-1990s.

Research studies by Stein and colleagues also show how anomalies in the neurology of visual processing can affect reading. See:

Miles, T.R. and Miles, Elaine. *Dyslexia. A Hundred Years On*, 2nd edn. Buckingham: Open University Press, 1999: 67–76.

See the following for an overview of research studies into the use of tinted lenses:

Whitely, H.E. and Smith, C.D. *Journal of Research in Reading* 2001; **24**(1): 30–40.

Note 3.3, page 29

The *Oxford Reading Tree Teachers' Guide 2* (Oxford University Press) has a short account of how to make a running reading record. For a more extended description see:

Arnold, Helen. *Listening to Children's Reading*. Sevenoaks: Hodder & Stoughton, 1982.

See also the teacher's manual of:

Arnold, Helen. *Diagnostic Reading Record* test kit, revised edn. Sevenoaks: Hodder & Stoughton, 1998.

Chapter 4

Note 4.1, pages 32 and 58

It has been observed by many teachers that dyslexic children can sometimes spell simple, regular words before they can read them. They seem to marshal their phonic skills more successfully to encode sounds, although this does depend on some ability to segment sounds in words that they want to write. On the other hand, they do not apply these skills to word attack, preferring instead to look at the word as a whole.

Research studies by Ellis and Cataldo looked at the way that the skills of reading, spelling and awareness of sounds interact in the early stages of reading development. They found that, as the children developed their phonological skills for spelling, this led directly to greater use of the same strategies for reading.

This is consistent with the models of reading and spelling developed by Uta Frith and others which identify distinct stages – logographic, alphabetic and orthographic – in the learning of these skills. These show that young readers first work through a whole-word approach. Spelling starts with an alphabetic strategy and this approach is transferred into reading so that this too begins to develop along a phonic route. Last to emerge in the development of basic literacy skills is the orthographic stage in which children learn different spelling patterns and irregular spellings. This begins in the spelling/writing domain and is transferred to reading. It can be seen that, after the first stage, word building and spelling have an important role in the learning process. There is a good deal of overlap between these stages and they should not be seen as 'water-tight' boxes. See:

Ellis, N.C. and Cataldo, S. Learning to spell, learning to read. In: Pumfrey, P.D. and Elliot, C.D. (eds). *Children's Difficulties in Reading, Spelling and Handwriting*. Basingstoke: Falmer Press, 1990.

Thomson, Michael. *The Psychology of Dyslexia*. London: Whurr Publishers, 2001.

Note 4.2, page 33

The Letterland pictogram system by Lyn Wendon uses a method that makes links between letter shapes, their sounds, and associated words or ideas, e.g. *s* is represented as a snake that hisses, and *k* has a kicking foot; *w* and *h* are characterised by roles that they play in spelling–sound patterns and become the Wicked Witch and the Hairy Hat Man. Each letter has a story that helps the young child to remember what it says and does. (Available from Letterland Ltd, Barton, Cambridge.)

Note 4.3, page 34

The term Linkages was used by Anna Gillingham and Bessie Stillman to describe the associations between the properties of each alphabetic letter – name, sound, appearance, and the movements for saying and writing it. They worked with S.T. Orton in America and developed a teaching programme:

Gillingham, Anna and Stillman, Bessie. *Remedial Training for Children with Specific Difficulty in Reading, Writing and Penmanship*, 7th edn. Cambridge, MA: Educators Publishing Service Inc., 1969.

Note 4.4, page 36

This method was devised and used extensively by a Russian psychologist C.D. Elkonin. For a short discussion of the approach see:

Clay, Marie. *Reading: The patterning of complex behaviour*, 2nd edn. London: Heinemann, 1979: 65–66.

The method is now used in the Literacy Hour teaching strategies.

Note 4.5, page 38

'Onset' and 'rime' together are an intra-syllable division of words which segments the word after the first consonant sound or consonant cluster. This is the onset of the word. The vowel and following consonant(s) form the rime, e.g. *sn* + *ap*. However, when word blending is attempted, if the first consonant is voiced it cannot easily be sounded without a following vowel and the alternative segmentation may therefore be easier, e.g. *ba-* + *t*.

The onset and rime theories were developed by Usha Goswami who argued that many readers approach new words by making analogies with words that they know. She showed that children were more able to make such analogies by using word endings than beginnings, e.g. they found it easier when given *beak*, to read *peak* than to read *bean*. This research underlies the PAT programmes and can be seen in, for example, the *Rhyme* and *Analogy* books of the *Oxford Reading Tree* and the *Rhyme World* reading series (Heinemann). Onset and rime are used as a key technique in the Literacy Hour phonics teaching.

Chapter 5

Note 5.1, page 49

Children's competence in rhyming tasks – the categorisation of sounds – when they enter school has been shown to be a good predictor of reading ability at age 8. Lynette Bradley and Peter Bryant found that training children in this skill was effective in improving reading skills, particularly when plastic letters were used to make the link between the sounds and their alphabetic representation.

An extensive programme of phonological training for children in early years of school has been developed by Peter Hatcher. This is a sequential programme which trains children's ability to segment initial sounds, then other sounds within words, to recognise and produce rhyming words and to categorise words by their sounds in different ways.

Bryant, Peter and Bradley, Lynette. *Children's Reading Problems*. Oxford: Blackwell, 1983.

Hatcher, Peter. *Sound Linkage*, 2nd edn. London: Whurr Publishers Ltd, 2000.

Chapter 6

Note 6.1, page 73

Although references are given to the *Bangor Dyslexia Teaching System*, lists of words for these points and all other phonic topics can be found in a number of teaching programmes, notably *Alpha to Omega* (Beve Hornsby) and *Remedial Spelling* (Violet Brand) (see Appendix II).

Note 6.2, page 78

Different accents have an effect on many vowel sounds and also on *r* – which is sometimes sounded separately, sometimes rolled. Vowels followed by *-re* can sound more like 'pure' long vowels when spoken by someone with a Scottish accent, e.g. *care*. A Welsh person might pronounce /ă/ in *car* more as a short vowel followed by a rolled /r/.

This may affect the order in which the teacher includes them in the spelling work.

Note 6.3, page 84

The spelling convention of double letters following short vowels is found mainly in words of Anglo-Saxon and Germanic origin. Many of the words that appear to defy this 'rule' derive from Greek words.

Note 6.4, page 84

Teaching word-attack and stress patterns by working systematically through a large number of examples is a method found in many American teaching programmes. *Solving Language Difficulties* (Amey Steere, Caroline Z. Peck and Linda Kahn) uses this method, although this is essentially a linguistic approach, which groups words according to their historical derivations (see Appendix II for full details). Lists of polysyllabic words for this kind of practice can be found in the *Bangor Dyslexia Teaching System*, Part 2 and also in *Solving Language Difficulties*.

However, there are pitfalls in over-emphasis on syllable division and blending and it should be treated with care. In spoken words, sounds and syllables do not divide neatly; they carry over from one to another. Detailed analysis of speech sounds shows that they are frequently affected by adjacent sounds. When we write them as separate letters, we impose artificial boundaries on them. The phonic spelling of young children, and some dyslexic learners, can show the effect of over-attention to segmenting phonemes, even when it looks bizarre.

To explore this, say some words carefully, feeling the positions and movements of the lips and tongue as they go from one speech sound to the next. This can help to explain certain spellings, e.g. -*tch* in *match*, and -*dge* in *hedge*.

Chapter 8

Note 8.1, page 109

When dyslexic children are tested on the *Neale Analysis of Reading* it is often found that their score for comprehension is greater than for accuracy. However, many need help to develop more advanced comprehension skills. See:

Oakhill, Jane and Beard, Roger (eds). *Reading Development and the Teaching of Reading*. Oxford: Blackwell, 1999.

for a discussion of the development of comprehension skills and the educational implications of difficulties in this area.

Note 8.2, page 110

Research studies into comprehension have provided much evidence that comprehension is dependent to a large extent on word-recognition skills, but there is still much that is puzzling about comprehension at a higher level. For a readable account of some research, see:

Oakhill, Jane and Beard, Roger (eds). *Reading Development and the Teaching of Reading*. Oxford: Blackwell, 1999.

Note 8.3, page 111

This method was tested in a research project by four teachers, reported in the *British Journal of Special Education*.

Moram H, Smith K, Meads J and Becks M. Let's try that word again in a new way. Helping failing readers to learn high frequency words. *British Journal of Special Education*, 1996, 23(4).

Note 8.4, page 119

Children who have had to struggle with words – and have perhaps developed good guessing techniques – can find it difficult to attend to details and to remember more than the outline of what they have read. An increasing amount of material is available to help the development of these skills (see Appendix II).

Note 8.5, page 119

The use of coloured overlays by school children was investigated in a research study by Wilkins et al. They found that many children in the study showed a marked improvement in reading speed when using the overlays.

Wilkins, A.J., Lewis, E., Smith, F., Rowland, E. and Tweedie, W. Coloured overlays and their benefit for reading. *Journal of Research in Reading*, 2001, **24**(1): 40–64.

Note 8.6, page 121

Many secondary schools have set up 'reading clubs' in which senior pupils listen to younger ones who need help and encouragement. The emphasis is on listening and support, not teaching, but it is important that the helpers are given guidance in the best ways to give support.

Paired reading projects are often set up by teachers or advisers, who provide background support and encouragement for the parents as they help their children.

Chapter 9

Note 9.1, page 127

For information about the Numeracy Hour and the syllabus for teaching, see the Department for Education and Employment publications.

Chapter 10

Note 10.1, page 144

The PAT programme (see page 14 and Note 2.5 above) was intended for use with a class or group.

Note 10.2, page 144

The Literacy Hour arrangements started being extended to secondary schools (Key Stage 3), beginning with Year 7, in 2001.

Note 10.3, page 148

Kipling's verse from the *Just So Stories* is a useful reminder of the question words:

> I keep six honest serving men
> (They taught me all I knew);
> Their names are What, and Why, and When,
> And How, and Where, and Who.

Note 10.4, page 150

The use of writing frames for literacy was investigated and developed by a research project in the University of Exeter. The outcome is described in:

Wray, David and Lewis, Maureen. *Extending Literacy.* London: Routledge, 1997.

In the first place, the method aims to support the way children use text by providing sets of questions based on the books they are using. This helps to ensure that they are reading with full comprehension. In Wray and Lewis's project the writing frames were used with young children aged 5 to 7. The method is also very suitable for older dyslexic children. It keeps the whole task in front of the child while he fills in the parts in an organised, sequential way. The content is his own.

Writing frames is one of the approaches used in the Literacy Hour and a number of publishers have produced this kind of material to support other parts of the curriculum.

Note 10.5, page 150

The technique of Mind Mapping was developed by Tony and Barry Buzan and introduced in a series of BBC television programmes, *Use Your Head*, in 1974. The technique allows ideas to be explored and developed in a web of ideas, unrestricted by the need for literacy expression or logic and using the method of notation that the student prefers. Dyslexic students – particularly if they have skills in graphics and design – often respond more strongly to images and colour than to words. For them a visual strategy can be more powerful than a verbal one for memory tasks, and they find the Mind Map approach an effective medium for thinking and preparing work, and for study and revision.

Note 10.6, page 153

The scaffolding approach is becoming a standard way to help students develop writing and comprehension skills. See:

Moore, P. Reciprocal teaching and reading comprehension: a review. *Journal of Research in Reading* 1988; **11**(1): 3–14.

Note 10.7, page 154

Young readers may develop a 'silent reading' technique of pronouncing words in their heads and 'listening in' to themselves. Skilled readers rarely do this unless circumstances demand it, e.g. if they encounter text that is complex or difficult to understand. Here it may serve to help overall comprehension, rather than assist the recognition of individual words. For a discussion of the role of phonology in word identification and in comprehension, see:

Perfetti, C.A. Cognitive research and misconceptions of reading education. In: Oakhill, J. and Beard, R. (eds). *Reading Development and the Teaching of Reading.* Oxford: Blackwell, 1999.

Note 10.8, page 158

The material in this section is based on the National Curriculum publication *English, Key Stages 1–4,* published by the Department for Education and Skills and the Qualifications and Curriculum Authority, and the parallel version published by the National Assembly for Wales.

In Wales, the National Curriculum requirements for English are similar but they are arranged under Oracy, Reading and Writing, and set out under the headings Range, Skills and Language Development. Welsh is a core subject and compulsory for all children from the first school years. It is assessed by SATS at the end of Key Stage 1, and there is no requirement for children to take SATS in English at this stage.

Chapter 11

Note 11.1, page 172

The publications on handwriting by Jean Alston and Jane Taylor include a checklist for identifying errors and troublesome features, and give suggestions for improvement (see Appendix II).

The Handwriting Interest Group is a forum for teachers and researchers to share ideas. It publishes a journal, *Handwriting Review,* in which issues such as handwriting styles and the speed of writing of children and students can be explored. The issue of writing speed is particularly important for dyslexic candidates in examinations (see Appendix II for details).

Chapter 12

Note 12.1, page 175

Verbal rehearsal, either aloud or subvocal, is an automatic technique for memorisation and learning and it develops spontaneously in children at around 8 years. Younger, and some older, dyslexic learners have to be taught how to make use of it. How effective it is may be related to the individual's speed of articulation – the faster speakers get more into the memory system in the time available. It has a central role in multisensory teaching. See:

Gathercole, Susan and Baddeley, Alan. *Working Memory and Language.* Hove: Erlbaum, 1993.

Chapter 13

Note 13.1, page 186

Dyslexic individuals are often considered to be 'right-brain' thinkers, i.e. although they are good at logical reasoning, their skills are visual and spatial and they prefer to take a global approach. (In contrast to this, 'left-brain' thinkers tend to use a more verbal, linear approach, with greater attention to detail.) This can often be seen in the way that dyslexic students prefer to work, although younger pupils may need encouragement to develop these skills. ICT and other technologies seem to be suited to the way that dyslexic students work and through which they can develop their sometimes innovative way of thinking. These ideas are explored by Tom West in his book:

West, Thomas. *In the Mind's Eye* 2nd edn. New York: Prometheus Books, 1997.

Note 13.2, page 203

In cases where extreme difficulties make the use of a word processor indispensable, parents and teachers should ask to have this included in a psychologist's report on the child's needs, and in the Statement of Special Need.

In such cases, it could also be useful for the Statement to make a recommendation for the use of word processors when the child takes SATs and external examinations.

Application to the relevant examination group must be made with plenty of time to provide evidence and enter into discussion. One year before the date of the examination would not be too early to start the process.

Chapter 14

Note 14.1, page 212

Leaving aside familiar reasons for anxiety such as examinations, there are many reports of children being afraid of certain lessons at school. (Maths seems to be particularly stressful, not only for children with specific learning difficulties.) A physical reaction – sweating or feeling sick – is not uncommon and mothers are familiar with 'morning tummy-ache' as a reason for staying at home on certain days. See:

Miles, T.R. and Varma, V. (eds). Dyslexia and Stress. London: Whurr Publishers Ltd., 1999.

Index